Managing the City

Edited by John Diamond, Joyce Liddle, Alan Southern and Alan Townsend

Routledge
Taylor & Francis Group

LONDON AND NEW YORK

First published 2007
by Routledge
2 Park Square, Milton Park, Abingdon, Oxon OX14 4RN

Simultaneously published in the USA and Canada
by Routledge
270 Madison Ave, New York, NY 10016

Routledge is an imprint of the Taylor & Francis Group, an informa business

© 2007 John Diamond, Joyce Liddle, Alan Southern and Alan Townsend for editorial
selection and material; individual contributors, their own contributions

Typeset in Perpetua and Bell Gothic by
Keystroke, 28 High Street, Tettenhall, Wolverhampton
Printed and bound in Great Britain by
Antony Rowe Ltd, Chippenham, Wiltshire

British Library Cataloguing in Publication Data
A catalogue record for this book is available from the British Library

Library of Congress Cataloging in Publication Data
Managing the city / edited by John Diamond . . . [et al.].
    p. cm.
Includes bibliographical references and index.
ISBN 0–415–38257–2 (hard cover) – ISBN 0–415–38258–0 (soft cover)
1. Urban renewal–Great Britain. 2. Community development, Urban–Great Britain.
3. Urban policy–Great Britain. 4. Local government–Great Britain. 5. Central-local
government relations–Great Britain. I. Diamond, John, 1954–
HT178.G7M26 2006
307.3′4160941–dc22   2006014544

ISBN10: 0–415–38257–2 (hbk)
ISBN10: 0–415–38258–0 (pbk)

ISBN13: 978–0–415–38257–1 (hbk)
ISBN13: 978–0–415–38258–8 (pbk)

Contents

Illustrations

FIGURES

TABLES

Contributors

Dr Jon Coaffee is Lecturer in Spatial Planning at the School of Environment and Development, University of Manchester. Specializing in urban regeneration management, he has undertaken numerous pieces of action research for European, national, regional and local government on the rescaling of governance processes and their relationship with wider regeneration agendas.

Dr Andrew Coulson has worked at the Institute of Local Government Studies since 1984, taking a special interest in local economic development, partnership working and the modernization agenda. Between 1990 and 2004 he was an elected Councillor on Birmingham City Council, closely involved in the regeneration of the city.

Dr John Diamond is based in the Centre for Local Policy Studies at Edge Hill University. He is on the management committee of ARVAC (Association for Research into the Voluntary and Community Sector). Within CLPS he has carried out a range of evaluations on behalf of a number of agencies, including the Cheshire Children's Fund, the NWDA, Voluntary Action Lewisham, regeneration initiatives in Manchester and the Youth Justice Board. John is co-author (with Joyce Liddle) of *Management of Regeneration*, published by Routledge in 2005.

Scott Dickinson has worked for many years on EU programmes, local economic development and regeneration in West Yorkshire, Birmingham and the West Midlands, and London. He was a senior manager at the Audit Commission for five years, where he led national value for money studies on neighbourhood renewal and sustainable communities. He now works in consultancy.

Paul Hoggett is Professor of Politics and Director of the Centre for Psycho-Social Studies at the University of the West of England, Bristol and is co-editor of the journal *Organisational and Social Dynamics*. He has over twenty years' experience researching welfare change and the politics of community life for funders such as the ESRC, the Home Office and the European Foundation. His books include *The Politics of Decentralisation* (1994, Macmillan, with D. Burns and R. Hambleton), *Contested Communities* (1997, Policy Press) and *Emotional Life and the Politics of Welfare* (2000, Macmillan).

CONTRIBUTORS

Lorraine Johnston is Research Fellow at the Institute for Political and Economic Governance (IPEG), University of Manchester. She is currently undertaking research funded by the Economic and Social Research Council (ESRC) which looks at the relationship between change management agendas, new localism and local government modernization.

Joyce Liddle is Associate Professor of Public Policy and Director of the MPA programme at the Nottingham Policy Centre, University of Nottingham, having previously worked at both the Universities of Sunderland and Durham. She is the editor of the *International Journal of Public Sector Management* and co-author of *Management of Regeneration* (published by Routledge in 2005). She has a special interest in strategic and stakeholder management within the public sector, and the implications this has for learning and skills within regional partnerships.

Dr Calum Macleod is Lecturer in Public Management at Queen Margaret University College in Edinburgh. He was formerly a national advisor on sustainable development for Scotland's 2000–2006 European Structural Funds Programmes.

Marjorie Mayo is Professor in Community Development at Goldsmiths, University of London. She has worked in the community sector, as well as in local government, and has experience of working internationally. With colleagues at the Centre for Urban and Community Research at Goldsmiths, her research interests focus on strategies for participation and empowerment, at the local level in relation to urban regeneration and beyond internationally. She is currently working on an ESRC-funded project on ethical dilemmas in contested communities with colleagues at the University of the West of England and on the evaluation of the Civil Renewal Unit's Active Learning for Active Citizenship programme, using participatory approaches. Her publications include *Cultures, Communities, Identities: Cultural Strategies for Participation and Empowerment* (2000, Palgrave) and *Global Citizens* (2005, Zed Books).

Ruth McAlister is currently employed as an Urban Regeneration Assistant with Belfast City Council. She is completing a Ph.D. investigating the extent to which regeneration processes in Belfast actively seek out excluded groups in society.

Neil McInroy has been the Director of the Centre for Local Economic Studies based in Manchester since December 2002. His particular interests include regeneration, local economic development, the community and voluntary sector, and poverty. He is currently working on a pilot project for the Neighbourhood Renewal Unit, focusing on assisting Local Strategic Partnerships and Neighbourhood Management Pathfinders in improving their evidence needs. He is also involved in work in the Republic of Ireland – assessing the role of the community and voluntary sector in addressing health poverty.

Christopher Miller is Reader in Health, Community and Policy Studies and Director of the Centre for Local Democracy, University of the West of England, Bristol.

X

Recent publications include *Producing Welfare: A Modern Agenda* (2004, Palgrave Macmillan).

Dr Andy Pike is Senior Lecturer at the Centre for Urban and Regional Development Studies (CURDS), University of Newcastle, UK. His research interests are in the geographical political economy of local and regional development. He is currently working on projects about place-dependent brands and local development, de-mutualization in the brewing industry and the economic viability and self-containment of geographical economies.

Dr Peter O'Brien is Regional Policy Officer at the Northern TUC, where he leads on all policy matters relating to economic development, governance and industrial relations.

Dr Mike Rowe was a civil servant before taking up research at Nottingham Trent University, and now at the University of Liverpool. Some of his recent work has been on the changing nature of accountability and governance in the public sector, particularly in the context of local partnerships. He also has research interests in the roles of commissions of inquiry in the policy process.

Dr David Silbergh is Senior Lecturer at Glasgow Caledonian University, based in the Centre for Public Policy and Management. His main research focus is public administration and sustainable development in Europe and his recent research work includes a study of the vertical and horizontal implementation of structural funds in Central and Eastern Europe for The World Bank.

Stuart Smith BSc MSc (DIC) is Director of Consultancy at the Wood Holmes Group. Stuart has several years' experience of working in environmental, regeneration and strategy development. He is particularly interested in understanding complexity in regeneration and the knowledge-sharing processes that are vital to regeneration success. Stuart has pioneered community-centric approaches to regeneration and future visioning.

Dr Alan Southern is Senior Lecturer at the University of Liverpool Management School. His recent research has focused on the processes of regeneration, and more specifically on sustainable enterprise in areas of deprivation. He has previously worked on a number of projects that have evaluated regeneration in the North-East and North-West of England.

Stuart Speeden is Head of the Centre for Local Policy Studies at Edge Hill University. He has worked widely in research and consultancy on equality, diversity and social inclusion. He is joint author (with Julian Clarke) of the *Equality Standard for Local Government*. Together with Mick Carpenter and Belinda Freda, he is currently co-editing a book for Policy Press entitled *Open to all? Labour Markets, Equality and Human Rights*.

John Tomaney is Professor of Regional Governance and works at the Centre for Urban and Regional Development Studies, Newcastle University. He is co-author (with Andy Pike and Andres Rodriguez-Pose) of *Local and Regional Development* (2006, Routledge).

Alan Townsend is Emeritus Professor of Regional Regeneration and Development Studies, University of Durham and Chair of Regeneration, Wear Valley District Council. He became Chair of his mining village Community Partnership, and then a local Councillor and Council Committee Chair, working on the Single Regeneration Budget and Neighbourhood Renewal Fund for his area. Much of his recent work, including city employment growth, Local Strategic Partnerships and multi-level governance is available at odpm.gov.uk, by searching for 'icrrds'.

Preface

In seeking to make sense of the experience of contemporary regeneration practice there appears to be a tension which remains unresolved: about whether it is possible to reconcile the competing interests of civic or managerial elites with those of local residents. Since 1997 the claim has been that these tensions are more apparent than real. In practice it is argued that it is possible to develop policies and models of engagement which bring together the perceived needs of local residents with those priorities set by central government agencies or regeneration professionals.

Whilst regeneration activity has been concerned with the physical and economic renewal of urban areas, more recent initiatives have focused on raising the social capital and neighbourhood capacity of local communities. This latter development is an acknowledgement of the need to embed change and to ensure that the 'life' or impact of regeneration measures survive the exit of specialist staff or specialist measures.

Despite the claim by present and past governments of concerns with the expectations and experiences of local residents, the evidence suggests that practice is patchy and uneven. More significantly, perhaps, there may exist a mismatch between the needs and aspirations of local residents and those of central government. Whilst the former may seek to ensure an improvement in the quality of the environment and their lives through cleaner neighbourhoods, safer communities and good quality public services, the latter may seek to redefine the neighbourhood in terms of securing inward investment, the creation of jobs and a revived economy. More crucially, local residents may wish to engage in a dialogue about the regeneration initiative and to shape its priorities. This may in itself raise potential conflicts between the processes adopted and the eventual outcomes or practice.

This snapshot of the competing needs that can give rise to localized conflicts and/or misunderstandings on both sides also conceals what has become a 'traditional' approach to regeneration. This model has certain characteristics which successive approaches have shared. These are:

- A spatial definition of the distinct area to be regenerated
- An externally set framework within which activities are funded and defined
- A specialist team brought in to deliver
- An emphasis on multi-agency approaches cutting across the public/private/voluntary sectors

- An externally set performance management system
- An externally set time frame
- Specific resources which are short term.

It is because of these features that we have brought together a number of academics and practitioners to examine current practices and to anticipate new demands. Thus it is the intention of this book to reflect on current experiences and discuss what we feel are significant gaps in practice. Whilst this is an edited collection, our concern has been to provide a shape and coherence for what follows. Whilst we are all writers on regeneration, we are also local residents and active, in different ways, in our local communities. We are, therefore, seeking to 'bridge' what is an artificial construct between those who observe and reflect upon change and those who live and experience the changes and challenges of city life.

The structure of this collection is informed by our collective sense that it is necessary both to reflect upon past and present practice and, more crucially, to anticipate some of the changes or challenges inherent in current initiatives. The stimulus for this collection came from the debate and discussions at the Fourth Regeneration Management Research Network event hosted by the University of Liverpool in June 2004.

The collection of essays is organized as follows:

Part One provides a context to contemporary practice and initiatives present in the UK. Scott Dickinson reflects upon policies and practice since 1997 and points to the difficulties in making sense of what has happened, and Neil McInroy sets out a case for including the concepts of complexity and management by way of understanding the challenges faced not only at a national level but also at a local level.

Part Two provides four essays examining current practice. A major policy since 1997 has been the emergence of 'partnerships' as a key delivery agent. Mike Rowe and Andy Pike and his colleagues examine this approach, pointing to real problems in generalizing this model across public and private sectors and assessing alternative models. Lorraine Johnston and Jon Coaffee discuss the nature of managing involvement and participation policies. Ruth McAllister draws upon her experience of working in Belfast to examine the practice of managing inclusion.

Part Three draws upon the work of Joyce Liddle and Stuart Smith, who review models of evaluation, and Andrew Coulson who examines partnership structures to explore how accountability is understood by different partners.

Part Four brings together a series of essays which examine the gaps in understanding and practice. It is in this section that we seek to extend our understanding of what has happened and what has been omitted from existing research and practice. Marjorie Mayo and her colleagues look at the capacity of community-based practitioners to learn from and influence local practice, Stuart Speeden addresses the significance of equality and why it is missing in much regeneration activity and David Silbergh and Calum Macleod reflect on the extent to which, and the importance of how, the EU has shaped current UK practice.

Acknowledgements

The editors would like to thank all those who agreed to contribute to this collection of essays. In particular, we want to thank Carole Brocken (at the Centre for Local Policy Studies office at Edge Hill) for her help and patience!

We would also like to express our thanks to Francesca Heslop and Emma Joyes at Routledge for their support, advice and assistance.

Introduction

The central argument explored in this book is that there remain significant gaps in UK regeneration practice and understanding. These 'absences' indicate, we suggest, that there are important implications for policy makers, regeneration practitioners and those involved in research and evaluation. At one level the absences can be explained by the sheer complexity of the regeneration process itself. It is self-evident that not all needs or expectations can be realized within a relatively short time frame which is the common model of regeneration initiatives, and it can also be claimed that in raising local people's expectations more will be lost than gained. Furthermore, the UK regeneration model has been shaped, until relatively recently, by short-termism and 'quick fixes'.

At another level the argument would be that these significant gaps in practice and understanding are not new. On the contrary, the importance of equalities and the professional and practice dilemmas faced by community-based practitioners were present in the earliest forms of regeneration initiatives in the late 1960s. The (contested) story of the Urban Programme and the Community Development Projects (CDP) (Loney 1983) illustrates how central the issues of race and class were to the introduction of the Urban Programme. The analysis of urban poverty by the CDP programme illustrated the relative powerlessness of working class communities. This approach became marginalized as policy elites and decision makers focused upon physical and economic changes rather than social or structural change.

Finally, on a tertiary level we could frame the discussion in explicitly theoretical and conceptual terms. In this model current practice, especially since 1997 and the 'urban renaissance' promoted by New Labour, has represented a continuity in thinking (rather than a dis-continuity) with its emphasis in making deprived urban areas 'safe' for investment and renewal. In other words urban regeneration practice has always been characterized by the needs of outsiders (the policy making/practice community) rather than the needs of the insiders (local people, local activists and community-based organizations).

In tracing the practice and experience of UK-based regeneration initiatives we have been aware of the need to recapture those potential absences and to put them in context. This edited collection is, therefore, organized so that there is explicit reference to learning and understanding. We think that the following themes help to frame what follows:

- Learning from the complexities of initiatives
- Making sense of practice
- Understanding the significance of accountability
- Defining the new challenges and gaps.

LEARNING FROM THE COMPLEXITIES OF INITIATIVES

The complex range of urban regeneration initiatives since the late 1960s can often obscure their shared approaches to regeneration management practice and we are aware that there is a need to situate each specific programme in the context of their time and are also, ourselves, advocates of investigating each programme's success or failure and examining their impact against the goals set at the time. We also want to take a broader view of these different programmes, because we think it important to engage in a more holistic approach. This not only attempts to measure their impact over a generation but also tries to identify their themes and approaches which are similar to the process leading up to New Labour's White Paper on Urban Policy in 2000 which was focused upon the former rather than the latter.

We think we can identify those key themes which are common and from 1997 an approach which whilst seeking a break from the past is, in practice, a continuity of approach.

The common themes are:

- An emphasis on physical renewal
- A concern with employment as a route out of poverty
- A failure to learn from experience.

The apparent breaks with the past are:

- A stress on multi-agency working
- A stated focus on collaboration between agencies and residents
- An emphasis on sustainability
- An emergence of user voices
- A recognition that the quality of measures is as important as measuring outputs.

These common themes illustrate the need to contextualize practice and to assess the barriers to learning. We want to suggest that the crucial factors in learning from regeneration practice are the absence of understanding of the particular local dynamics present in an area and the imposition of a set of practices from the outside. Whilst many regeneration initiatives have been labelled as short term this is, in our view, to miss the point. If you do not fully engage with the processes of analysing and understanding the local circumstances it follows that your 'solution' will be incomplete. The structure of the UK government policy-making process is itself geared to centralized decision-making, whilst the scope for local discretion in decision-making has become narrower over the past 30 years. In practice regeneration initiatives have always sat outside local politics and local decision-making. We are suggesting that an inability to learn, to generalize that learning and then to apply the lessons learnt was inevitable given the organizational and structural arrangements which existed. However, as we explore in Part One of this book, it is necessary to reflect upon practices and to interpret that learning.

MAKING SENSE OF PRACTICE

Since 1997 there has been an explicit emphasis on partnership and collaboration. In many ways, as we have indicated above, these represent 'new' or 'innovative' approaches to regeneration practice which imply both a break with the past and evidence of learning from previous policies.

There can be no doubt that the proliferation of partnership working does represent something new. The question as to whether this dates from 1997 is something we explore in Part Two of this collection. At this stage, we want to highlight why partnership working and collaboration represent the potential to share learning and to inform current practice and why this represents some real challenges for regeneration professionals.

The debate about what constitutes a partnership is not a semantic one. Whilst the language of partnership working is in danger of being debased we can identify some pre-conditions which might help us in making sense of practice. These pre-conditions might encompass the following:

- Explicit recognition of difference in power and status
- Commitment to learning and reflection upon practice
- Practice which actively seeks alternative perspectives
- Multi-agency working which is informed by a recognition of different approaches
- Evidence of learning from practice.

In Part Two of the collection we explore the ways in which different models and approaches have (or not) engaged with these 'pre-conditions'. In our view the evidence still remains patchy and uneven, but an essential prerequisite for applying the lessons learnt or for making sense of practice is an emphasis on professional development and enhancing the capacity of professional agencies to engage with local communities. In our view it is the absence of both a strategic and practical emphasis on learning from practice and experience which limits the potential of regeneration practitioners as well as limiting the access of local community activists to regeneration initiatives.

UNDERSTANDING THE SIGNIFICANCE OF ACCOUNTABILITY

The ways in which contemporary (and past) regeneration initiatives are held to account illustrate our concern with the gaps and absences in practice which need to be 'reclaimed'. It is evident in a number of reports (NRU 2002, 2004) that the ways in which regeneration projects demonstrate their accountability are open to interpretation. Whilst formal structures do exist and local regeneration managers often describe the burden of demonstrating their progress to different interest groups, it is the information processes which are themselves hidden.

The formal mechanisms are, largely, reactive. They require local managers to place an emphasis on meeting defined outcomes. The scope for review and reflection which can then influence practice is limited. Formal evaluations, as we discuss, are often unused and become yet another policy paper which has no life beyond meeting an internally defined requirement.

The trend since 1997 has been to establish new forms of local governance (and accountability) as part of the succession strategy of local initiatives. The extent to which local managers or local people (who may find themselves part of local boards) are prepared for their roles and responsibilities is mixed. Here too new forms of accountability are being developed which often do not take account of the immediate needs of local board members, nor do they place the new board in context.

We want to explore these developments and suggest that the composition of local boards often under-assesses the needs of local board members and fails to take account of the potential risks those boards pose for local democracy and decision-making.

DEFINING THE NEW CHALLENGES AND GAPS

A primary purpose of this collection is to bring together writers and practitioners who are actively engaged in the processes of learning from and working with local regeneration practitioners. In this context it is evident that the external policy environment has a significant role to play and it is in this context that we want to understand the impact of the European Union (EU). Whilst it does have a significant role in terms of providing resources through its various funding regimes, it is in the models and conceptual understanding of regeneration that its significance lies.

Perhaps the two key absences in the discussion of regeneration practice rest upon:

- Equalities and regeneration
- Community practice.

In the area of equalities, whilst we can trace the significance of these back to the Urban Programme in the 1960s they have remained largely absent in contemporary initiatives.

Despite the emphasis placed upon mainstreaming and the promotion of diversity the issues of race and equality practice remains controversial. By exploring its significance we hope to bring it back to the centre and examine its absence in a broader theoretical and conceptual sense.

The role of community practice has been seen as a centrepiece of the New Labour Neighbourhood Renewal Strategy (NRS), yet the support given to community-based workers and the expectations placed upon them are often in direct conflict. We want to explore the current context and to reframe their experience in a new way. Developing professional and ethical guidelines for community practitioners would, we believe, place their role in a different and much more important context. It would have direct implications for training and employment rights and place more responsibility on commissioning agencies to provide supervision and support. It can also provide a point of direct engagement with local people and local agencies.

CONCLUSION

These themes are discussed below. We hope that what follows will act as a contribution to further debate and will, also, help to frame a much wider discussion on training, staff development and practice for both regeneration professionals and local community-based organizations. As you will see each section contains a focused statement of its purpose and structure. We start by providing a more detailed context to current practice.

Context

KEY THEMES

- Developing a sense of current and anticipated practice.
- Emerging trends in UK regeneration management.
- Defining the complexity of regeneration management.

LEARNING POINTS

By the end of Part One we hope that you will be able to:

- Develop an understanding of the competing models of regeneration management in the UK.
- Identify the key trends in regeneration management practice.
- Reflect upon the ways that different approaches have addressed regeneration activity.
- Begin to develop a sense of the impact of regeneration management approaches on local areas.

CONTEXT SETTING

The three chapters in Part One provide a necessary context to the practice of regeneration management in the UK and the ways in which such practice is subject to change. In the first chapter (by the editors) the primary focus is on the context of current practice. In part we provide an overview and, at the same time, seek to sketch out what we believe are the key developments in regeneration management practices. This context is necessary because it demonstrates that the 'story' of regeneration management is both contested and open to change. We are not arguing that the outcomes of regeneration activity can be anticipated in specific detail. On the contrary, as this collection of essays suggests, the complexity of activity, the presence of competing interests and the broad political, social and economic factors which shape much regeneration activity change over time. What we do suggest is that these complex interrelationships can lead to significant differences between local regeneration initiatives over time and within local initiatives.

Scott Dickinson's chapter is an attempt to rehearse some of the competing policy debates over the last decade and to point to the current trends in regeneration management practice. In particular, he describes the ways in which different initiatives have resulted in unintended outcomes, which have, in turn, shaped the next phase of regeneration management activity. He identifies the ways in which central government departments and/or agencies have developed different performance management systems both to increase their capacity to gather appropriate data or intelligence and to define the scope of regeneration initiatives. These attempts to understand what is happening within very localized initiatives and to benchmark the activity against externally defined indicators illustrate a recurrent tension in regeneration management practice. This tension is one in which the needs of localities are often set against those who fund or initiate regeneration activity.

Neil McInroy explores these competing tensions by examining the ways in which regeneration management is, itself, informed by management practice which acknowledges both the political tensions inherent in initiatives and the capacities of agencies to respond to such complexities. As a consequence his essay is, essentially, a demand to accept the complexity of the interactions and processes and to place more significance on the experiences and knowledge of local practitioners and residents.

Chapter 1

Context

Marking the transition

*John Diamond, Joyce Liddle, Alan Southern
and Alan Townsend*

INTRODUCTION

Regeneration practice in the UK has entered a significant phase in its development. It is now possible to think of this phase as a process of transition. This phase can be understood by reference to the fact that it is nearly 40 years since the launch of the Urban Programme, 25 years since the urban disorders of the early 1980s and nearly 10 years since the New Labour government introduced a range of initiatives (including the New Deal for Communities) and established the Social Exclusion Unit (SEU). Whilst the New Labour administration have initiated a range of policy reviews and new developments since 1997, it is possible to identify a number of recurring themes:

- A willingness to target resources from the centre to 'deprived' neighbourhoods
- A reluctance to accept pre-existing structures of governance and service delivery as a given
- An insistence that collaboration across the public, private and voluntary and community sectors is a prerequisite
- An expectation that successful regeneration initiatives have the potential to renew civil society.

TARGETING RESOURCES TO 'DEPRIVED' NEIGHBOURHOODS

Since 1997 the Labour government has experimented with a range of different approaches to ensure that resources are linked to the achievement of specific outcomes. This process of seeking to target resources to realize highly specific outputs has not always been well received, but in seeking to explore the significance of this, and its impact upon regeneration processes as well as the management and governance of cities, we need to note the following:

- The introduction of targets and those associated with the Neighbourhood Renewal Strategy (NRS) signalled a new departure in terms of the conventional relationship between the centre and local government. The NRS set out a number of Public Service Agreements (PSA) which linked funding to the achievement of targets associated with education, health and community safety.
- Such targets indicated a desire by central government to set their priorities for local communities irrespective of whether they were congruent with the priorities of local agencies.
- The implications of this target-setting (which has undergone change and revision over the last few years), was that without such targets the priorities of the government could not be achieved.

This process is not without its problems and has had a number of unintended consequences, such as giving a greater priority to meeting the target and a lack of awareness (at all levels of government) that this might result in poorer service delivery within communities.

In addition, the effect of target-setting placed the onus of responsibility on service professionals to manage their departments or agencies, sometimes at the expense of enhancing local accountability or local responsiveness. As we explore in some of the subsequent chapters, the role of partnership managers and/or regeneration professionals assumed a greater significance in the lives of local people than the institutions of local government or local democracy.

THE REJECTION OF PRE-EXISTING STRUCTURES AS A GIVEN

A feature of the Labour government's programme since 1997 has been its willingness to establish new agencies or reform existing systems to meet their targets. This approach has had a direct impact on the structures and organizational framework of local government. We can see, over time, how their approach has altered the relationships between locally elected members, professionals and local residents or service users.

The eagerness to embark on this programme of reorganization implies that the new government was not convinced that the structures before 1997 were capable of delivering its social, economic and policy objectives. We can assume that the combination of organizational change and a shift in the way services were expected to demonstrate their effectiveness has had a destabilizing effect on local governance systems and processes.

In some respects this desire to reform the structures as well as defining specific targets suggests a link with the reforms introduced by many Labour-run local authorities in the 1980s. At that time there was an introduction of specialist units or agencies to promote local economic development, tenant and community participation, equal opportunities and service decentralization to local neighbourhoods. This reform was predicated upon the belief that the existing systems were incapable of responding to the priorities set by local councillors. Specialist units were expected to act both as providers of new services and as change agents within local authority structures. Over a decade or more later the new Labour government created a range of units to promote change across a wide spectrum of central and local government activity. The consequences of these changes are difficult to assess. However, we can see how they have added more complexity to the local management of services and the decision or resource allocation processes.

THE NEED FOR COLLABORATION ACROSS DIFFERENT SECTORS

The most useful example to illustrate the approach of the government after 1997 is its promotion of 'partnerships' to effect its reform programme. We are not suggesting that partnership working is new and that it was invented after 1997. On the contrary the Conservative administration of John Major had, since 1990, introduced a number of regeneration initiatives which took as their starting point the requirement for local partnerships to be established as a pre-condition for funding. New Labour's approach was a continuation and expansion of this idea.

The sheer number of partnerships across a range of different initiatives represents something slightly different. The difference is that the period after 1997 marks a transition from partnerships being 'new' to their being the 'norm' at regional, subregional, local and neighbourhood level. As a consequence the task of mapping the changing governance frameworks within which services now sit becomes more complex and challenging. At times it is difficult to identify where accountability or decision-making rests. Whereas with large scale infrastructure or capital building arrangements (involving the public and private sector) the need to agree contracts provides one route for exploring accountability, this is not the case with other forms of service delivery. Across a wide range of services it is harder to pinpoint the place where decisions are taken. We can conclude that partnerships are a given but it is much more difficult to assess their long term impact.

REGENERATION INITIATIVES HAVE THE POTENTIAL TO RENEW CIVIL SOCIETY

The assertion made by Labour in its NRS was that their approach to neighbourhood renewal would enhance the status, vitality and significance of local communities and civil society. This claim was underpinned by the creation of Community Empowerment Networks to work with Local Strategic Partnerships. In addition successive initiatives from the Home Office and the Office of the Deputy Prime Minister (ODPM) have focused upon the reform of the voluntary sector. The importance of engaging the voluntary and community sector as service partners or providers of services and in the funding and promotion of capacity building for the voluntary and community sector was emphasized. The NDC initiatives (a key regeneration initiative introduced earlier on in Labour's first term), included elected resident representatives on NDC boards.

Against this background of initiatives, programmes and commitments we can see how the Labour government sought to assert its desire to revitalize local civil society. The questions we explore in the chapters which follow seek to address the extent to which such claims can be justified.

MARKING A TRANSITION

We want to suggest, in this chapter, that this point of transition represents an important opportunity to reflect upon the lessons learnt from previous phases of regeneration in the UK and to set down some important markers by which we can assess the next decade of regeneration practice. We think that it is helpful for practitioners and policy makers to think of the present wave of regeneration activity as marking a transition for the following reasons:

- The local organizational and structural context within which regeneration initiatives are located has changed significantly
- The discourse of partnership and collaboration has become the norm by which initiatives are both described and assembled
- The decline of party political activity has accentuated the significance of regeneration initiatives as potential sites for renewing local political activity institutions.

We discuss each of these below.

CHANGES TO THE LOCAL ORGANIZATIONAL AND STRUCTURAL CONTEXT

The landscape or architecture of local governance has altered significantly since 1997. Alongside the changes discussed above there have been very significant changes in the management and political structures of local government. From 1997 onwards the Government have reformed (or 'modernized') the systems and structures of political decision-making at the local level. There are two changes which we think are worth noting. First, the Government has allowed for the election of local mayors with some responsibility to act as the lead political voice in local areas. Second, the Government have reformed the systems of local political decision-making by creating 'cabinets' of leading politicians and giving remaining councillors a scrutinizing role in monitoring the administrative process at a local level.

These changes, by themselves, do not radically transform the local context within which decisions are taken, they need to be seen as part of a wider picture of change. The importance attached to partnership working (discussed below) and the overall reform of the ways in which public services are managed raises much more fundamental challenges to the ways our cities and communities are managed and governed.

Since 1997 the Government has reinvented or reconfigured the role and function of local councillors. In part this has been achieved through changing the decision-making processes, but it has also been accompanied by diverting responsibility for a range of services away from local authorities either directly to service providers (schools) or by promoting the transfer of services to trusts or stand-alone agencies (housing). These changes have impacted directly on the political/community role of local councillors. They may be recast as neighbourhood champions, but in many towns and services they have little or no voice when it comes to setting local priorities or meeting locally defined needs.

This transformation of local government signals a key part of this phase of transition. We cannot know what the consequences of these changes will be. What we can assert is that the context, content and priorities of local regeneration initiatives now sit outside forms of local political accountability. We can, also, assume that these changes will become embedded over the next decade and that the map of local government, in a political sense, has been changed profoundly.

THE DISCOURSE OF PARTNERSHIP AND COLLABORATION

A second element which signals this process of transition can be seen in the language or discourse within which partnership working is discussed and conceptualized. We have already made the point that partnerships are seen as the preferred model of service delivery. Our concern here is to explore the implications this particular model has for institutions and processes of local governance and accountability.

We can expect that the precise label of partnerships may, over time, disappear to be replaced by the 'trust' model (as with the new Children's Service agenda). But regardless of the organizational or legal entity used there are four trends we can discern:

1 Multi-agency working is seen as the most effective way of organizing or configuring services. This has implications for staff and professional development both in terms of identifying the needs of specialist staff and ensuring that services are appropriately managed or coordinated. This, in turn, has significant implications for the leadership and direction of these services in terms of the skills and competencies expected, as well as the status and authority which senior managers will acquire.

2 An additional trend we can observe is the increased separation of such multi-functional teams or services from local political authority. New forms of

13

accountability will emerge over time, but we are witnessing a further distancing of service professionals from the authority and culture of local government institutions and working practices.

3 The priority afforded to partnerships or collaborative provision also has profound implications for service users. The isolation of agencies from structures of accountability at the local level shifts responsibility for involving local users to service professionals. We cannot assume that these shifts in responsibility will improve access to decision makers without structural changes in the management and organization of services.

4 The Labour government are, themselves, engaged in a reflection of how the structures of local government might change. These changes are predicated upon the assumption that some power will be devolved to neighbourhood fora. It is too early to comment, but these proposals indicate the significance of this transition phase.

THE DECLINE OF PARTY POLITICAL ACTIVITIES HAS ACCENTUATED THE SIGNIFICANCE OF REGENERATION INITIATIVES

As we have suggested the renewal of civil society has been claimed by the Government as one of their key objectives. The extent to which this claim can be justified is explored in a number of the chapters which follow. At this point we want to note that regeneration initiatives have the potential to be places where new forms of local democracy may emerge. There are two separate but interrelated processes under way at this time. Again, whilst we cannot anticipate their actual outcomes over time, we can observe new trends and developments which suggest this is yet another indication of this process of transition.

First, where they work effectively, regeneration initiatives are constructed around partnership across the public and voluntary and community sectors. Most regeneration initiatives have local residents as board members and a number are exploring ways in which they can transform themselves into local trusts with local residents having majority representation. This is resulting in new layers of activists being encouraged to participate directly in the monitoring and supervision of initiatives. Their local knowledge will be enhanced by the development of their skills and growing experience. Over time it may be possible to anticipate shifts in the relationships between professionals and residents so that local users are able to exert influence rather than being passive receivers of knowledge or decision-making.

The multiplicity of initiatives in localities is raising the significance of these programmes so that they do provide opportunities for local engagement and participation. At the same time the capacity of paid voluntary organizations to provide a leadership role may be under threat but again, over time, we cannot anticipate the nature and quality of outcomes for local residents to challenge or to exercise local neighbourhood leadership.

Second, the decline both of party political organizations as the site of local activity and the reduction in significance and authority of councillors creates a policy and political vacuum. It is here that empowered resident/community organizations can occupy the spaces left behind.

Whilst this may seem an over-optimistic reading of future trends, we note the resurgence of interest in community development processes and practices may indicate an additional element in this process of transition. The emergence of a form of 'localism' as part of discourse indicates the potential for change.

SUMMARY

We are suggesting that a reading of the current trends in regeneration practice and local or city management indicates that we are living through a period of transition. We are not ignoring the global or structural forces at play here, but we are suggesting that at the local or neighbourhood level there are some significant trends which need to be explored, debated and reflected upon. In the chapters which follow we examine these in more depth and point to the gaps in our knowledge and understanding. In particular we are concerned to examine and to reflect upon:

- The impact of initiatives on the capacity of local organizations and agencies to cope with the pressure for change.
- The ways in which the capacity of professionals, politicians and local residents has been stretched to absorb the demands for monitoring and evaluation.
- The implications for local governance of these changes and the emergence of local partnerships as the new sites of local decision-making.
- The 'absence' of an equality perspective and the ways in which the lived experience of regeneration and local management approaches can capture and hold this central dimension.
- The need for professionals to be aware of and responsive to the ethical and emotional demands those changes represent.
- The need for professionals to recognize the importance of measuring the impact of initiatives on the lives of local people.

Chapter 2

Urban regeneration

UK practice

Scott Dickinson

INTRODUCTION

Urban regeneration, by its very nature, is both a part of and a response to economic, social, technological, environmental and political changes. It mitigates the negative effects of the changes on an area and it remakes (or attempts to remake) an area's economic, social, technological, environmental and political infrastructure, so that it meets the revised demands of society. Local leaders have to decide how best to respond to the changes and then choose the 'tools' to do it. The tools may be based on the state or the market or mutual and voluntary action, or combinations of the three. The legislative and policy environment in which they are deployed varies over time (Appendix 1).

Recent guidance on how to assess government initiatives provides a reasonable working definition of what constitutes 'regeneration' in the UK. It says:

> *Regeneration* can be defined as the holistic process of reversing economic, social and physical decay in areas where it has reached a stage when market forces alone will not suffice. *Renewal* covers many of the same issues but has an additional focus on communities, the most disadvantaged areas and the quality of services they receive. Renewal objectives may be wide ranging but will seek to deliver improved work and business opportunities, improved residential attractiveness and improved public services. *Regional economic development* is the remit of the regional development agencies and involves regeneration and renewal but also other areas of activity (skills, innovation etc.) which are less area focused but contribute to the way the region is to develop.
>
> (ODPM 2004: 41)

This quotation shows that by definition a 'venue' for regeneration is also a venue for state intervention, as opposed to market solutions and/or voluntary action operating on their own. Indeed, there is little in UK regeneration that is not either initiated by the state or very quickly becomes focused on influencing the state's activities. However, as is argued below, the role of the state, the areas in which it seeks to intervene and the timing of those interventions has changed and is changing. To understand regeneration practice in the UK, one needs to keep an eye on these changes and work out how best to respond to them.

This chapter focuses on the development of regeneration policy and practice in England since New Labour took office in 1997. It looks at the interaction of state, market and voluntary and mutual activity, which in the UK is more often than not coalescing into a 'partnership approach' that frames and contains the tensions and conflicts of interests between different organizational forms and the groups that operate within them.

The chapter has three further sections. The next section outlines some of the social, economic and political changes that have affected both the need for continuing regeneration activity and the nature of that activity. The subsequent section outlines some of the state's responses to the changing landscape. The final section summarizes the main arguments and sets out the challenges facing local leaders and regeneration practitioners.

RECENT TRENDS: SOCIAL AND ECONOMIC CONTEXT

The introduction noted the relationship between regeneration and wider changes in society. This section looks at key economic, social and political changes that have affected regeneration, and the role of the state. In doing this, it also looks at the changing nature of the relationship between the individual and society.

GLOBALIZATION AND THE STATE

The role of the state has changed profoundly over the last 35 years. Globalization, as a theory and concept, has been used to frame people's understanding of the nature of social, technological and economic changes.[1] It has also produced an ideological paradigm that has been used to produce policies to discipline economies and states by restricting their perceived room for manoeuvre. This has led to a reconfiguration of the state's role in the economy to what has been termed 'the competition state', where the state intervenes to create competitive advantage, either at a general level or within specific sectors or locations. The process has been described as one where 'State managers . . . intervene in a growing range of economically relevant practices, institutions, functional systems and domains of the lifeworld to enhance competitiveness' (Jessop 2002: 233). Resulting in a level of complexity that 'renders the sorts of top-down intervention typical of the postwar KWNS [Keynesian Welfare Nation State] less effective – requiring the state [to] retreat from some areas of intervention and reinvent itself as a condition for more effective intervention in others' (Jessop 2002: 233).[2]

GROWTH OF SERVICE INDUSTRIES AND POLARIZATION

As the economy has restructured it has become more reliant on service industries which emphasize people, rather than capital equipment, as the key input in to the production process. The focus of state intervention has, therefore, moved accordingly to activities that seek to ensure people's employability, adaptability, skills and experience, in other words to build human capital (Cameron and Palan 2004: 133).

The service sector has bifurcated into high value added industries (e.g. finance, advertising, media and legal services) and low value added industries (e.g. hotels, catering and retail). This has resulted in polarization of the labour market, between well paid 'MacJobs' and low paid 'McJobs', with a disappearing middle, producing an hourglass or egg-timer shaped labour market (Goos *et al.* 2003: 70). This in turn has been accompanied by a twin-track approach to state interventions in the labour market, based on what has been termed 'flexploitation' for the low paid and unemployed, as a means of maintaining the supply of low paid labour; and 'flexicurity' for those in work, who are seen to 'add value' rather than costs to a firm, but who need to be transferable to new jobs, as the economy changes (Jessop 2002: 225).[3]

The changes in the labour market have a spatial impact that can be seen in regional and local disparities. At the regional level, the Government has focused on the disparities in regional gross value added (GVA) per worker.[4] The disparities in GVA per worker in different regions form the backdrop to much regeneration activity.

While showing its economic heels to the rest of the country, however, London provides the UK's primary example of localized social polarization, where the bottom end of the labour market lives cheek by jowl with the high end of the pay and value added scales. It is a city where life expectancies can vary by 10 years within the same local authority district, Camden. It includes areas with the lowest rates of participation in employment of any region in the UK: proving proximity to opportunities is no guarantee of access, ability or motivation.

It is this physical manifestation of inequality at regional and local levels that has informed much recent policy on regeneration and renewal. However, the paradox at the heart of the socially responsible competition state is that, in order to promote competitiveness, each region has to be free to maximize its economic growth, which means disparities can grow.

Thus, the changes and disparities in labour productivity and wealth may be driven by global economic forces but they are experienced as a localized phenomenon, and the points of reconnection (that is state intervention) are more often than not also local.[5] The period since 1997 has seen the state restrict its role in terms of macroeconomic activity, and grow its role in microeconomics, e.g., through competition policy; its relationship with the individual, e.g., through the skills agenda; and the management of the spatial implications of change, e.g., through the devolution agenda. This is the context in which regeneration operates. It offers opportunities, but it also carries certain risks, as it takes regeneration into sensitive areas. The next section looks at cultural changes that provide the context in which these localized and often personalized interventions occur and highlights some of the risks associated with the changes in regeneration policy and practice.

WIDER SOCIAL CHANGES: ATOMIZATION, INDIVIDUALIZATION AND NARCISSISM

The process of economic and political change has interacted with other social and cultural factors, where individuals have experienced the break-up of traditional collective identities.[6] Sennett, Beck and Beck-Gernsheim, Furedi and Lasch have captured aspects of this process's movement in different and insightful ways.

For Sennett, businesses are now characterized by three features. First, *discontinuous reinvention*, where, rather than reforming the way they operate, loose networked corporations reorganize themselves through breaks in the way they do things, in an open-ended experiment to gain productivity and/or shareholder value. Second, they are characterized by *flexible production/specialization*, with supply chains providing diversity in products and increased speed to market. Third comes *the concentration of power without centralization*, where islands of work lie offshore of a mainland of power, with the centre setting targets and carrying out audits of the responses (Sennett 1998: 47–57).

Sennett argues that these changes promote discontinuity, rather than loyalty and persistence, as the norm of working life. The new model, he suggests, mistakes movement for improvement and tends to alienate the person from their work and the work environment, rather than providing a space for creativity and fulfilment. It also tends to require geographical mobility and a lightness of ties to area and family, as the diktats of firm and market require flexibility from workers at all levels of organizations. In some cases this makes people value stability and community, as a refuge; in others it produces acquiescence to isolation and atomization with benign or malign indifference to one's neighbours.

The process of social disruption, however, has been seen by some to have positive aspects. The breakdown of traditional group identities, based around class, nationality, gender, race etc. opens up a process of individualization, where people are (forced to be) free to create their own biographies (Beck and Gernsheim 2002: 23). It has also been described as a negative process that leads to the disempowerment of the individual and reinforces a heightened sense of fear, and disengagement from politics as a means of making social progress (Furedi 2005).[7]

For Lasch, this movement is part of an unhealthy trend towards narcissism, with an over-heightened importance of a limited self, that is increasingly losing its sense of self-reliance, because capitalism 'has evolved a new political ideology, welfare liberalism, which absolves individuals of moral responsibility and treats them as victims of social circumstances,' and 'has evolved new forms of social control, which deal with the deviant

19

as a patient' (Lasch 1979: 218). The solipsist wrapped in their sense of victimhood and modern pathologies is susceptible then to both corporate marketing – 'it's all about you', 'because you're worth it' – and the state's creeping authority over personal behaviour and conduct – diet, exercise, parenting etc. – once considered private matters.

The atomization and alienation experienced in society interact with people's experience of the places they live in, work in and travel through. In the UK, the trend has been for increased anxiety over crime to an extent that changes consumption patterns (Hubbard 2003). The UK approach has been to draw heavily on the American neo-conservatives' response to crime and disorder, which developed the 'broken windows' thesis in 1982 and produced the now familiar zero tolerance and neighbourhood approach to policing (Wilson and Kelling 2004).

Thus, cultural changes have been Janus-faced: allowing the individual the fluidity to break out of traditional, limiting definitions of identity, while dislocating the previous forms of socialization and solidarity, leaving the individual susceptible to surrogate forms of authority from the state and the corporate world. These forms are based on a thera-peutic impulse, usually mixed with the state's and businesses' utilitarian and bureaucratic reflexes (Nolan 1998: 283). The practical implications of these cultural shifts, when mixed with the economic trends outlined above, mean that regeneration practitioners often hold a double-edged sword: working with people as individuals or communities to overcome depressing and debilitating circumstances, but at the same time, potentially policing and controlling them, as they react to the circumstances in which they find themselves. Circumstances that often no longer include self-help organizations, such as trades unions or educational associations, providing moral and practical leadership, but do include professionals who provide therapy and impose order, potentially undermining long-term self-reliance.

This section has set out in broad terms the economic, political and cultural changes that have affected contemporary regeneration practice. The next section provides a framework within which regeneration can be understood. It acts as a precursor to the chapter's conclusions, which outline the challenges and ethical questions regeneration practitioners face.

RESPONSES TO THE CHANGING ECONOMIC AND SOCIAL LANDSCAPE

This section sets out the basic framework within which policies are framed and the objectives they traditionally try to reach. It argues that regeneration and mainstream services are commingling, producing changes in each other and in the relationship they have with each other.

TYPES OF STATE INTERVENTION

This subsection looks at the basic framework for state intervention and the mix of options the state has at its disposal when attempting to promote regeneration activity. Where state intervention is considered appropriate, i.e., where there is said to be a market failure or a non-self-correcting inequality, it can take broadly three forms:

1 Legislation, regulation, and non-statutory guidance and norms, such as planning laws and guidance;
2 Taxes, tax exemptions and transfer payments/benefits, such as pensions and income support; and
3 The provision of facilities and services for use by residents and businesses, such as libraries, public space etc.

These interventions may be based on communities of interest/client groups, such as the retired or small firms, or they can be based on geographical areas, for example, enterprise and regeneration zones. They may take the form of mainstream policy and practice or special and area-based initiatives. It is these initiatives that have, to date, formed the core of what has traditionally been thought of as urban regeneration. They have had a range of (official) purposes, including to:

■ Address a specific problem for which normal budgetary allocations to agencies in an area are inadequate, such as the cost of land decontamination, much of which is currently covered by the quango English Partnerships;
■ Address a time-sensitive issue, such as a mass redundancy or community tensions, such as the Task Force to deal with the impact of Rover's closure on the West Midlands;
■ Experiment with the design and delivery of public services, such as the Neighbourhood Management Pathfinder Programme;
■ By-pass ineffective organizations, for example, City Challenge and Urban Development Corporations ignored local authorities considered not up to the job; and
■ Anticipate problems and intervene 'upstream' to prevent them or minimize their impact, such as the Sure Start initiative.

There have also been a number of unstated, but oft suspected purposes of these types of interventions, such as the 'policing' of areas with persistent problems in order to contain the situation, and the production of an image of action and concern with nothing more than placebo effects anticipated.

FROM THE PERIPHERY TO THE MAINSTREAM

The previous subsection set out a schematic framework to characterize state intervention for regeneration. This one looks at recent changes in the operation of the state in relation to regeneration. The state is increasingly acting like Sennett's corporation: it is characterized by punctuated activity and periodic reorganizations. Special initiatives have become the lingua franca of the mainstream service provider, and government has metamorphosed into an administrative core that sets targets and outsources delivery to an archipelago of managing agents and providers. This change allows nimble(ish) negotiation and experimentation in a dynamic operating environment. It also requires regular monitoring, audit and inspection, and evaluation in order to check on performance and to allow room for reflection on what is happening. Thus, mainstream activity is increasingly provisional and contingent, not unlike much regeneration work. Furthermore, with policy initiatives such as the National Neighbourhood Renewal Strategy and the Sustainable Communities plan, regeneration is becoming part of mainstream public service provision. This is perhaps exemplified by the Neighbourhood Renewal 'floor targets', which set targets for central government departments (and their delivery agents) to improve conditions in the most deprived areas in England. The targets are a significant subset of the public service agreement targets set by the Treasury for central government departments (whether targets are an effective tool is another issue; they are the Government's current preferred tool).

This commingling of regeneration policy and practice with the mainstream public services can be traced back to the drive for joined-up government/public services (Perri 6 1997; PIU 2000). It contains a mix of utilitarian and therapeutic impulses based on the rational argument that complex problems needed to be understood in sufficient (local and personal) detail, in order to deliver coordinated responses across a range of public services.

The drive for new solutions to complex problems has led to a plethora of new bodies and quasi-market approaches to delivery, which it is the task of another chapter to explain. It has also led to a process of mutual colonization among people working in the field, a process that is changing the nature and purposes of traditional professions. This process was highlighted by the Egan Review, which identified seven groups of 'core' occupations required to deliver the sustainable communities agenda:

1 Decision makers and implementers, such as local authority leaders;
2 Built environment occupations, for example, planners and urban designers;
3 Environmental occupations, including environmental health officers;
4 Social occupations, like housing and social services;
5 Economic occupations, embracing developers, investors and economic development professionals;
6 Community occupations, among them, neighbourhood wardens and professional and volunteer workers; and

7 Cross-cutting occupations, i.e., neighbourhood renewal and regeneration practitioners.[8]

Regeneration and neighbourhood renewal were identified as peculiar, cross-cutting occupations. Two further groups were identified as essential for delivery of sustainable communities: 'associated occupations', such as educators, the police and health service managers; and 'the wider public'. It is difficult to see any act of physical, economic or social regeneration not involving the occupations on these lists. The Egan Review concluded that, as far as specialisms were concerned, skill levels were pretty much OK. It was in the generic skills, such as leadership, communication, team work and project management that gaps were identified. The next subsection looks in more depth at leadership; however, it does not treat leadership simply as a skill.

LOCAL LEADERSHIP AND GOVERNANCE

This subsection looks at the role of leadership in regeneration. It does so by focusing on the strategic questions local leaders face and the arrangements they have for tackling them, rather than reviewing the tricks of the trade.[9]

Local leadership – involving business, public sector staff and elected members, trade unions and other voluntary sector and community representatives – operates within a system of local governance that is made up of vertical and horizontal networks (Stoker 2004: 9–27). Within these networks, local leaders have to manage the trade-offs and exploit the synergies between economic, social and environmental interests in order to promote the well-being of their areas. They do this either by seeking to cope with or to drive a set of dynamic processes that are only partially known and understood. They ask consciously or unconsciously: Are we trying to manage within constraints or are we trying to exercise choice over constraints? If they wish to exercise some choice over constraints, they need to identify the parameters they face and select which ones they wish to change (Dickinson 2005: 224–9).

The local authority and the local councillors are formally treated as *primus inter pares* in local arrangements, but with the decline in the membership of political parties and poor turnouts at elections, there is a perceived need to earn more than ballot box legitimacy. In practice this means elected politicians have increasingly had to work with other local leaders to develop participatory and deliberative democracy, through public consultations, neighbourhood fora, citizens' panels and locally run service delivery organizations. They have done this to help create coalitions to pursue local priorities, and to development a sense of community with some common purpose.[10]

The creation of Local Strategic Partnerships (LSPs) is a somewhat inappropriate response to the need to develop deliberative and participatory approaches to local decision-making. It is inappropriate, in that the Local Government Act 2000 does not require LSPs to be established, nor does it compel any body to participate in one. The

23

national evaluation of LSPs highlighted significant gaps in effective vertical and horizontal networking – one-third of LSPs had no links with their regional development agency, a fifth had no links to subregional partnerships and around one in seven had no links with their local learning and skills council (ODPM and DfT 2006: 69). In other words, after five years of the legislation many partnerships were not well placed to pull the 'levers of change', even if they had identified the changes that they wished to make. However, the evaluation also found that many local strategies were not grounded in evidence; that is they did not demonstrate an understanding of the constraints the area faced and, therefore, could not ask the strategic questions or set out the strategic options for regeneration in their areas. Thus, in many places the key challenge for regeneration practitioners is to get local leaders and publics to understand the situation they face and the options they have and then to develop the capacity to respond to them.

CONCLUSION

This chapter started by noting that regeneration practice is intertwined with wider changes in society. It suggested regeneration has changed to reflect the development of the competition state and its response to regions' divergent economic performance and to social polarization. It noted wider cultural changes that have seen the loss of traditional institutions of socialization and self-help and the twin processes of atomization and individualization. It argued that the state has used therapeutic and authoritarian interventions that often appear to empower the individual and communities but may in fact undermine self-reliance.

The chapter noted also that regeneration and mainstream services increasingly till the same soil and adopt the same methods. This commingling brings opportunities for influence over significant amounts of collective resources that could be used to intervene in areas to the benefit of those suffering as a consequence of globalization and social polarization; but it also contains the risks of co-option into interventions which may cut across the aims of many practitioners – whether they are economic development specialists who want robust independent firms that don't need state subsidies, or community development workers who want to develop active independent organizations that are not reliant on grants and are not compliant to the needs of the market or the state. Having set this risk-ridden scene, what are the options for those who want to make a difference?

Notwithstanding the messiness of the picture, it is possible to piece together a framework from current practice that could be used to inform local decision-making for progressive interventions.[11] The changes outlined earlier in the chapter highlighted the importance of *human capital* to the competition state; it is therefore inevitably a requirement of any contemporary regeneration activity to understand the make-up of local skills, employability and adaptability and the best routes to get people in to work (given that the economy is currently regularly producing new jobs within a 45 minute commute for most people). The ethical point for local leaders and practitioners alike is how best to negotiate the consequences of a two-tier labour market on the one hand and the enervating and socially debilitating effects of benefit dependency on the other. The need to improve the quality of local education is the common ground where all agree that gains can be made, but while education is a public good in and of itself, it is the supply of well-paid jobs that is the essential side of the equation: leaders and regeneration practitioners need to focus on the quality of the jobs, as well as the quality of the human labour going in to them.

The chapter also identified recent social dislocation. Local leaders and regeneration practitioners need to build their knowledge of the area's *social capital*, i.e. the levels of trust and interaction within and between different communities of interest and/or place. Where there are signs of fracture, they need to develop strategies to cope with or break the constraints. These strategies may include some local adaptation to a more mobile, consumerist society where benign indifference to one's neighbours and good service provision brings social stability – the locality as a well-run hotel. It may require practical interventions to promote trust and build bridges between communities – the locality with a sustainable, healthy, diverse community with equality of opportunity.[12] A further alternative is practical interventions to police communities through authoritarian and coercive interventions, such as criminalizing antisocial behaviour through the use of zero tolerance policies. The ethical and political issues suggested in this chapter are the extent to which state action is further undermining local communities' ability to generate and promote self-help and self-reliance, and to what extent it is genuinely building independence of spirit and action, where real esteem is earned from others by deeds judged against high standards. The question for practice is how to ensure regeneration activity enables people to exercise power, rather than engage in processes with predefined limits to the power available.

If the local economy is to grow, local leaders need to understand the quality and quantity of *private capital* in the area – that is the scale and competitiveness of financial, physical and intellectual capital available – that set the scope for wealth creation. They also need to appreciate and cater for the likely future needs of private capital, if a thriving economy is to be achieved and maintained. This means local leaders need to understand and seek to steer the development of the externalities produced by business activity, i.e., the impacts that firms have on their external environment. For example, local leaders could seek to promote the positive externalities of easy access to supply chains and a pool of skilled labour through the co-location of firms that operate in the same sector by supporting the development of science parks. They may also have to introduce business-friendly ways to manage the negative externalities of business operations, such as traffic congestion, e.g., through congestion charging. The question for leaders and regeneration practitioners here is to what extent the needs of business should override those of other groups, such as those forced off the roads by toll charges or those adversely affected by business friendly planning policies that squeeze the availability of land for housing.

25

The final piece in the jigsaw is an understanding of the quantity and quality of *public capital* in an area. Since 1997, the role of public services in improving economic performance and in improving the life chances of individuals living in deprived areas has been stated and restated, from the 'post-neoclassical endogenous growth theory' of Messrs Ball and Brown, to the work of the Social Exclusion Unit (SEU 2001). And it is true to say that with an increasingly mobile workforce (in both tiers of the labour market) good housing, health, education, transport and environmental amenities are required if an area is to attract and retain the workforce a strong, diverse and robust economy needs. So, local leaders need to marry the grand visions and strategic choices to the routine tasks of delivering clean streets, decent schools and humane social services. And they need to find ways to do this that do not undermine individuals' and communities' self-reliance and power of agency.

The concern for progressive local leaders and regeneration practitioners is two-fold: how to act so that inequalities are reduced, not managed or made palatable by the promise of mobility, and how to make sure that interventions promote independence, based on mutual respect rather than dependence on outside authority figures, bringing either solace or 'order', based on pity for the 'beneficiaries'.

These concerns are explored in the chapters which follow.

NOTES

1 This is not the place to review the process of globalization, nor the literature it has spawned. For the positive history see M. Wolf, *Why Globalization Works: The Case for the Global Market Economy*, London: Yale University Press, 2004; and for a contra view, see B. Kargarlitsky, *New Realism, New Barbarism: Socialist Theory in the Era of Globalization*, London: Pluto Press, 1999.

2 The existence of relatively high levels of demand for labour in the period 1997–2005 has also removed traditional bottom-up pressure for large scale macro-interventions.

3 It should be noted that minimum wage legislation has ameliorated some of the negative impacts of the UK's relatively unregulated labour market.

4 While the disparities that exist say between London and the North East to some extent reflect the different skills of the workforces in the two regions, they also reflect different industrial structures and London's 'urbanization economies' (based on public investments and the location of so many significant firms and decision makers).

5 The discourses around globalization and social exclusion began around the same time, the early 1970s, and can be seen to have similar triggers (Cameron and Palan 2004: 19). The discourse around sustainability also emerges at this point, out of the Club of Rome. However, the interaction of these discourses and their shared heritage founded on economic and environmental limits is beyond the scope of this chapter.

6 It has also seen the growth of 'identity politics' of race, faith and 'tribes' of one kind or another. This chapter does not address these issues, due to the confines of space.

7 This may also push the fearful into the arms of reactionary group politics – the 'dark side' of social capital – not covered in this chapter.

8 The Review set out to look at skills in the built environment, but it expanded its remit to fill the space implied by the sustainable communities agenda.

9 The literature on leadership is broad and deep. The approach used here reflects a bias in favour of understanding leadership in terms of situations and behaviour, rather than character traits or possession of an office.

10 Indeed this is now identified by the Audit Commission as the essence of good community leadership (Audit Commission 2003).

11 The Conclusion uses the terms human, social, private and public capital as shorthand. It is accepted that the terms are slippery and subject to debate and to some eyes have reactionary connotations.

12 Views may differ as to both how social capital is measured and its economic, social and political application and implications (e.g. PIU 2000). It may, of course, be used to confront governments and business, as well as provide self-policing of communities.

APPENDIX 2.1 A SELECTED HISTORY OF REGENERATION INITIATIVES IN ENGLAND 1960–2005

1960 *Employment Act* designates development districts

1961 Skelmersdale new town development designed to take 'overspill' from Merseyside

1963 Plans for a growth zone development in the North East; the Location of Offices Bureau encourages location outside London (most of it goes to the South East); Dawley new town to be established West Midlands

1964 *South East Study* projects 3.5m population increase from 1961–1981, (due to natural growth and immigration), leads to proposed new town/growth initiatives in Milton Keynes, Northampton, Peterborough, and Southampton-Portsmouth; Redditch new town starts in West Midlands; Washington new town designated in the North East; the Department for Economic Affairs sets about developing a National Plan based on indicative (spatial) planning

1965 Regional Studies of the West Midlands and the North West that conclude there is a need for new towns to take 'overspill' from the conurbations: *Control of Office Employment Act* restricts office development (not retail, etc.) in London and Birmingham; regional economic planning councils and boards established

1966 *Industrial Development Act* scraps development districts in favour of larger Development Areas and gives grant aid worth 40 per cent of the value of investments in development areas; the Selective Employment Tax favours manufacturing over service jobs (nationally); Royal Commission (Redcliffe Maud) established to look at local government in England: four attributes for 'units' sought: efficient use of resources, effective provision of services, communal consciousness and whole area planning issues – the attributes prove not to be coterminous

1967 Maud Committee recommends a new management structure for local government, based on a few policy committees and a central policy making committee; Regional Employment Premium (REP) offers grants to manufacturing firms creating jobs in development areas

1968 Dawley is renamed Telford as a further new town development begins in order to take account of the 1965 West Midlands Study; Warrington and central Lancashire (Preston and Leyland) are designated as new town developments for Manchester's 'overspill'

1969 Community Development Programme; *Hunt Report* on the needs of 'Intermediate Areas'

1971 *Town and Country Planning Act* introduces 'planning gain'

1972 Club of Rome produces *Limits to Growth* and UN Stockholm Conference on Human Environment puts environmental issues on the agenda and provides a narrative of limits and negative unintended consequences of man's action; Inner Area Studies

1973 UK accession to the EU sees the introduction of EEC Regional Policy

1974 Local Government reorganization – Metropolitan Counties and National Parks committees; the term social exclusion makes its appearance in its modern guise, it is used to describe those without social insurance in France

1975 European Regional Development Fund (ERDF) is established

1976 REP abolished due to EEC rules

1978 Urban Programme (7 areas) and Inner Urban Partnerships (15 areas)

1979 Assisted Areas map cuts coverage from 43 per cent to 25 per cent of the UK population; the focus shifts from regional to urban policy, as depopulation of cities grows; Priority Estates for housing; ERDF reform

1980/81 *Local Government Planning and Land Act* establishes competitive tendering for certain local authority services; Urban Development Corporations (UDCs) and 11 Enterprise Zones (EZs) given freedom from local property taxes and planning rules; 1981 London and Liverpool Docklands UDCs started

1982 Financial management initiative in civil service: devolves budgets, establishes performance indicators and value for money reviews; Audit Commission established

1983/4 13 more EZs announced

1985 *Local Government Act* abolishes the Greater London Council and six metropolitan county councils; Estate Action starts

1987 Large scale voluntary transfers of housing stock from councils to registered social landlords

1988 Urban development grant and urban regeneration grant merged into city grant; reform of the EC's structural funds: principles of concentration, programming and 'additionality' drive regional programmes; *Local Government Finance Act* replaces domestic rates with the community charge

1989 *Local Government and Housing Act* introduces a new capital finance system and gives local authorities explicit economic development powers; Estate Management Board and Tenant Management Organizations established

1990 Rio Earth Summit triggers pressure to promote environmentally sustainable development; Local Training and Enterprise Councils (TECs) are established to deliver government programmes for business and workforce development under the leadership of local business people

1991 Competing for Quality Initiative introduces market testing into the civil service; City Challenge sets up integrated area-based interventions based on need and competitive bidding

1992 *Local Government Finance Act* replaces community charge with council tax; *Local Government Act* creates more unitary authorities in England

1993 *Delors White Paper* on *Growth, Competitiveness and Employment*; fourth reform of the EU Structural Funds sees return of some power to nation states, and the introduction of a community economic development strand to encourage 'bottom-up' activity; Estate Renewal Challenge Fund

1994 Integrated Regional Government Offices established: Single Regeneration Budget launched to promote cross-cutting interventions by partnerships in geographic areas of varying sizes, with money allocated on the basis of competitive bidding; and English Partnerships a single, national development agency to undertake significant regeneration projects

1995 Thames Gateway Regional Planning Guidance sets out a 30-mile long regeneration zone of areas for development to accompany the Channel Tunnel rail link

1996 Select Committee on Relations between Central and Local Government is established, in order to build joint-working between central and local government

1997 Kyoto Climate Change Conference; Scottish and Welsh vote in favour of devolution; *Building Partnerships for Prosperity* White Paper on regional development; Social Exclusion Unit established; independence of Bank of England from Government direction

1998 Education/Health/Employment Action Zones and New Deal for Communities, with a philosophical shift to resource allocation based on need rather than competitive bidding; *Bringing Britain Together: A National Strategy for Neighbourhood Renewal*; *The Learning Age: A Renaissance for a New Britain*, Green Paper, sets out the lifelong learning agenda; *Fairness at Work*, White Paper; Crime and Disorder Act; *Modern Local Government: In Touch with the People*, White Paper; National Minimum Wage Act; Human Rights Act; Home Office publishes *Supporting Families* consultation; Regional Development Agencies Act; DTI publishes *Our Competitive Future: Building the Knowledge Driven Economy*, White Paper

1999 RDAs take responsibility for SRB and over time a new 'single pot', with oversight from the Department of Trade and Industry; Sure Start Programme trailblazers; Crime and Disorder Partnerships start; Lord Roger's Urban Task Force sets out urban renaissance initiatives to respond to projections of 4m new households, while protecting greenbelts and greenfield sites; *Local Government Act* introduces 'best value'; *Greater London Act* establishes the framework for Greater London's governance of police, fire, transport and development; *Better Quality of Life, A Strategy for Sustainable Development in the UK*; Department of Health publishes *Our Healthier Nation*; Employment Relations Act (inc. right to trade union recognition); Youth Justice and Criminal Evidence Act; Immigration and Asylum Act

2000 Rural White Paper; Urban Regeneration Companies; Drug Action Teams;

Neighbourhood Renewal Unit (neighbourhood wardens and management schemes, plus neighbourhood renewal and community empowerment funds) starts operating; Thames Gateway Partnership established; *Local Government Act* introduces the power of well-being, requiring community strategies for an area and new political structures; mayors and cabinets with scrutiny committees and area committees; Cabinet Office Performance and Innovation Unit criticize poor coordination and delivery on 'the regional agenda'; HM Treasury (HMT) publishes *Productivity in the UK: The Evidence and the Government's Approach*

2001 *New Commitment to Neighbourhood Renewal Action Plan*; riots in Oldham, Burnley and Bradford (reports on the events indicate racial segregation and rivalry over the allocation of regeneration funds as causes); Learning and Skills Councils and Small Business Service replace TECs; *Urban and Rural White Papers*; Arms Length Management Companies for council housing; HMT publishes *Productivity in the UK: Progress Towards a Productive Economy, Productivity in the UK: Enterprise and the Productivity Challenge* and *Productivity in the UK 3 – The Regional Dimension*

2002 English Partnerships remit changed to focus on strategic sites; Audit Commission reforms best value regime to introduce Comprehensive Performance Assessments of local authorities; Regional Co-ordination Unit recommends a reduction in area based initiatives (ABIs) and a new process for initiating them

2003 *Sustainable Communities: Building for the Future*: £22bn of spending over three years including nine Housing Market Renewal Pathfinders in Birmingham/Sandwell, East Lancashire, Hull/East Ridings, Manchester/Salford, Merseyside, Newcastle/Gateshead, North Staffordshire, Oldham/Rochdale and South Yorkshire; Growth Areas in London and south east England (including new UDCs in Thurrock and the Thames Gateway); introduction of Regional Housing Boards; HM Treasury introduces the Business Growth Incentive scheme, allowing the retention of a proportion of the Business Rate produced in an area, based on business growth; Core Cities network publishes government sponsored research on *Cities, Regions and Competitiveness*, starting to make the case for city-regions; DTI publishes *Prosperity for All*; Home Office publishes *Building Civil Renewal*, HMT produces *Productivity in the UK 4 – The Local Dimension*

2004 *Making it Happen: The Northern Way*, outlines ways to promote economic growth in the north of England, followed by equivalent regional strategies for the rest of the England; Planning Bill to speed up planning processes and to ensure that community strategies have a spatial expression in Local Development Frameworks (replacing Unitary Development Plans) that fit with Regional Spatial Strategies (replacing Regional Planning Guidance); Egan Review reports on *Skills for Sustainable Communities*; ODPM publishes *Mainstream Public Services and their Impact on Deprived Neighbourhoods*, noting some bend of the spend, but gaps in quality of life measures

2005 *People, Places and Prosperity* updates the Communities Plan, supported by documents on *Homes for All*, *Why Neighbourhoods Matter* and *Vibrant Local Leadership*;

areas involved in the Northern Way initiative produce city-region strategies on improving economic performance; Local Economic Growth Incentive Scheme introduced by HM Treasury; Regional Assemblies (and London Mayor) to take over regional housing boards, also regional planning boards; Prime Minister's Strategy Unit publishes *Improving the Prospects of People Living in Areas of Multiple Deprivation in England*, noting there was a long way to go.

Chapter 3

Working with complexity

The key to effective management of the city?

Neil McInroy

INTRODUCTION

The management of cities and regeneration activity is driven by a need to manage effectively a complex range of factors, which are made increasingly complex by the policy framework. Complexity is seen by many as a problem, a barrier, a hindrance to more effective working. In short it's a negative. Complexity on the ground is commonly expressed in a sense that there are too many partnerships and meetings, many and competing views on the way forward and too many targets and difficulties in proving the real quality worth of activity. Thus, it is argued that because of this complexity, there is not enough 'doing' and not enough effective delivery. However, on the other hand it is important to recognize that this complexity is not going to disappear and in many respects is just the 'way of the regeneration world', and a necessary feature of good governance and effective interventions.

In this chapter, I wish to touch upon and recognize how the study of complexity[1] is a new and exciting interdisciplinary approach that can challenge traditional academic and policy divisions, frameworks and paradigms. There is a respected body of thought, which has been developing solidly over the last couple of decades, which has evolved from work in the physical and biological sciences into how complex systems work. This thinking, now being applied to human systems and to organizations, is gradually being incorporated into mainstream policy-making. As such this paper attempts to bring together this area of study with the practice of regeneration. We wish to explore these issues of complexity, by first looking at the factors that make the field of regeneration complex, exploring some arguments for reducing complexity, and some recent activities such as Local Area Agreements which in my view will reduce or at least set parameters to this complexity. However, the key message in this chapter is that we need to acknowledge and work with this concept so that we can both reflect upon our practice and anticipate potential barriers to effective working

WHY THE FIELD OF REGENERATION IS COMPLEX

Wicked issues

First, and quite simply, the field of regeneration is complex because it is dealing with 'wicked' issues. By wicked issues I am referring to problems that have many dimensions and as such are not easily solvable. For example, in unpacking worklessness, it is clear that an attempt to socially regenerate an area which is subject to a high proportion of people who are on job seekers allowance and incapacity benefit, is not a simple case of providing jobs, as in many locations the supply of jobs is not a problem. Instead, it is evident that regeneration of certain areas requires a range of interventions that aim to tackle an individual *and* collective culture of worklessness, reflected in a second or third generation of long-term unemployment, and a set of pernicious issues which mean that many, whilst unfit for work at present, could (through assistance) be fit and ready for work. However the process of getting individuals ready for work and creating a context in which this could work is not easy. Indeed, it is a 'wicked' task, requiring a sophisticated and complex interweaving of interventions and solutions. For instance, interventions would need to focus on:

- Increasing the supply of jobs through inward investment and/or business development activities
- Demonstrating to employers that local employees or employees from a particular area are ready and willing to work
- Assistance in getting people into work, through intermediary labour organizations and brokerage
- Assistance with developing and increasing self-esteem and understanding the concepts behind work
- Support whilst in work, ensuring that the new employees stick with it.

Clearly then the ability to manage this involves a range of planning and associated partnerships. Thus there is a complexity to the nature of the issues we face.

Interrelated factors

Second, one of the key reasons why the field of regeneration is complex is that the issues we deal with are all interrelated. For example if we look at the problems we see in regeneration – failing local economies, poor local environments, declining housing markets, low employment, crime and poverty – they are all very complex. What we see is that they are all interrelated, and are created by a range of social, economic, cultural, historical, environmental and physical factors. As a result of this interrelatedness nobody can be certain of the ideal starting point for a regeneration programme: it is impossible to know which factor is most important (e.g. are social factors more important than economic ones, and if so why and why is it not the reverse?) or how a blend of interventions that complement one another can be created.

This is particularly common in the field of health. For instance the problems of coronary heart disease are in many instances seen as being rooted in the individual and their lifestyle issues and choices, such as alcohol, smoking and lack of exercise. However, many health professionals recognize that to solve some of the concentrated geographical pockets of coronary heart disease, one needs to look at wider societal factors associated with poor housing, unemployment, stress and poor local facilities.

In an effort to solve this complicated set of interrelations, social scientists and those working on policy assume two main perspectives. First, they isolate policy areas, linking well-defined causes to well-defined effects. Thus those in the policy and regeneration fields are increasingly tending to look for solid links between policies and outcomes. Policy areas have been separated off, for example transport or housing, and policies are created under these banners. As a result of this perspective, driven by a desire for positive change, a range of funding streams have been developed. These funding streams are there to fulfil a particular function, or nuance, of a particular issue. Nevertheless they have created a heady brew of initiatives and funding pathways which are complex in terms of steering a path through the regeneration terrain.

Third, to accommodate this interrelated set of factors, a range of structures, including partnerships and other mechanisms for deciding on strategy, have been set up. In attempts to draw the interrelated factors together, each of these encompassing structures has its own strategy or plan, which frames interventions and brings together the aims of individual partners.

A multidisciplinary approach increases complexity

Regeneration covers many disciplines and policy areas because of the complex nature of the problems and their range. This breadth of policy means that many individuals come at the issue from different disciplines and perspectives. This multidisciplinary basis to regeneration means that it has many traditions and schools of thought and many perspectives that have a different emphasis. This creates tensions and increasing complexities, for instance the ongoing tension which emerges between those who favour social approaches to regeneration as opposed to economic approaches. Indeed these debates are consistently played out within agencies, in planning strategy and in discussing the best way forward.

In response to this, from a local government perspective, we see some areas creating departments and directorates which are at the corporate centre, giving regeneration a holistic view across a range of services and policy areas. In this local policy context for social and economic development, the interface between local strategies is of paramount importance. This agenda can be summarized as widening the focus of activity; as a result more divergent areas of policy making are being brought together.

Regeneration is a process

Regeneration is a process, and a complicated one at that. There are many issues that need to be considered. In reducing unemployment for example, it is not just a case of providing jobs. Many other elements are in play due to the number of interrelated factors, such as skills, providing the context to local investment, transport infrastructure and type of jobs. In addressing unemployment a set of interventions needs to be put in place and then the process of these interventions taking effect takes time.

These interventions attempt to tease out the many facets relating to the issue, and monitoring of these various strands of activity is required. There are now many sophisticated performance management systems being set up which gauge both quantitative and qualitative change, and ensure there are feedback and feedforward mechanisms in place. Monitoring and evaluation toolkits have been developed to better inform the policy process and bring together the information required to better direct any intervention. When used correctly this 'knitting' process can work: when it does it is a truly 'radical' project in that it attempts to provide a comprehensive policy mix and a solution to poor places and people.

ARGUMENTS FOR REDUCING COMPLEXITY

As regards how to reduce complexity, many answers are posited. Both practitioners and residents in the field of regeneration make the following suggestions:

- Fewer funding streams. There is a particular emphasis on central government joining-up budgets, and clearly there is some work to be done, but the government has started this. Bending the mainstream central and local government resources to meet the needs of people living in deprived neighbourhoods appears to be a reaction against the explosion in area-based initiatives, which have added to the complexity in the field of regeneration.
- Simple solutions, which focus on single issues. By trying to address one problem at a time regeneration would not get drawn into the complexities we come across now.
- Banks of best practice spread out across the country, a whole range of proven 'off-the-shelf' products could be applied to problems in any locality.
- Interventions that have predictable outcomes and results should be used, interventions that do not get bogged down in process.

There is a case to be made for reducing complexity, but there is a crucial caveat to these simple solutions to reducing complexity, which is that the relationship between policy and outcome is not always linear. It is not as straightforward as we would want or hope.

Regeneration policy and outcome is not straightforward

When you look at areas that are being regenerated, they are usually in a state of flux. There may be a churning of population, a changing picture of local health and education, pockets of enterprise alongside pockets of deprivation. When we have this highly localized scenario, it is not always that easy to discern what the issues are, or are going to be, and how they need to be addressed.

Thus the clear linear relationship between policy and outcome is confused due to the internal context. For instance, in an area which is socially changing, but where there are low levels of community activity, do you invest in a community centre when the demographics and picture of need is changing? If not, what do you do with the existing problem of low levels of community activity?

Furthermore, if what is considered a simple policy is introduced, it may be that it creates different actions and consequences. For example the development of a new community park in an inner city neighbourhood abutting the city centre, whilst intended for young and old people, with play facilities and areas for quiet contemplation, may attract a host of street drinkers who had been displaced from the central city centre squares: as a result the park becomes a different issue for the local community. Policies can consist of a large number of elements which in themselves can be simple, but they need to interact dynamically by exchanging energy or information if they are to solve even simple problems like the example above.

Similarly, thinking about the wider external context, including the global economy, it is very difficult to predict what is going to happen. It is chaotic, change is inevitable. Thus whilst complexity can be reduced in some instances and simple measures will work, it is increasingly difficult to create a tight link between policy and outcome. Of course in areas of social and economic stability things are easier: however, in many cases we are left with situations in which we need to work with complexity.

WORKING WITH THEORIES AND CONCEPTS OF COMPLEXITY

Complexity theory

Governments and organizations across the world are starting to think about what application complexity theory can have to the work that they do. Many large commercial companies are already using this complexity paradigm to inform the way that they conduct their business and to tackle complex issues within their organizations. Complexity thinking offers an explanation for why many of our current approaches to regeneration don't have all of the desired impacts and gives insight into the best way to tackle complex issues.

In looking at complexity in regeneration, it is evident that regeneration is not the only complex environment. Coming from a tradition in the natural sciences, theories of complexity are beginning to be applied more consistently to a range of other disciplines, including the social world. Therefore, complexity theory tells us, whether it is changes in the weather, traffic flow patterns, epidemics, the behaviour of groups of people on a Saturday night, that everything is interrelated. Continuously changing and unpredictable results and interventions are the norm.

There is, however, no need to embrace complexity just for the sake of it. There is no point in aiming for a situation in which people try to devise sophisticated techniques and means to solve problems when it may not be needed. However, whilst we should strive for simplicity and not over-complicate issues, we also need to work with complexity, recognizing that in some situations complex issues will need complex solutions. In working with complexity, we need to recognize three key things. In particular there is a need to:

1 Recognize different shapes of policy and types of adaptation
2 Use the local
3 Ensure creativity is supported.

Different shapes of policy and types of adaptation

It is important to recognize that adaptation can happen at a variety of scales whether neighbourhood, community, local authority area, subregional or regional. Thus the ability of mechanisms to create different processes, structures and styles should be recognized and supported. It is only through this structural and procedural adaptation that measures to address issues can be identified. The desire for institutional neatness and the blind application of best practice from elsewhere only serves to constrain adaptation, local knowledge and thus the abilities to address the issue. Mechanisms that can create different processes and structures in different places are providing a way forward, a way for policy to be more adaptive to local context. This is an emerging feature of the British policy landscape and is the key to a progressive agenda, which allows for complexity and difference between various places and people.

Use the local

A community, neighbourhood or area of a city is composed of thousands of individual needs. If we want to change the city for the better by changing its land use, its travel patterns, or its use of public spaces, for example, complexity tells us that top-down intervention, or implementing an a priori rigid plan, will either not make much of a difference or have an unpredicted or even counterproductive effect (as the example from the inner city park highlighted). There is a lack of adaptation to local circumstances from a top-down intervention or an off-the-shelf product: local information is required to put policy interventions in context.

Thus the community and local practitioners who know the local area best are the most valuable, as it is these local people and organizations which are most adaptive, most capable of dealing with the issues. The people involved in living with and within the system are the people best placed to improve it, since they often are in a position to see the problem, and have the greatest amount of direct information relating to that problem. This is all information which is likely to be above and beyond that provided by simple monitoring: we need to involve local people where appropriate and ensure that local knowledge from people working with local communities is captured.

Supporting creativity

Regeneration is akin to an art form, in that it involves creative thinkers and innovators. Creativity is a vital part of dealing with the complexity within regeneration: it is vital for positive change that we have people involved in regeneration who have the abilities and skills to think cross-sectorally, think differently, and think in the context of the problem. In this, more effort must be made to increase and retain regeneration skills within the sector. Many regional centres of excellence are looking at this sort of thing, though it must be ensured that they don't just focus on traditional skills but also set in train methods for developing innovative and creative skills as well. The Egan Review recently looked at the skills and training required by urban regeneration professionals, planning authorities and developers and how they need to work together in achieving measurable improvements to the communities they serve. It also considered how any skills gap can best be bridged. The review calls for a cultural change in the skills, behaviours, knowledge and training of more than 100 occupations involved in delivering sustainable communities.

The use of Local Area Agreements

Local Area Agreements (LAAs) were introduced in a government prospectus in July 2004 with the primary aim of improving the relationship between central and local government and Local Strategic Partnerships (ODPM 2004a). LAAs are expected to reach agreements that achieve local solutions by meeting local needs, whilst also contributing to national priorities and standards set by central government. Originally, the prospectus hoped to pilot nine LAAs, one for each of the English regions. However, as a result of unexpected demand by local and county authorities, 21 pilot LAAs[2] were announced across the country in October 2004. By March 2005 each of the chosen pilots released their visions, development and delivery prospects for their own individual LAA[3] and these were then signed off by the Local Government Minister, Nick Raynsford.

Background and context

Since their return to power in 1997 the Labour government have actively sought to reduce the amount of bureaucracy that exists between local and central government, with an emphasis on increasing the powers of local authorities. In recent years in particular, many local authorities have been taking a lead role in creating private and public partnerships which are delivering change locally and meeting central government targets. However, there is further recognition of the need of central and local government and their respective partners within LSPs, to do more in order to overcome disadvantage and improve quality of life.

The Local Area Agreement initiative is situated within the broader considerations of the Office of the Deputy Prime Minister as regards local government, local democracy and partnership working. In 2004, the ODPM released its 10-year vision for the future of local government (ODPM 2004b). This document is based around the key themes of improving leadership, citizen engagement and service delivery within local authorities as well as attempting to reduce the bureaucracy that exists between central, regional and local government.

The principles of Local Area Agreements

LAAs will require a step change in the way in which local and central government relate to each other in order to achieve priority outcomes at the local level. Figure 3.1 highlights a model of how each LAA pilot operates:

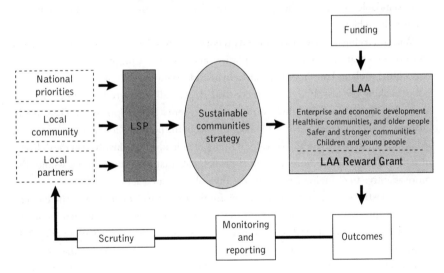

Figure 3.1 *The process of Local Area Agreements*

The Local Area Agreement package highlighted in the ODPM prospectus is based around four key elements as well as establishing the pilot LAAs. The four key elements are:

1 Simplified funding for safer and stronger communities
2 Strengthened local public service agreements

39

3 Strengthened National Strategy for Neighbourhood Renewal

4 A stronger role for government offices.

With regard to national outcomes and priorities and their relationship with the priorities set out by local authorities in their Local Area Agreement, the emphasis will be on delivering national outcomes in a way that reflects local priorities. The Community Strategy, for example, will play a key role in reflecting these local priorities as they reflect the aims set out in specific service plans. In terms of agreeing exactly what sources are involved in the Local Area Agreement, the Government Office (GO) for each region will play a key role in negotiating and signing off each agreement.

CONCLUSION

The field of regeneration is complex, but it is only a reflection of the complexity of the real world. Complexity needs to be embraced as a concept if we are to produce lasting impacts in regeneration. Complex solutions are a fundamental and key feature of good governance and healthy democracy. The search for simplicity in policy making is understandable, but if the policy process is to be improved, then a deeper understanding needs to be achieved.

What this refined model of complexity theory tells us is that we need to have processes and systems that are capable of adaptation and change. Complexity theory offers conceptual tools and methods that can help in understanding the complex nature of the policy making process. It argues that controlled, centrally delivered top-down policies are least effective because their very nature prevents adaptation to the continually changing world in which we live. On the other hand the potential for an inclusive nature in bottom-up strategies means a greater number of individuals are involved in the delivery of policy aims, and the more individual participants that contribute to the whole, the more adaptive to changing circumstances the policy-related actions will be.

The questions we need to reflect upon are the extent to which (even if the current initiatives through LAA are an attempt to simplify the process) they, in turn, generate unintended outcomes and, if so, whether they have the skills and capacity to adapt? At its most basic this refined model of complexity is an attempt to illustrate the extent to which local practitioners and residents hold valuable experience and knowledge which needs to be embedded in the policy and practice decision-making process. The risk associated with the LAA model is that the layer of decision-making is, itself, too distant from the site of intervention.

NOTES

1   Complexity is a broad term for describing and understanding a wide range of chaotic, dissipative, adaptive, and non-linear systems and phenomena.
2   The 21 LAA pilots are: Greenwich, Hammersmith and Fulham, Dorset, Devon, Kent, Brighton and Hove, Suffolk, Peterborough, Derby, Derbyshire, Telford and Wrekin, Coventry, Wolverhampton, Wigan, Knowsley, Stockton-on-Tees, Gateshead, Barnsley, Sheffield, Doncaster, Bradford.
3   The majority of Local Area Agreement Pilot documents are available at: http://www.idea-knowledge.gov.uk.

Part Two

Practice

KEY THEMES

■ Competing models of partnership working.
■ Developing alternative approaches to practice.
■ Managing participation and community involvement.
■ Managing practitioner and local interests.

LEARNING POINTS

By the end of Part Two we hope that you will be able to:

■ Identify the different models of partnership working present in regeneration initiatives.
■ Reflect upon the theoretical debates which inform partnership practice.
■ Develop an awareness and informed understanding of the practical and managerial issues raised by practitioner and resident participation in regeneration activity.

CONTEXT SETTING

These four chapters draw upon empirical work which has focused upon seeking to identify the different experiences of practitioners, residents and managers in regeneration initiatives.

In their different ways each chapter offers a snapshot of experiences from which the authors have attempted to draw conclusions. All of the chapters provide a context to their work and a review of the theoretical and policy literature.

In his chapter Mike Rowe provides an important and necessary contribution to the partnership debate by offering a set of definitions from which we can imagine partnership in practice. His analysis represents a very valuable set of perspectives on much of the contemporary literature. We feel that his approach stressing the relationships present in partnerships can provide an insight into practice which is generalizable from the particular.

Andy Pike and his colleagues describe another approach to imagining alternative sets of relationships. The presence or absence of trade unions in partnership working raises another set of necessary questions for regeneration practitioners. In particular, there remains a need to revisit the implications of their work in terms of how we make sense of training, professional development and the local knowledge trade unions can bring to local regeneration initiatives as well as their contribution to national policy development.

Jon Coaffee and Lorraine Johnston draw upon their knowledge, experience and understanding to identify the tensions present in local regeneration initiatives and, in particular, the tensions which exist between elected members, residents and practitioners. The role of elected members (as we discussed in Chapter 1) still remains a contested issue. This chapter highlights not only the theoretical and conceptual debates but also the practical implications of these tensions.

Ruth McAllister draws upon her experiences in Belfast to trace the policy and practice issues present in large regeneration initiatives with multiple aims and aspirations. She sets out the ways in which local regeneration initiatives seek to address a potentially diverse set of aims and the extent to which these can be met. She not only provides a sense of place in her chapter but also identifies the ways in which local regeneration managers and offices need to negotiate differences between competing interests.

Chapter 4

Partnerships

Models of working

Mike Rowe

A number of models of public policy focus upon the translation of ideas and proposals into practice. In all of these models, a key concern is that the theory that underpins any policy (that policy A will have effect B) should be clear and uncontested. There should also be few (if any) external factors that interfere in this simple and clear relationship (e.g. Hogwood and Gunn 1984: 199–206). That this simple, not to say obvious, idea is highly problematic is well captured in the frustration expressed in the title of Pressman and Wildavsky's (1973) book on implementation. One can easily imagine ministers and civil servants expressing similar frustrations as they survey the ruins of the now scarcely mentioned flagship programme, New Deal for Communities. Partnership after partnership has experienced problems and scarcely any are unblemished by accusations and/or open rifts. In part, this is to be expected. It is in the nature of regeneration that programmes will not please everyone and will provoke a degree of criticism, even hostility, whether warranted or not. However, the problems go far beyond questions about the appropriateness of individual funding decisions or other such local disputes. There is something about the link between policy and effect that needs examining in greater depth. Elsewhere, I have sought to outline some of the competing understandings of much used concepts (Rowe 2003, 2005) and here I turn to partnerships. The chapter will describe the forms that different partnerships take before going on to consider the understandings that these represent.

THE IDEA OF PARTNERSHIP

Partnerships can be located in the literature associated with networks (Newman 2001; Rhodes 1997). Thompson (1993) sketches out the key concepts underpinning networks: solidarity, altruism, loyalty, reciprocity and trust. They represent a more collaborative form of relationship compared to bureaucratic rationality and the competitive marketplace and, as such, networks are presented as an alternative to these traditional forms of governance (Rhodes even going so far as to redefine governance to mean networks). More recently, and particularly since the election of the Labour government in 1997, networks and partnerships have become central to the language of modernization in public services. Recognizing the rigidity and inflexibility of bureaucracy and the inequities that arise through competition, the government has sought to bring the strengths of networks to everything from health to capital investment.

It is in urban regeneration that the idea of partnerships has most currency. Fundamentally, the government argues that by working across organizational and sectoral boundaries, better value will be derived from public spending, particularly at a local level (Cabinet Office 1999; Department of Transport, Local Government and the Regions 2001; Social Exclusion Unit 1998). At the same time, the business sense of the private sector would be tempered by the social agendas of the public, voluntary and charitable sectors. More specifically, the benefits to be derived include:

- Greater sharing of information and resources between public agencies, and between the public, charitable, voluntary, community and business sectors;
- Better coordination of public services, securing efficiencies both in terms of cash savings and improved delivery;
- Engagement with local communities to better plan and design service provision, thus improving take-up and outcomes;
- Through participation, build capacity and 'social capital' in excluded communities;
- Allowing for experimentation and learning from small-scale initiatives, mainstreaming these where they prove effective;
- More effective interventions to deal with complex social problems (the 'wicked issues');
- Greater accountability and oversight of public services; and
- Improvements in local democratic life, both through participation in decision-making and in elections.

Local Strategic Partnerships, Community Strategies, Community Empowerment Networks, Neighbourhood Renewal Funding and a host of other initiatives have sought to develop the local infrastructure to enable these key benefits.

However, to suggest that networks are simply an alternative to hierarchies and markets is to simplify understandings of governance. Definitions of bureaucracy and models of perfect competition describe forms of organizational structure, relationships and of resource allocation that are not to be found in practice in such pure forms. The marketplace is heavily regulated because of market imperfections and information asymmetries. Hirschman (1970) has argued that, as an ideal type, markets would, in any case, be undesirable and self-destructive. On the other hand, it is all too easy to caricature organizations as archetypal bureaucracies. Rhodes (1996) suggests that the Benefits Agency was such an organization, yet there is substantial evidence of discretion and of flexibility in the manner in which it responds both to individual needs and to local circumstances (Huby and Dix 1992; National Audit Office 1991). Indeed, even security guards use discretion in the manner in which they perform gatekeeping duties (Rowe 1999, 2002).

Furthermore, the evidence of forms of competitive behaviour within bureaucracies is substantial (Niskanen 1971; Tullock 1965; Dunleavy 1991).

Within and between these complex combinations of bureaucratic and competitive forms of governance exist networks. Even where there is the opportunity for competition, Granovetter (1992) suggests that embeddedness, forms of long-term network relationship, are to be found in markets. At the same time, networks are to be found throughout the public sector (Flynn et al. 1996). Indeed, it is far too simplistic to talk of forms of governance replacing others, of markets replacing bureaucracy in health or education for example. At the same time, networks continue to exist and to operate regardless of the efforts to alter forms of governance. To see networks as a new paradigm for the public sector, replacing hierarchies and competition, is to misinterpret the nature of networks and of governance (Rowlinson 1997).

Perhaps more fundamentally, networks and partnerships are generally discussed, certainly as an ideal type, in a voluntary context. Those organizations and individuals involved wish to enter into the relationship for a clear and shared purpose. The necessary characteristics of a successful network (solidarity, altruism, loyalty, reciprocity and trust) cannot be imposed or artificially created (Kooiman 1993). Nor can networks simply be broken or replaced with some new form of governance. Despite changes to the forms of governance in the health care system, the professional networks continue to shape and undermine government intentions (Flynn et al. 1996).

Finally, in many cases, networks are far from the idyllic, trusting groupings described by their advocates. The medical profession has a history of concealing its members from external scrutiny and of protecting its own interests against others. Post Enron, the accounting profession's close relationship with clients has been exposed. In seeking to engage different sectors and individuals in partnerships, to ignore the potentially closed and exclusive character of networks is foolhardy.

In the context of regeneration partnerships, these points have particular relevance. Members of partnerships are not simply engaged in some form of new governance. Those from organizations, whether public, private, voluntary or community, are normally also engaged in some form of market, hierarchy, or both. Indeed, this is almost certainly the environment within which their future lies, having implications for their motivation, objectives and behaviour in any partnership context. Divorcing partnerships, and members of them, from the contexts within which they work is to fail to grasp some key influences and challenges to new ways of problem-solving and working. To separate partnerships as a new governance, operating separately from more traditionally understood forms of governance, is to both idealize the concept and to set it up to fail.

Far from being a simple way of tackling the complex problems of urban decline, partnerships bring additional problems. At the same time, government publications only set out a broad picture of what it is that partnerships are intended to achieve and what a good partnership might look like. Practitioners are left to develop their own detailed understandings and approaches. In essence, the connection between theory and effect is highly problematic and prone to the interference of many actors along the way,

47

each with a different interpretation of the theory and with interests that might conflict with the interests of the partnership. What is, perhaps, surprising is the lack of response to the problems of partnership working in practice to be found in government publications and guidance. Recent criticism from the National Audit Office (2004) has prompted some reflection on standards of governance (Neighbourhood Renewal Unit 2004), but not on the causes of problems. The remainder of this chapter will focus explicitly upon the nature of partnerships and the relationships that underpin these, situated as they are in a wider context of local politics and power.

THE PRACTICE OF PARTNERSHIP

Each of the narratives draws upon features and practices to be found in different partnerships and locations, none being simply an anonymized account of one.

The narratives of partnerships related below sketch out the ways in which agencies respond to the arrival of a new policy initiative. In each case, I have assumed, for the sake of consistency, that the local authority is the lead statutory agency. Similar stories emerge from regeneration programmes led by health authorities, such as Health Action Zones, or in which other agencies have a more significant profile, such as Crime and Disorder Reduction Partnerships. At the same time, the narratives presented here are not dynamic. They describe partnerships at moments in time while, in practice, they may move between the different models presented below over a period of time. There are certainly instances of shotgun partnerships developing, after a period of conflict, into partnerships of convenience. The nature of these narratives is that they seek to abstract some general observations from a range of detail in a form that communicates basic ideas rather than seek to elaborate in detail upon a range of specific cases. To a degree, the lack of any real effort to get beyond studies of individual partnerships to look at the broader patterns is a weakness of evaluations and academic studies that this work begins to address.

Infantilizing partnerships

In many cases, the local authority will understand itself to be responsible for the way in which regeneration and renewal resources are used. As the Accountable Body, they are answerable financially and any programme success or failure will reflect upon the authority. Partnerships complicate the task at hand and bring to the table people with no appropriate experience or skills. The local authority knows best and can voice the needs of the community. Furthermore, to ensure that the programme stays on the right lines, it is natural to seek to ensure that appropriate Accountable Body arrangements are established and that a partnership is formed with adequate staff support. In large part, this might reflect a genuine concern that the programme succeeds. The partnership's internal rules and procedures will begin to reflect the rules and culture of the local authority. The offer of human resource management and IT support, and the secondment of staff to a partnership, might reflect genuine generosity. Together with local authority representation on the board of such partnerships, meetings and subgroups might soon become dominated by the organization. In some cases, the voice of the community might also be heard through elected councillors rather than some form of wider engagement with consultation, representation and debate. These partnerships become professionalized and, as a consequence, are unlikely to generate or be receptive to different perspectives or approaches to solving the complex social problems they are created to confront. Indeed, because of the dominance of the local authority, they are more likely to augment the poor services in education, youth services etc. that have failed in the past. Perhaps they will fund new initiatives, but these will be largely dominated by statutory agency projects shelved for lack of funding in recent years.

The communities served by such partnerships will generally experience regeneration as something being done to them remotely. In the voluntary and community sectors, for whom the burdensome rules and procedures set by the Accountable Body will appear as an almost insurmountable obstacle between them and the funds, the experience will breed frustration and anger. However, this will all too readily be addressed by awarding a sum of money to them. If they are in charge of deciding which organizations get funds from this finance, the sector will soon be embroiled in internal conflicts and arguments. At the same time, other statutory agencies will raise no concerns so long as some of the funding comes their way. Yet such partnerships are not necessarily deliberate and conscious attempts to control the funds. In some cases, this is undoubtedly the case. However, in others, local authorities might act out of a genuine wish to avoid the lack of professionalism that has dogged other partnerships. 'Their' regeneration programme will not operate without proper financial procedures, asset registers, job descriptions and other basic organizational requirements. To avoid this, they take over and do it for the community rather than use it as an opportunity to develop local skills and capacity.

Shotgun partnerships

Rather than engage in genuine consultation to develop a strategy and define priorities as required by central government as a condition of funding, some local authorities will seek an easier route. Informed again by the belief that they know best, many authorities' experience of consultation is that they learn little and hear nothing but criticism. It is understandable that they should not relish the prospect of another round of public flagellation. Instead, using the information they already have regarding performance and drawing upon political definitions of priorities, they develop a strategy internally. In most authorities, there are ideas that have been floated before but, for lack of funding, have never been taken forward. Every new funding stream is another opportunity to try to secure resources, regardless of the fit with the objectives of the funding stream or with the needs of intended beneficiaries. For some public agencies, successfully securing funds is a key indicator of the effectiveness of officers. The strategy is then presented to a hastily

49

convened gathering of other partners. The need for urgency is impressed upon those present because deadlines are fast approaching and the local authority's own strategy is presented as a generous solution to the new partnership's need for a strategy. The vast majority of funding is to be committed to the local authority.

The communities served by the programme will experience this in much the same way as the infantilizing partnership. Community and voluntary groups will be excluded from any meaningful engagement with the programme and begin, from the very outset, to act as an opposition to the actions of the local authority. Other statutory agencies will disengage from the partnership and, perhaps, other partnership opportunities that might subsequently arise. Why waste time and energy when the nature of the game has been so clearly set out to them? The programme will, again, largely fail to deliver anything but additional resources to the local authority while actively undermining efforts to engage with the communities intended to benefit.

Partnerships of convenience

In other contexts, local authorities may find themselves obliged to engage in a more meaningful relationship with partner agencies and the wider community. However, partnerships are regarded as a necessary evil, a route to funding, and not something to be embraced. Rather than open itself up to genuine challenge and risk losing control of resources, the local authority hand-picks the partners to be involved. Ideally, they all have a direct financial interest in services as providers. In such an environment, additional funding might be cosily divided between existing agencies with few questions asked. The local authority would receive the lion's share, but key statutory agencies and potential critics, such as the voluntary sector, would receive a sum proportionate to their level of influence and not necessarily the quality of the service they provide. None would be asked for genuine projects and all would collude with the use of the funds simply to augment or extend existing services and projects. In some circumstances, the degree of calculation is evident from an analysis of the patterns of spend. In one case, the proportion of spending on groups that classified themselves as serving black and minority ethnic communities almost exactly mirrored their proportion in the population as a whole. As an indication of the degree to which the investment represented innovation, brief descriptions of projects included the following phrases: 'the fund will supplement . . .'; 'fund money will be used to continue paying . . .'; 'the project aims to enhance existing . . .'; and 'allow the centre to keep running to full capacity . . .'. Resources are not used to challenge or change current mainstream standards but to plug gaps in or augment existing services.

These partnerships present the image of participation and innovation but providers dominate and real change is limited. The processes are opaque and each participant, being complicit, will not challenge the failures of the others. In this sense, it is a more deliberate and manipulative approach to partnership, requiring collusion on the part of others and, in some cases, the betrayal of the interests of a wider constituency. It shares many characteristics with what have been called the 'dark side' of partnerships – those associated with exclusivity and exclusion, secrecy and complicity – that are to be found in, for example, the Mafia and other criminal networks.

Abusive partnerships

Perhaps rarer, abusive partnerships take a number of forms which may include features to be found in the first three. However, they are characterized by a degree of conflict that indicates a loss of local authority control. Some outside voices are to be heard on the board, challenging decisions, demanding changes to the management of funds and seeking greater involvement from the community. But the loss of control is only partial. Others on the board, who may be averse to conflict, are persuaded that those disruptive voices, often using intemperate language, are the ones seeking to distort the agenda to their own interests. For statutory agencies, troublesome local residents may merely be conforming to their stereotype and any views they express may be automatically disregarded. Whatever the case, those who voice concerns, which may or may not be legitimate, are labelled as troublemakers and isolated, disciplined and expelled. While the partnership focuses upon overt conflict, the work of approving projects and spending money continues apace.

In these partnerships, the local authority will concentrate on controlling resources through the Accountable Body. For them, the presence of dissonant voices on the partnership only underlines the degree to which they know best. If you give too much control to the community, you are asking for trouble. Similar views will be expressed by other statutory agencies and other partners, so long as they are in receipt of funding. For the community, the experience is more destructive than the previous forms because, to some degree, they have believed the language of 'communities in the lead'. The experience of trying to make this work will leave some feeling more excluded from the decisions that affect them than they did before the programme arrived. For all partners concerned, the lesson will be that partnerships and genuine engagement with the community do not work.

Polygamous partnerships

In many instances, partnerships will not consist simply of a board responsible for all decisions. There will also be an array of working groups, theme groups or other such forums in which specific issues and, very often, funding proposals are discussed. Each of these subgroups might take on the form of one of the models already outlined. Particularly where the theme covered by the group relates clearly to the work of one agency, such as health, housing or crime, membership of the group is likely to look like a subgroup of the Primary Care Trust or equivalent, not unlike an infantilizing partnership. Where other voices are represented, the group often takes the form of a partnership of convenience, bringing the key service deliverers together in a complicit relationship.

51

The main partnership board, meanwhile, will be concerned to approve decisions taken by subgroups. This main board may be operating in the same ways, concerned to agree the decisions of each subgroup for fear of all subgroups being subject to challenge. Partners are bound together in a second relationship with an unspoken rule that the detailed workings of the sub-relationships should not be discussed. In this sense, all involved know of the other relationships but avert their gaze. In some such partnerships, there may even be room for the community, with their own subgroup, responsible for public events and outreach for example, and with its own funding. The connection between the work of this subgroup and the decisions taken by other subgroups, such as ones on health or community safety, may be less than clear but at least the voice of the community is heard.

ATTITUDES TO PARTNERSHIP

In all of these forms, there is no shared understanding of partnership. Instead, what is clear is the dominance of other factors in determining the attitude of participants. In describing some of the attitudes towards partnership, the discussion below focuses upon those sectors and partners with some real power to shape the terms of the debate. Other sectors, notably business and the community itself, are involved to the degree that other partners allow them to be. In this context, it is not surprising that business involvement is on a self-interested basis. As for the community, where they are involved at all, it will tend to be on the sidelines.

Local authorities

The local authorities receiving neighbourhood renewal funding, through whatever stream, are, for the most part, Labour controlled. These authorities have experienced twenty years of central constraints on funding, the imposition of compulsory competitive tendering and other measures intended to reduce both their resources and their scope for action. During these years, a culture of crude budget-maximizing developed in which securing resources for the authority was an indicator of a successful officer (Niskanen 1971; Dunleavy 1991). It did not matter what the funds were meant to be for, each new stream represented an opportunity for the authority to try to do the things it wanted, to bend the funds to meet its needs. If that meant presenting the appearance of conformity while actually bending the rules, so be it. And, in some instances, this could be justified by ideological differences with central government.

The election of a Labour government in 1997 was meant to end all of that and be the starting point for a revival of local democracy. However, what new monies have filtered down to the local level have, in the main, come with strings attached. Specific client groups, geographical constraints and clear targets all limit the options available. At the same time, Best Value turned out to be a tighter regime of control than had been anticipated, and now partnerships require the authority to open itself up to criticism and challenge from other statutory agencies and the local community and to relinquish some of its control over spending decisions. Rather than actively engage with this new agenda, many authorities have continued to operate in the way that has become familiar to them over the past twenty years. For them, then, the idea of partnership is to be paid lip-service to rather than genuinely engaged with. Partners represent a potential threat to control over and a drain upon resources that needs to be managed to the benefit of the local authority so far as possible.

Local councillors

While this may represent the views of the authority, in the shape of the political leadership and officers, local councillors will sometimes have a very different perspective, particularly those excluded from cabinet roles. Without a clear position in decision-making structures, such councillors may view the role of the community on partnerships as a further threat to their status. Having been formally elected, they consider themselves the legitimate voice of that community. At the same time, a seat on the partnership gives them some control over funding and an opportunity to pursue some of their projects and issues without having to argue the case in the local authority. While this attitude may not be necessarily at odds with the concept of partnership, it can lead to the exclusion of voices from the wider community that might represent a more powerful challenge to the status quo.

Other statutory agencies

In some cases, the attitudes to be found in health services and the police will be similar to local authorities. Additional resources will be treated as 'theirs' and the additional constraints as obstacles to circumvent. So Health Action Zones and Crime and Disorder Partnerships will be largely health or police-led, in much the same way as the models of partnership outlined above. When asked to engage with a partnership for which they have no sense of prime ownership, such as Local Strategic Partnerships, their attitude will be largely shaped by what they are likely to get out of their involvement. The greater the rewards available, the more likely they are to engage. However, given that their understanding of reward will generally be a narrowly financial one, engagement does not necessarily imply a positive attitude towards the partnership agenda.

Voluntary and community organizations

Dependent on contracts and grants for survival, voluntary and community organizations will tend to perceive partnerships as another opportunity to acquire resources. They are more likely to interpret the agenda as a challenge to the mainstream and argue that they should be the beneficiaries as providers of alternative services (Rowe 2005). However,

53

for many small local organizations, the majority of their funding will come through the local authority and other statutory agencies. To challenge them directly might jeopardize those resources (Craig and Taylor 2002). At the same time, to genuinely engage in partnership would open voluntary and community organizations up to challenge from their client groups just as much as statutory agencies. This would not just be difficult to hear but would also undermine their right to speak on behalf of those client groups. Thus, there is a tendency to engage in complicit relationships that maintain the status quo.

REFLECTIONS

The idea of partnership as a tool for change at a local level is a powerful and apparently simple one. It offers prospects for genuine challenge, experimentation and change in order to tackle some of the more intractable social problems. However, as a policy, it is imposed upon institutions with particular attitudes, experiences and pre-existing relationships. Unlike theoretical understandings of partnerships, those associated with regeneration are not voluntarily formed around a shared understanding of purpose. Rather they are formed by organizations and individuals with a history, sometimes positive and sometimes negative, with different interests and with varying levels of power. Each will have different organizational objectives and, as a consequence, their understandings of partnership will vary. Instead of coming together to share resources and information, to work collaboratively and to focus upon service improvement, they engage in a process of compromise to adapt the policy to the pre-existing interests of the key partners. To external audiences, the processes and structures will look right but the relationships underneath this impression remain little changed.

In this sense, partnership as a policy intervention fails to fit with the most basic requirements of 'perfect implementation'. The term is itself a contested one. There are numerous external institutions and actors that will affect the way in which the policy is interpreted and enacted at a local level. More fundamentally, there is not a simple cause and effect relationship. It is not just that policy A does not have effect B. On the contrary, policy A can, in some contexts, have the effect −A and −B. That is, the attempt to introduce partnerships in a specific local context can undermine the very concept of partnership in and beyond that local context. At the same time, by alienating and excluding those the partnership is intended to help, the policy might have an actively negative impact on the wider agenda of social exclusion and neighbourhood renewal.

Throughout this chapter, the term partnership has been applied in a deliberately ambiguous manner. The metaphors have been of marriages, of very human relationships. This metaphor helps to understand the form that partnerships take in practice and to begin to diagnose the problems, getting beyond an analysis of structures and processes. But the metaphor can be stretched a little further. In the discussion so far, the focus has been upon failure and destructive partnerships. Turning to the metaphor, we might also ask what a more constructive partnership might look like.

Mature partnerships

An effective partnership would be characterized by a range of possible permutations of relationship, there being no one size fits all approach. Just as in human relationships, there would be some recognition of the strengths and weaknesses of each partner such that, together, they are a more effective whole. There would be a clear and shared sense of purpose to which all were freely signed up. There would also be a recognition that this purpose could not be delivered by any one partner alone but that all were mutually dependent. There would be sharing of resources to make best use of what was available, focusing upon joint priorities rather than the individual pet projects of one partner or another and upon the impact of investment rather than who got the money. Conflicts and disagreements would be pre-empted, where possible, or resolved in an active and constructive manner where they arose.

Chapter 5

'Coming in from the cold'?

Trade unions in local and regional development

Andy Pike, Peter O'Brien and John Tomaney

INTRODUCTION: 'COMING IN FROM THE COLD'?

The role of trade unions in local and regional development is beginning to find a place in the labour movement and the strategic development of organized labour. In the context of recent membership decline, trade union renewal may be furthered by 'looking beyond the factory gates' of the workplace and the employment relation to build progressive alliances and to work for economic and social justice and development with local and regional interests and institutions (Wills 2001). This new-found interest in the role of trade unions in local and regional development connects with the broader feeling that trade unions have been 'coming in from the cold' in the UK since the election of New Labour's first administration in 1997 (CLES 1999; Heselden 2001; Pike *et al.* 2002, 2004).

From a position of relative isolation, significant changes are evident. At the national level, trade unions have seen their involvement grow in the new institutions of governance (e.g. Low Pay Commission, New Deal Task Force) and a renewal of their role in shaping legislation within existing governance arrangements (e.g. employment rights, information and consultation and health and safety). At the subnational, regional and local levels too, a similar thaw is evident as the uneven decentralization of political and administrative structures has opened the doors to trade union participation in local and regional development and governance (Bache and George 1999; UNISON 2000; Heselden 2001; Pike *et al.* 2002; TUC 2002a). The extent and nature of these changing relations with Government and within the public realm have to be viewed carefully, however, and are markedly different from the previous heyday of organized labour influence during the 1970s experiments with national level corporatism in the UK (Pike *et al.* 2002). In addition, while some aspects of recent developments could be interpreted as the adoption of the European model of decentralized governance and plural, inclusive social partnership (Streeck 1992), substantial differences remain.

56

The emergent opportunities for participation in local and regional development raise daunting challenges for organized labour and trade unions. Alongside other economic and social partners in the private and voluntary sectors, trade unions are increasingly being asked to become credible partners and to make substantive and effective contributions – to a much greater degree than hitherto – in local and regional development. In this chapter, we seek to deepen our conceptual understanding and examine some of the ways in which trade unions are participating in local and regional development, and the strategic and organizational challenges that result. Our argument is that trade union engagement is conditioned by the interrelations between labour movement concerns of economic and social justice mediated by the particular nature, type and interests of trade unions, their degree of autonomy and decentralization within their national structures, and the openness of local and regional development institutions to meaningful trade union engagement. Trade unions are building a strategy and making interventions that attempt to reconcile the traditional welfarist 'politics of redistribution' with the 'politics of recognition' in the more complex pluralism of the multilayered and partnership-based system of governance of local and regional development in the UK.

TRADE UNIONS IN LOCAL AND REGIONAL DEVELOPMENT

The role of trade unions in local and regional development has only recently received conceptual, theoretical and empirical attention (Heselden 2001; Pike *et al.* 2002; Baccaro, Carrieri and Damiano 2003; O'Brien, Pike and Tomaney 2004). Industrial relations' traditional focus upon the social relations, institutions and politics of the workplace and, often national, corporatist concertation arrangements has often neglected the geographical dimensions of organized labour or reduced them to particular, contextual factors – notwithstanding important work on the 'regionalization' and decentralization of industrial relations systems (Perulli 1993; Teague 1995; Ellem and Shields 1999).

Building upon the traditions of labour (Cooke 1985) and trade union geography (Massey and Painter 1989), recent work has focused on how economic, social, political and cultural geographies are shaping and are shaped by the agency of labour – individually and collectively through social institutions such as trade unions – across and between interrelated scales. Explicit attention has focused upon such geographically embedded social institutions which recognize that while they: 'are unlikely to be the sole cause of geographically uneven development they enable, constrain and refract economic development in spatially differentiated ways' (Martin 1999: 6). Analytical levels include the workplace (Wills and Cumbers 2000), community (Tufts 1998; Wills 2001), local (Herod 2001), regional (Sadler and Thompson 2001; O'Brien *et al.* 2004) and supranational (Wills 1998; Sadler 2000; Herod 2001). Such work forms the basis of a potentially fruitful dialogue between industrial relations and economic geography, since: 'raising the gaze over the factory gates calls for a *theoretical* understanding of the roles of

57

space, place and uneven geographical development in the perpetual reconstitution of labour–capital relations' (Herod, Peck and Wills 2002: 2).

In the context of recent decline and stabilization of trade membership at the national level in the UK (Figure 5.1), debate has focused on whether it is a cyclical downturn to be followed by further growth or a structural change. This discussion underpins the debate about trade union renewal, especially the need to organize and recruit in areas of employment growth, particularly the service sector and atypical jobs as well as women and black and minority ethnic groups. In addition, for several commentators, the articulation and mobilization of trade union interests beyond the workplace is pivotal to trade union renewal (Wills 2002). By developing into more inclusive 'social movements', rather than narrowly labourist guardians of workplace and members' interests, trade unions may 'achieve the political cachet and social respect – as carriers of the "general interest" – needed to secure supports for their own organization' (Rogers Hollingsworth 1995: 368).

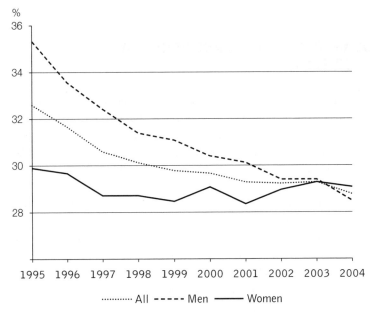

Figure 5.1 *Trade union density in the UK 1995–2004*

Yet emergent roles for trade union interests beyond – but still crucially relevant to – the employment relation and the workplace raise significant challenges:

unions in many countries today are faced with new, more divergent, more specialized and more 'qualitative' demands by their members and clients. This is reflected in growing pressures to participate in production- and supply-related policy areas which are difficult to conceive in terms of traditional, labor-market and distribution-centred trade union ideology.

(Streeck 1992: 100)

Wolfgang Streeck goes on to argue that when large and encompassing trade union organizations – including the emergent 'super-unions' and federations such as the TUC – are brought into production politics, for example industrial policy: 'they usually perform poorly, not least reason being that they find it difficult to deal with the internal divisions of interest among their members that immediately emerge on such occasions' (Streeck 1992: 98). Organized labour is manifest in a multitude of different institutional forms, including trades councils, trade unions – general, craft, professional and so on – and federations, each of which is capable of adding further layers of institutional complexity and process onto the social construction of labour interest definition, organization, mobilization, opportunity and collective action (Kelly 1998). Moreover, in an allegedly 'post-socialist' era, such interests are extending beyond traditional labour concerns with the 'politics of redistribution' to incorporate the 'politics of recognition' of communities of interest and identity organized around disability, ethnicity, faith, gender and sexuality (Fraser 1995). Institutions of organized labour can, then, struggle to act, articulate and coordinate conscious affiliate interests concerned with progressive, solidaristic and value-based principles such as economic and social justice, equity and equality in this more complex context.

In response to charges of token involvement, organized labour now faces the challenge of making effective use of the new opportunities for engagement. Notwithstanding the complexities of labour movement interest representation (Hyman 1994), organized labour has a central role to play in local and regional development in four closely related ways. First, demonstrating and establishing credibility and consolidating their participation by delivering government policy objectives (e.g. learning and skills and productivity agendas). This role has potentially positive knock-on benefits for trade union recruitment and renewal (Manning 2002). Second, broadening the issues addressed in mainstream debate (e.g. social inclusion, equalities, diversity) and underpinning the more balanced and holistic approaches to economic, social and environmental prosperity and well-being characteristic of the new centrism in local and regional economic development policy (Geddes and Newman 1999). Third, providing the focus for debate around more localized and welfarist alternatives to the 'narrow optic of "globalisation-competitiveness"' (Lovering 2001: 352) that currently dominates the local and regional development agenda in the UK. For example, developing and articulating alternatives to public–private partnerships, private financing and contracting-out (Foley 2002). Last, organized labour can provide a means for other formerly marginalized agents in local and regional civil society, such as the voluntary and community sector, to mobilize around a broadly progressive local and regional agenda. The challenge for organized labour has been to learn how to achieve and deliver on such potential contributions.

59

BUILDING AND ORGANIZING CAPACITY AS 'ECONOMIC AND SOCIAL PARTNERS'

The rapidly growing opportunities for participation in local and regional development have severely stretched the organizational resources of trade unions. In the context of tight financial constraints and declining or static membership, trade unions have been focused on organizational survival, often involving amalgamation and merger. Engaging in local and regional development has received a lesser priority. Yet when given a seat at the decision-making table it is crucial for trade unions to have something substantive to contribute, bringing their distinctive contributions to the fore. Organized labour and trade unions have therefore had to build and organize capacity as a means of learning how to participate as more broadly based 'economic and social partners' rather than just narrowly based representative bodies for their members. In particular, trade unions have had to recognize that their voice is now one amongst many from more plural sets of institutions, contrasting with their historically privileged role within tripartite corporatist structures alongside business and the state.

Often involvement in the burgeoning administration of local and regional development falls upon a relatively limited number of individuals. While these participants have had to engage in learning by doing, they can become overloaded and relatively detached from the broader labour movement through the accumulation of specialized knowledge and networks. Mechanisms to report back and account for the activities of participating trades unionists have been underdeveloped. Moreover, while trade unions strive to move closer to the ideal, the participating individuals often have some way to go to match the diversity of the localities and regions they govern (Robinson and Shaw 2000). The need to broaden and deepen the pool of capable individuals able and willing to participate has become paramount.

Analytically, it is helpful to distinguish between internal and external governance and between horizontal and vertical institutional relations. Table 5.1 illustrates examples of organizational inputs and relations evident at a range of geographical levels: supranational, national, subnational/regional and subregional/local. The inputs and relations work both internally and externally inside and outside the institutions of organized labour. For example, members and branch activities provide grass roots inputs to trade union policy; national governments frame the legislative context within which trade unions work. Such inputs and relations impinge upon the roles and strategic opportunities for trade union agency in local and regional development. In addition, strategic relationships are being recast vertically – between the different geographical levels – and horizontally – across levels – in the internal and external governance arrangements of organized labour. For example, EU-level legislation can change the context for national legislation; devolution has reorganized the institutions of government and governance at the national and subnational levels in the UK. Managing the articulation and balance between such potentially aligned and/or conflicting internal and external interests is an ongoing process faced by the institutions of organized labour.

Table 5.1 *Organizational inputs and relations*

Level	Internal	External
Supranational	European TUC European Works Councils	European Commission European Parliament International trade unions

National	Federation
	Trade union affiliates
	Officers
	Members
		Parliaments and/or
		  Assemblies (committees,
		  members)
		Government departments
		Government agencies and
		  NDPBs intergovernmental
		  committees

Subnational and/or regional	Federation (conference,
	executive and council)
	Trade union affiliates
	Officers
	Members
		Devolved Parliaments
		  and/or Assemblies
		Government offices
		Government agencies and
		  NDPBs
		Business associations
		Voluntary and community
		  sector associations
		Communities of interest and
		  identity (e.g. black and
		  minority ethnic, women's,
		  faith groups)

Subregional and/or local	County associations
	Trades councils
	Trade union branches
	Members
		Local and municipal
		  government
		Regeneration partnerships
		Neighbourhood and
		  community groups

Source: Adapted from Pike, O'Brien and Tomaney (2006)

The geography of trade union membership and organization plays an integral role in shaping the available capacity of organized labour within trades councils, trade unions and trade union federations. In membership terms, clear regional and subnational heartlands exist within the UK in Northern Ireland, Wales, the north east, north west and Scotland (Table 5.2) (Martin *et al*. 1996). Where membership levels are relatively high, trade unions have traditionally had more prominent roles in public affairs and consciousness through having a substantial number of members on the ground. This provides a potential pool of contributors to participate in local and regional development, although their willingness and capability to get involved remains an important question.

The organizational geography of labour institutions adds a further layer of complexity to the task of building and organizing capacity to participate in local and regional development. A highly differentiated organizational structure exists at the national, regional and local levels amongst the institutions of organized labour (Martin *et al*. 1996).

Table 5.2 *Trade union membership expressed as percentages*, autumn 2002*

Region/Nation	All employees
United Kingdom	29
North east	38
North west	34
Yorkshire and the Humber	32
East Midlands	28
West Midlands	30
East	23
London	25
South east	21
South west	26
England	28
Wales	40
Scotland	34
Northern Ireland	41

* As a percentage of all employees in each region, excluding the armed forces and those who did not say whether they belonged to a trade union.

Source: Labour Force Survey

Trades councils are highly localized. Different types of trade unions have different historical roots and geographies. The trade union federation the TUC provides a distinct example. At the national level, with its historical grounding in the local activism of Trades Councils and Scottish affairs, the Scottish TUC is an independent organization following the 1897 split from the emergent 'national' TUC in England and Wales (Aitken 1997). In the English regions, the TUC and Government Office (GO) regions are not aligned, creating severe strain upon the respective TUC secretariats: six regional TUCs cover nine GO regions (including London) (Figure 5.2). The situation is particularly acute at the regional level for the Southern and Eastern Region TUC (SERTUC) which has to deal with three different sets of Government Offices, RDAs and Regional Chambers as well as the Mayoralty and Authority in London. This is not even to consider the diversity of bodies at the subregional and local levels. In northern England too, the institutional picture is complex. The Northern TUC work jointly with the North West TUC and RDA because Cumbria remains part of the NTUC's regional structures but is within the north west GO region. Some RDAs have also introduced subregional partnerships, opening up another tier for potential trade union involvement.

Building and organizing capacity to act as social and economic partners and to engage in the emergent landscape of local and regional development is, as a result, highly challenging. Internally, many trade unions and confederations have sought to develop a more policy-oriented approach and focus upon clear priorities. Given that they cannot actively respond to all that is being asked of them, many seek to work where they see potential or gaps. Internal governance has also been reviewed drawing upon the Scottish TUC experience that emphasized the need for rapid and transparent decision-making to

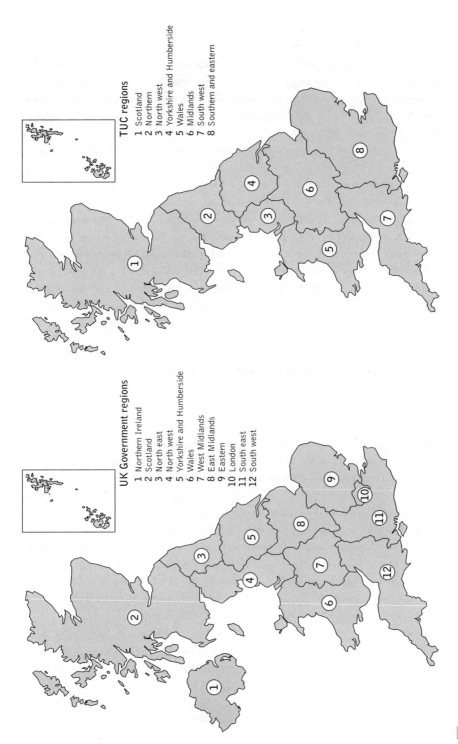

UK Government regions
1 Northern Ireland
2 Scotland
3 North east
4 North west
5 Yorkshire and Humberside
6 Wales
7 West Midlands
8 East Midlands
9 Eastern
10 London
11 South east
12 South west

TUC regions
1 Scotland
2 Northern
3 North west
4 Yorkshire and Humberside
5 Wales
6 Midlands
7 South west
8 Southern and eastern

Figure 5.2 *TUC regions and UK Government nations and regions in the UK*

facilitate engagement (McKay 1999). Reforms have included encouraging greater participation and developing more sophisticated communication strategies and mechanisms for their legitimate policy-making bodies (Executives and Councils), membership and beyond to local and regional institutions. Examples include media and press strategies, web sites, newsletters and contacts directories. External funding for additional posts has also played a key role, for instance from RDAs and LLSCs, as well as capacity building courses for relevant staff.

Other innovations have sought to strengthen the research capacity of trade unions, to a degree building upon the independent and historical traditions of national organizations and movements such as Counter Information Services (CIS) and Alternative Economic Strategies as well as shop steward and combine-based resources such as the Tyneside-based Trade Union Studies Information Unit (TUSIU). Research capacity is central in supporting trade unions to make meaningful contributions to regional debates and improve their perception as credible partners. Developments include joint projects with universities (Copeland and Philo 2000; O'Brien 2001), the establishment of local and regional development policy task or working groups, and academic networks to bring together trade unionists, academics and local and regional policy makers to support engagement, for example the union research networks in London and Scotland.

BROADENING ECONOMIC AND SOCIAL DEVELOPMENT STRATEGIES

Broadly based international evidence – including The World Bank (Aidt and Tzannatos 2002) – suggests that trade unions can promote rather than inhibit regional and national economic prosperity and the social and territorial equity of growth through contributions to learning and skills development, employee involvement, productivity and the equalities agenda (Dunlop 1994; CEC 1996; Etherington 1997). This growing body of work has eclipsed the discredited arguments that high levels of trade union membership caused poor local and regional economic performance (Minford 1985). Such work tended to confuse correlation with causation, provide crude analyses based upon a narrow reading of neo-classical economics and carry the suspicion of 'New Right' political bias. Organized labour and trade unions have a central role to play in broadening the terms of debate about the fundamental questions of 'what kind of local and regional development and for whom?' (Pike, Rodríguez Pose and Tomaney 2006).

There are several dimensions in which trade unions might make substantive interventions. First, trade unions can emphasize the need for more appropriate balances in local and regional development strategies between economic, social and environmental concerns. Trade unions can act as promoters and custodians of more sustainable forms of development. This can, for example, underpin the need for economic inclusion as a necessary complement to economic competitiveness, and a concern with the quality and sustainability of job creation activities. Second, organized labour can encourage the

64

promotion of more context-sensitive local and regional development strategies tailored to the specific conditions and concerns of particular places. This can entail ensuring that locally and regionally appropriate balances are achieved between promoting services and manufacturing, traditional and new industries, knowledge and labour-intensive activities and indigenous and exogenous sources of growth. Third, trade unions can play a key role in emphasizing the local and regional development dimensions of public service modernization. This has included civil service unions engaging in and responding to the Lyons Review of public sector relocation and the Gershon Review of public sector efficiency, each of which has potentially significant implications for different localities and regions in the UK. In positive ways, UNISON, GMB and the TGWU have sought increased investment in publicly owned services, fair employment clauses in contracts let by public bodies and safeguards on employment transfer. Last, trade unions can promote the role of labour movement history in culture-led regeneration strategies, particularly in old industrial regions in the UK. The Northern TUC, for example, funded work such as part of Newcastle-Gateshead's unsuccessful 'Capital of Culture' bid.

Wales TUC's experience demonstrates just such an approach to local and regional development. WTUC has promoted its 'agenda for prosperity' based upon a more holistic and sustainable vision of developing the economy, promoting life-long learning and improving health and well-being:

> a successful economy is one which is technologically innovative, ecologically sustainable and socially inclusive, an economy characterised by high levels of employment, based on fair terms and conditions for all employees, supported by public services which are properly funded and effectively managed.
>
> (Wales TUC n.d.(a): 1.2)

Underpinning this approach is a commitment to a 'partnership economy' in which 'social partners jointly seek to address the barriers to innovation and productivity' (Wales TUC n.d.(b): 3.1). WTUC's economic strategy has developed proposals on environmental goods and services, public procurement and infrastructure, particularly rail. As we noted at the outset, however, tensions can exist amongst the myriad interests of organized labour as trade union member interests may diverge from the intentions of the broader local and regional development strategies promoted by organized labour. Members may be focused on workforce development, safeguarding jobs and the needs of the employed, unionized workforce and less concerned about wider local and regional issues of social exclusion and environmental protection for example.

Trade unions face different kinds of economic and social development challenges depending upon their particular local and regional contexts. The marked regional and local economic and social disparities in the UK, in particular, provide a challenging backdrop for articulating trade union interests (Table 5.3). In London and the south east, unemployment is relatively low and employment rates are high, increasing labour's bargaining power in tight local labour markets but potentially encouraging poaching,

Table 5.3 *Unemployment, gross value added and household income by region and nation*

Regions/nations	Unemployment*	Gross value added***		Household income****	
	Rate**	Per capita (£)	Index (UK = 100)	Per capita (£)	Index (UK = 100)
North east	6.4	11,019	76.1	9,018	89
North west	5.0	13,011	89.9	9,501	94
Yorkshire and the Humber	5.4	12,468	86.2	9,325	92
East Midlands	4.2	13,268	91.7	9,409	93
West Midlands	5.7	13,070	90.3	9,541	94
East	4.1	13,926	96.2	10,638	105
London	7.0	22,607	156.2	12,207	120
South east	3.8	15,908	109.9	11,055	109
South west	3.8	12,880	89.0	10,073	99
Wales	4.4	11,396	78.8	8,870	87
Scotland	5.6	13,660	94.4	9,870	97
Northern Ireland	5.3	11,311	78.2	8,998	89
United Kingdom	5.0	14,470	100.0	10,142	100

* ILO Unemployment for Spring 2003; ** Denominator = Totally economically active; *** Provisional headline gross value added (GVA) (workplace basis) per head for 2001. **** Gross disposable household income (GDHI) for 1999. UK excludes GDHI for Extra-Regio.

Source: Labour Force Survey, Office for National Statistics

stoking wage inflation and undermining longer-term training and development. Recruiting new members may be tough in the context of relative local and regional prosperity. In this context, trades unions have to confront the issues of uneven local and regional growth, and its myriad challenges from organizing black and minority ethnic as well as immigrant service labour to encouraging the development of affordable housing for key public sector workers. In contrast, in north east England, unemployment remains stubbornly high and above the national average with significant concentrations and even higher levels of 'hidden unemployment' (Fothergill 2001). In terms of wealth and prosperity, the north east has the lowest gross value added per capita, almost 25 per cent lower than the UK level. At just over 10 per cent lower than the national level, gross disposable household income is level with Northern Ireland and only just higher than Wales. Given the magnitude of such enduring economic problems, organized labour, especially the regional TUC, has been a willing partner in the strategies and institutions of economic regeneration. But current local and regional economic strategies seeking higher-value added activities and higher productivity are problematic in the context of high unemployment and the need for job creation. Sharpened inequalities at the subregional and local levels further complicate the local and regional contexts of trade union agency.

DELIVERING THE LEARNING AND SKILLS AGENDA

The connection of the traditional trade union concern of workplace training with national and regional economic strategy and the drive to increase productivity has placed trade unions at the heart of government policy (HM Treasury 2001; DfES 2003). Given their membership, workplace-based organization and intermediary role between employer and employee, trade unions are seen a key delivery agents in the learning and skills agenda (Clough 1997). Places with relatively poor education levels, lack of basic skills, limited aspirations and perceptions of job prospects by both potential employers and employees have fostered acute 'low skills equilibriums'. Trade unions are interpreted as a potential means to address such problems. The national level learning and skills drive has seen a substantial growth in activity and funding, often through the LLSC or equivalent bodies, at the regional, subregional and local levels. National level funds, for example the Department for Education and Skills' Union Learning Fund, have been complemented by statutory rights for Union Learning Representatives on the ground.

In strategic terms, learning and skills has become embedded within broader trade union contributions to economic and social development strategies. WTUC, for example, recognize the persistence of basic skills deficiencies and its implications in their analysis of the offshore relocation of low value, price-sensitive activities to lower cost regions in Europe and beyond:

> The conventional response to this problem from the WDA and the Assembly is to say that Wales needs to 'move up market' into the 'knowledge-driven economy'. But the big question is how Wales gets from here to there when one in four of the Welsh population is functionally illiterate and two in five non-numerate?
>
> (Wales TUC n.d. b: 4.1)

The strong equalities theme in the Government of Wales Act and the ability of trade union organizations to raise demands for learning among under-represented sections of society has underpinned WTUC's growing contribution to learning and skills in Wales. Indeed, the Labour Welsh Assembly Government is providing over £1.4 million grant assistance to WTUC Learning Services until 2006 (Wales TUC 2003). WTUC is the key facilitator of learning and skills on behalf of the trade union movement in Wales.

Elsewhere, trade unions and their regional federations are building records as credible and capable delivery partners for RDAs and LLSCs, embedded within local and regional strategies and, albeit unevenly, brought into the relevant institutions. For example, the Regional Skills Partnerships recently established in the English regions as well as other employer training pilot initiatives for basic skills. Internally, some trade unions and their federations have established regional level Education, Learning and Skills Forums, integrating the work of TUC Education and TUC Learning Services, and bringing together trade unionists sitting on the RDA, LSCs and Lifelong Learning Partnerships, as well as Regional Education Officers and TUC Education Course providers. Local and regional networks of Union Learning Representatives are also emerging.

PROGRESSING THE EQUALITIES AND DIVERSITY AGENDA

Organized labour is struggling with the strategic issues raised by the need to reconcile its traditional concerns with the politics of redistribution and the politics of recognition in the equalities and diversity agenda. Tensions exist in the context of scarce resources and organizational priorities within particular trade unions that may be more comfortable and used to focusing upon 'harder', less ambiguous and clearer cut issues of jobs and terms and conditions of employment. Yet the concerns of wider social movements are reflected through the trade union membership and impinge upon such basic trade union concerns including discrimination and fairness at work. Trade unions have tried to institutionalize such concerns through organized groups given legitimate roles within union organizations, including black and minority ethnic networks, environmentalist coalitions, lesbian, gay, bisexual and transgender groups, and disabled workers.

Nonetheless, extending such unresolved and ongoing issues into the realm of local and regional development has been a huge challenge for organized labour institutions. There are examples where trade unions and their federations have been developing a role as custodians of the equalities and diversity agendas in the context of local and regional development. In north east England, for example, the northern TUC has utilized European Social Fund resources to support work on barriers to employment and training for women and ethnic minorities that has shaped social inclusion strategies in the region (TUC 2002a). The legislatively embedded equalities commitment in the Government of Wales Act is also providing opportunities for trade unions to progress this agenda.

PARTICIPATING IN THE GOVERNANCE OF LOCAL AND REGIONAL DEVELOPMENT

The burgeoning opportunities for engagement in local and regional development have, albeit highly unevenly, brought elements of organized labour into local and regional governance institutions. During the cold climate of the 1980s under successive Conservative governments, trade unions maintained a vestige of institutional involvement, especially in the labourist heartlands of northern England, Northern Ireland, Scotland and Wales. This often took the form of seats on the boards of public bodies (e.g. universities and colleges) and the increasingly prevalent quangos (e.g. Regional Development Organizations, Training and Enterprise Councils and Urban Development Corporations). Often this engagement took the form of the nomination of senior individuals with unclear representative responsibilities for themselves, their sector, their union, their federation, organized labour or the wider labour movement. In the hostile political atmosphere of the 1980s, trade unions were still blamed for the 'British Disease' of national economic underperformance and regarded as part of the failed 1970s national corporatism. Often compounded by their weaknesses in developing distinctive contributions to local and regional development, trade unions remained marginal agents in local and regional decision-making during the 1980s and much of the 1990s.

New Labour's election in 1997 radically changed the policy agenda and institutional architecture of local and regional development. At the subnational and regional levels, devolution established the Scottish Parliament, National Assemblies in Northern Ireland (currently suspended) and Wales, and the Mayoralty and Greater London Authority in London. These constitutional changes ushered in a new and broad range of policy and institutional fora, such as committees and task groups, many seeking trade union input (Pike, O'Brien and Tomaney 2006). Politically and symbolically important memoranda of understanding agreements have been agreed between the Welsh and Scottish Executives and the Welsh and Scottish TUCs. The Government of Wales Act has legally entrenched the duty to consult economic and social partners on policy and legislatively embedded the Business Partnership Council involving three 'pillars' of structured representative organizations (Business Wales, WTUC and 'not-for-profit' companies; Welsh Council for Voluntary Action and local government) (Pike, O'Brien and Tomaney 2006). Economic and Social Partners are also encouraged to engage with the Assembly's Subject and Regional Committees.

Regionalization in England has meant the adaptation of existing organizations, including the regional GOs, and the establishment of RDAs as the new lead local and regional economic development institution. While modest institutional innovations with somewhat limited powers and resources relative to their responsibilities, the Act gave trade unions a statutory seat on RDA boards alongside other regional interests. Trade unions have continued their involvement in the Regional Industrial Development Boards and Programme Management Committees disbursing national and European funds through the GO and RDA. The Regional Chambers involve trade unions as 'Economic and Social Partners' alongside business and the voluntary and community sectors (currently involving five trade unionists, including the Group's Vice Chair). Organized labour interests were supportive and engaged in the campaigning for the ultimately rejected plans for an elected regional assembly in north east England.

At the subregional and local scale the institutions of local and regional development have continued to multiply, creating acute problems for trade union capacity in providing able, willing and capable representation. Subregional partnerships and Local Learning and Skills Councils in England have each sought trade union involvement. The local level presents even more problems, encompassing a myriad of organizations and partnerships such as the Single Regeneration Budget (SRB) and 'New Deal' Steering Groups, Employment Tribunals Groups, ICT Steering Groups, Local Strategic Partnerships and New Deal for Communities regeneration partnerships to name but a handful just from the English context. Broadly, regional trade union and NTUC officers tend to be part of the corporatist elite in regional and subregional bodies while rank and file representatives and members participate in local level partnerships. The development of trade union capacity to engage has cohered at the regional level but is attempting to reach the local level, albeit with some difficulty given the sheer number of local institutions.

Participation in the institutions of local and regional development has tangibly, if unevenly, changed perceptions of trade unions and what they can bring to the decision-making table. In north east England, the experience is illustrative:

> Trade unions are seen not as bodies to be kept outside the camp and occasionally told what's going on, but organizations that should be brought into the new structures being developed.
>
> (Director, Government Office North East,
> authors' interview, 2000)

Engagement in the governance of local and regional development raises a number of strategic issues for organized labour and trade unions. First, to what extent does involvement represent incorporation and capture, potentially compromising trade union independence and autonomy as they become party to the aims and outcomes of local and regional development institutions and their strategies? Second, are trade unions being asked or securing participation as a result of tokenism in a more plural, partnership-based governance system? Third, how can trade unions effectively work within a more complex, multilevel institutional context?

> Like other organizations, the trade union movement has to learn to come to terms with the emerging system of multi-level governance in post-devolution Britain. This multi-level governance system – embracing local, regional, national and supranational levels of government and governance – poses a wholly new set of threats and opportunities for trade unions.
>
> (Wales TUC n.d. b): 6.1)

Last, how much meaningful influence are trade union interests having on the form, nature and practice of local and regional development, particularly as they are now one 'economic and social partner' amongst many within the new institutional context?

CONCLUSIONS AND STRATEGIC ISSUES

This chapter has sought to deepen our conceptual understanding and to examine the strategic issues raised by the participation of trade unions in local and regional development. Trade union engagement is shaped by the interrelations between broader labour movement concerns of economic and social justice and the nature, type and interests of trade unions, their degree of autonomy and decentralization within their national structures, and the relative degree of openness and receptiveness of local and regional development institutions to trade union engagement.

Traditional corporatist modes of collective action have been reshaped through the introduction of more decentralized, plural and partnership-based forms of governance at the subnational, regional and local levels. The national, centralized collective bargaining history in the labour movement often constrains national trade union organizations and limits their willingness to support decentralization amid fears that it may diminish national trade union power and influence. Emergent decentralized local and regional development institutional forms in which trade union interests are involved range from formalized, legislatively embedded and supported institutional structures to informal, ad hoc and largely voluntary arrangements. For some, recent changes might:

> not necessarily eliminate corporatism as a form of interest organization and policy coordination . . . but points to it assuming a more fragmented, decentralised and functionally specialised structure ('local', 'sectoral' or 'policy area' corporatism).
>
> (Streeck 1992: 79)

While mirroring the concern with the articulation of trade union activity at different levels in Europe (Waddington and Hoffman 2000), the experiences of local and regional engagement suggest trades unions in the UK are moving toward but remain some way from the degree of power and influence afforded by the legislatively embedded role of trade unions in more devolved governance systems such as Germany.

Organizational inputs to the institutions of organized labour have become myriad in the realm of local and regional development. Internal and external pressures raise acute challenges of coordination. A clear division of labour may well be required to cope with the demands of such multilevel governance:

> In the field of regional development and regeneration this multi-level system is already well advanced, with policy-making functions split between Brussels, London and Cardiff, which means that the trade union movement will need to devote more time to co-ordinating its activities – especially as regards *who* does *what* at *which* level.
>
> (Wales TUC n.d. a: 6.2)

Substantive interest definitions emerging from the labour movement have shaped trade union strategy and interventions. Trade unions have attempted and, sometimes, struggled to reconcile the traditional welfarist politics of redistribution and the politics of recognition in the context of membership and federation concerns in the more complex pluralism of post-devolution UK. As Streeck (1992) acknowledges, however, while complex, the integrative capacity and ability to forge consensus of the dialogic and democratically founded mode of organizational process within the labour movement should not be underestimated.

Several strategic issues emerge from our analysis. First, trade unions need to find and strengthen their voices at the local and regional level by considering how they represent, mobilize and articulate their collective interests (Kelly 1998). Enhancing the sophistication of local and regional public policy development requires a clear understanding of local and regional labour movement concerns and independent research capacity to provide evidence to support the identification of priorities, interventions and responses to consultations. By articulating well-supported arguments, trade union bodies can demonstrate credibility and capability as civic institutions integral to the public realm and contribute to progressive local and regional economic, social and political development. Second, trade unions need to balance their position as a 'critical friend' with constructive and positive relations with key local and regional institutions as well as a channel for dissent and discussion of alternatives. Such a stance might counter accusations of co-option and capture. Third, while much trade union activity in local and regional development is evident, it remains too early to say whether and to what extent it can contribute positively to the core trade union renewal agenda. An inclusive approach within and beyond the workplace may have the – as yet largely unrealized – potential to contribute to trade union renewal by fostering a consensus between the industrial and political arms of the labour movement and making common cause with the voluntary and community sector, and other relatively marginalized youth, women, black and minority ethnic, environmentalist and faith groups. Developing such plural alliances may be a more complex and demanding way of working than the historically class-based struggles of tripartite corporatism.

ACKNOWLEDGEMENT

This paper draws upon joint research between CURDS and the Northern TUC that examined the engagement of trade union federations in local and regional development and governance in the north east and north west English regions and Wales. The project involved over 70 interviews with trade union officers, activists, politicians, public officials and private sector representatives, secondary source analysis and non-participant observation in meetings, seminars and conferences between 1999 and 2002.

Chapter 6

Managing involvement

Lorraine Johnston and Jon Coaffee

INTRODUCTION

The New Labour Government, elected in 1997, actively pursued an overall modernization and reform agenda, which had widespread implications for the direction and management of regeneration policy, and in particular the evolution of 'community planning' – the development of a community-owned process, led by the local authority with the aim of creating a shared vision of intervention to address priorities identified by local communities and expressed in a place-based action plan which demonstrates the commitment and support of the multiple stakeholders involved. This is an agenda which continues to evolve and refocus on both the development of creative and innovative policy, which should be community-led, as well as ensuring that adopted policies are cost-effective and target driven. These aims of regeneration reform, as will be demonstrated in this chapter, are often in conflict.

Early experiences from the New Labour regeneration regime are mixed with more recent acknowledgements emphasizing that more should be done to empower local government and develop community infrastructures. In October 2005, the Minister for Communities and Local Government, David Milliband, highlighted that:

> Local government has a key role in building this new community infrastructure.
> A strategic local authority will ensure that institutions and activities do not just take place *in* the community but are *of* the community. A strategic local authority therefore seeks to shift the balance of power towards communities, through neighbourhood management and governance, through individual voice and choice, and through partnership with the voluntary sector.
>
> (Milliband 2005, our emphasis)

Within this context, this chapter examines how local actors in recent years have increasingly sought to be involved in regeneration initiatives. It specifically examines the roles of locally elected politicians and the extent to which they have, on the one hand, become active community leaders and on the other hand felt that they have become marginalized in certain aspects of the community planning process.

This chapter is divided into five parts. The first will briefly outline the historical experience of community and councillor roles in regeneration management. Second, the way in which community and councillor involvement in community planning has been facilitated since 1997 will be unpacked. This sets up an analysis of the workings of both strategic city-wide partnerships (Local Strategic Partnerships) and sub-local neighbourhood governance arenas (area committees) that have developed in many English cities as a result of policy developed from the 2000 Local Government Act. The chapter concludes by drawing out key lessons from these community planning initiatives as well as the highlighting inherent tensions that have emerged from the development of such initiatives as a result of the conflicting experiences and aspirations of different regeneration actors.

PREVIOUS ATTEMPTS AT MANAGING THE INVOLVEMENT OF COUNCILLORS AND THE COMMUNITY

In the UK, local decentralization initiatives are now seen as integral to new patterns of urban governance and partnership working, as well as to overall projects of city-wide restructuring (Coaffee 2004; Johnston L. 2005). However, such attempts are not without precedent within urban regeneration management. The Community Development Projects of the late 1960s and early 1970s (see for example Loney 1983) and a number of 'localism' experiments in the 1980s, which attempted to decentralize the power of local government to local neighbourhoods, are perhaps the starkest historical examples of attempts to empower local communities and local councillors in the decision-making process and defend the collective provision of services in the face of public expenditure cuts. For example Boddy and Fudge in *Local Socialism* cite the then leader of Sheffield City Council and later key architect of the New Labour project, David Blunkett, who highlighted how such experiments saw a new future emerging in local neighbourhood management and community planning:

> Changing people's awareness, changing structures to make things possible, opening up the political process to people down the ladder, all those things are taking place. And at the same time we are trying to delegate, to decentralise services into the community, to bring the community into the process with tenants, works department shop stewards and councillors, for example, meeting together and forming working groups, trying to get people involved in the running of social services at local level. All this is happening at once and that is a very difficult process to manage. There is a danger of it collapsing under its own its own momentum. But it has benefits. If you are challenging people then you bring them alive. You are increasing the potential for dynamic change, and people will begin to respond.
>
> (Boddy and Fudge 1984: 249)

74

These early experiments in community development and decentralization occurred against a backdrop of the rise of the New Right and Thatcherism and an increase in central government control and direction. In broad terms, under such an approach local government was marginalized and mistrusted and had its funding reduced and hence local councillors had a much-reduced role. Notions of partnership were reshaped from one where central and local government worked together to one where central government actively began to court the private sector as development partners.

During the late 1980s and early 1990s, academic observers and policy makers began to explore notions of transformative management change related to the governance of localities, particularly linked to the devolution of power and responsibility from national to city governments, and how this might make local public service delivery more efficient. Such an approach, linked strongly to regimes of 'challenge funding' such as City Challenge and the Single Regeneration Budget, adopted at least on paper elements of both 'citizen participation' and 'new public management', and was referred to, by some commentators, as 'new localism'. This market-led approach was, in part, criticized by political opponents for its focus on private investment opportunities, a lack of true community involvement and the decentralization of responsibility, but not power, from the national to local level. By contrast, at this time the opposition Labour party argued for an enhanced role for local autonomy and community participation per se in regeneration decision-making arenas alongside a move towards integrated public service delivery.

In the local government context highlighted briefly above, elected councillors performed a critical intermediary role, linking local government to local communities. This role is however multifaceted, and councillors were expected to balance a variety of overlapping responsibilities – as a representative policy maker, manager, ombudsman, scrutinizer, resolver of local conflict and a community leader, as well as being accountable to their electorate. However, over time the relative power of councillors in decision-making processes has ebbed and flowed. For example Bailey (1975: 86) saw councillor representation as 'merely a device for activating and refurbishing what politicians take to be a mandate for all decisions'. Through the early Conservative era of government the power and influence of local councillors was eroded significantly, becoming one characterized by 'consensual corporatism'. More recently, Copus (1998) has also highlighted how political affiliation of councillors can influence the degree to which they see themselves as a local representative or part of the overall governing regime. This can be most notably be expressed in council committees which have become an important arena where the democratic accountability of councillors meets the expertise of council officers. As Wilson and Game (2002: 93) note, 'committees can be seen as a council's workshop, where councillors' local knowledge and their political assessment of local needs have been brought together with officers' professional and expert advice to produce, hopefully, democratically responsive and implementable policy'.

However, in 1997 the New Labour administration sought to recast the traditional council committee system and to reinvigorate local democracy and the local accountability of councillors. In *Modernising Local Government: Local Democracy and Community Leadership* (DETR 1998b) it was argued that the way local authorities tended to work was inefficient and opaque and that a councillor's most important role – that of a community representative – was not prioritized. Wilson and Game (2002: 101) further noted that traditional committees were also 'a poor vehicle for communicating and demonstrating community leadership. They confuse the executive (policy-making) and representational roles of councillors. It is not always clear who is taking the decision and therefore who should be held to account.'

MY VOICE: MY PLACE – RE-IMAGINING INCLUSION AND REPRESENTATION UNDER NEW LABOUR

After 'New' Labour was elected in 1997 the twin ideas of participation and efficiency of service delivery became central drivers of regeneration management, resulting in a series of policy initiatives under the guise of the 'modernization of local government'. The approach adopted was seen as symptomatic of the emerging concept of 'third way' politics – a programme for permanent revisionism involving the development of a strong civil society and active government. The third way was embodied within a host of complex policies linked to reshaping the relationships between national and local government and between local government and its communities (Coaffee 2004). At the local level, this double-tension governance transformation has been articulated as a shift from local authorities having a traditional self-sufficient and providing role to play in service delivery to that of enablers, where local authorities, rather than provide all services themselves, facilitate and co-opt other organizations, often from the private sector, to act for them (Wilson and Game 2002: 23).

Such transformation in the public sector has occurred amidst the increased complexity and fragmentary nature of public policy. Local government, as key cornerstones of the third way, have been asked to develop a flexible enabling role, with changing mana-gerial positions reflecting pragmatism, accountability and transparency, alongside wider consultation with citizens/customers. In short, bottom-up approaches are favoured over top-down directive approaches, with central government providing both the funding and encouragement for locally focused strategies to take root and embrace principles of subsidiarity. This tenet argues smaller and simpler organizational forms are preferable to a larger and more complex organization and that if possible activity should be performed by a more decentralized organization, as opposed to many post-war reforms which saw large-scale centralization and bureaucratization characterize the public sector.

This approach amounted to what many have referred to as national government steering rather than directly controlling public service provision. However, despite such subtle guidance about partnership formation from national government, many have argued, in effect, that local authorities and locally elected councillors are being left to work out the practicalities of such a complex task for themselves with insufficient training and support.

The UK provides a radical example of how local political management structures have been reformed in recent years. Such change was particularly pronounced after the Local Government White Paper *Modern Local Government: in touch with the people* (DETR 1998a) and the subsequent Local Government Act (2000) which required all local authorities to modify their existing, and often entrenched, political management systems. The Act introduced changes to the local authority decision-making process and, in particular, focused on the creation of executive arrangements which were argued to be more efficient, accountable and transparent. The traditional committee system was arranged so that decision-making processes could not be delegated to individual councillors but taken by full council or by committee. This was because all elected councillors were accountable for decisions made. The Act for the first time separated the making and implementation of policy from its scrutiny.

As a result, the role for councillors was re-imagined with a clear separation in the majority of local councils between executive (Cabinet) and non-executive (backbench) councillors.[1] Backbench councillors in particular were expected to become community leaders and hold the executive to account through an overview and scrutiny function. However, many local councillors were concerned that power was being concentrated in the hands of the executive and that the majority of the elected representatives would be marginalized in the policy-making process. Non-executive councillors were therefore left with three key roles – members of full council, overviewers and scrutineers and as representatives of their ward on appropriate committees and forums.

For all councillors, importance was placed upon strong community leadership roles being established at a local level. Elected politicians became the conduit by which local community voice should reach the upper echelons of a local authority. These roles were to be advanced by the development of strategic cross-cutting partnership, the development of community strategies, and through the development of social capital in communities which would also allow 'communities to lead themselves' (Audit Commission 2003). The local councillors' new roles and responsibilities were in facilitating and developing community engagement and reconnecting citizen with council. However, as Copus (2003: 48) highlights, whereas councillors accept and encourage community voices to feed into the decision-making process, they also retain the view that they, as democratically elected, should make the final decision. This he further argues acts 'as a barrier to their community advocate role and to greater citizen involvement'.

In short, the 2000 Local Government Act paved the way for today's explosion in new styles of strategic partnership, area-based initiatives and networking at the local level, but also articulated a need for, and the development possibilities of, sub-local governance structures (Coaffee and Healey 2003) with traditional approaches to the management of place increasingly challenged by the call for more flexible arrangements with decentralized decision-making powers and wider participatory structures.

THE SEARCH FOR A NEW LOCALISM?

Importantly, these changes in local government management drew from a critique of previous local government reforms of the late 1960s and early 1970s,[2] most notably those introduced by the Conservative government who in the 1980s had championed theories of New Public Management (NPM) with an emphasis on effectiveness, streamlined decision-making processes, customer service and executive managerial control.

Equally, recent UK local government modernization has been influenced by North American experiences where public sector reform was embedded within a belief that private sector change management principles could be increasingly utilized in the management of the public sector to improve the quality and performance of delivery and, fundamentally, to 'reinvent government' (Osborne and Gaebler 1992). The aim was to create 'lean and athletic organizations with fewer management levels and greater responsiveness to change'. In short, NPM pointed to the possibilities of organizational change 'from unresponsive, paternalistic and leaden bureaucracies to the customer driven, flexible, quality orientated and responsive organizations of the future' (Powell and Hewitt 2002: 119).

In the late 1990s, the criticism of NPM by the incoming New Labour government was that it had a tendency to separate out the management and policy functions of local government and exacerbate policy complexity through further fragmentation. New Labour's approach was an attempt to knit together these two critical stands of public sector management. It did this, in large part, through an overarching programme of what became known as 'new localism'.

Contemporary new localism – a policy directive developed by the New Local Government Network (an influential public policy consultancy with close links to the New Labour government) as a response, and in relation to, third way thinking – has become an umbrella term for many of the policy changes enacted by New Labour linked to both managerial and political devolution. It is essentially a framework by which the relationship between the centre and local authorities and between local authorities and their communities have been refashioned and reshaped with the emphasis being placed on the government to take 'a leap of faith' and 'let go' (Corry and Stoker 2002).

New localism represented a new pragmatic ideology at the centre of government and, in theory, for local authorities. At the local level, the crucial question has been the extent to which the centre trusts localities to embrace such pragmatic change-management and offer the appropriate support to achieve this task, without localism being misused. This question is set against a tendency for national government to prescribe policy to localities in either a controlling and centralized way, or through subtler types of steering. That said, the much-debated and contested new localism has influenced the policy and practice of local government regeneration management in a number of fundamental ways:

1. Through *strategy devolution* – offering re-imagined concepts for joining up different tiers of government;

2. Through *alternative service management frameworks* which permit local authorities to focus on improvements through developing increased levels of efficiency and effectiveness;

3. Through *enhancing and empowering the community voice* within decision-making processes;

4. Through *democratic renewal* – with attempts to reform local authorities as community leaders rather than as service providers. This was facilitated in many areas by the development of a new model of executive cabinet and backbenchers;

5. Through *area decentralization* giving local authorities a clear opportunity to decentralize service delivery to the sublocal level and give local communities a voice in decisions about their place through the setting-up of area committees or area forums.

In many localities these new localism principles reflected uncertainties over the appropriate spatial scale at which to roll out governance and regeneration policy. This rescaling debate has been under scrutiny in recent years through the complex, and often contradictory relationship at a local level between area-based and city-wide policies, and the shifting national government emphasis between these two spatial levels of restructuring. Such rescaling has also led to the emergence of new institutional arenas such as Local Strategic Partnerships (LSPs) and area committees in order to bring together these key elements of new localist policy with a focus on both improving citizen engagement and ownership over local decision-making and the targeting of locally specific public service delivery.

RESCALING GOVERNANCE, STRATEGIC THINKING AND MULTI-STAKEHOLDER PARTNERSHIPS

Since the 1990s UK urban policy, and the networks through which it operates, has been transformed by wider cultural, economic and technological changes which in many cases have had dramatic restructuring and rescaling effects, both materially, and in terms of existing governance structures. In general, there has been an increasing emphasis placed on strategic reorganization and the development of joined-up or holistic governance especially at a local level with the establishment of a plethora of multi-stakeholder partnerships. Subsequently, multiple partners, partnerships and initiatives have come to the regeneration table with different agendas, timescales, resources, ways of working and, importantly, spatial operating scales, which have continued to cause problems for collaborative arrangements through the further broadening of local partnership structures that attempt to coordinate the splintered institutional environment often found in particular localities.

As such polices which attempted to take a more strategic overview of planned partnership intervention at a local authority level were developed (Apostolakis 2004).

79

This has provided a series of complex challenges for local authorities, especially where embedded governance regimes are being required to transform and develop new organizational cultures that foster coordination between different partnerships and between traditional top-down and new bottom-up approaches. Since 2000, in line with the Local Government Act, a particular solution to this tension was seen to be the development of city-wide LSPs which aimed to:

> bring together at a local level the different parts of the public sector as well as the private, business, community and voluntary sectors so that different initiatives and services support each other and work together.

> (DTLR 2001: 7)

Specifically, one of the key objectives of LSPs has been to develop a vision for an urban area, which would unite fragmented area-based partnerships and provide a more strategic framework in which they could develop and collaborate with other regeneration initiatives. This was to be presented in a coherent document – the Community Strategy.

These LSPs were initially to be established in the 88 most deprived areas to develop a vision for how the locality should develop as well as provide a conduit for Neighbourhood Renewal funding to flow – that was if the LSP could gain accreditation and prove that community engagement was more than tokenistic. For many local authorities attempts to develop an LSP were fraught with difficulties given the quick timescale imposed by national government for such accreditation. In many areas LSPs, as originally conceived, were highly focused upon creating an inclusive partnership through the mechanism of making the partnership as large, and hence representative, as possible with the local authority attempting to stack the board with the 'great and the good' from local business networks and assign the key role of community input to local councillors. As such, there was much concern over the large and unwieldy size of the overall LSP board. As a *Regeneration and Renewal* Editorial noted:

> On paper the partnerships look worryingly unwieldy. Accommodating representatives of all the key service providers, as well as the business people and community groups that also need to be involved, will require an extremely long table.

> (Garlick 2001)

A particular worry that many in the community and voluntary sector expressed at the outset of the LSP development process, despite Government guidance which made it clear that they would be non-executive, was that LSPs would just appoint another exclusive board that would function in isolation to other partnerships and concentrate power in the hands on an elite group of decision makers. This fear in many localities came to fruition with the executivizing of LSP boards with the local authority as lead agent – a similar process to how, in many areas, full councils had transformed to a backbench and cabinet model in line with Government guidance. For example in

Newcastle upon Tyne, the LSP board was reduced from 41 to 18 with the justification that the LSP should function as a fluid network and that individuals, especially local councillors whose representation had been markedly reduced, were IN the network not ON the partnership (Johnston L. 2005). The adoption of this controversial concept – 'you're in it not on it' – is ideologically reminiscent of Putnam's (2000) work on social capital and the importance of social networks not just for formal participants but also for the wider community.

As LSPs have developed local communities appear to have been relatively disengaged – either by design or due to a lack of capacity to play a meaningful role. The tension here also concerns who represents the community – the local councillor in their newly acquired *representative* role as community leaders or local citizens in a more *participative* role. Many LSPs are now developing associated area structures (see next section) that if formally connected to the LSP could provide a participative vehicle for local residents to inform and influence strategic decision-making. That said, the evidence from current research conducted upon such structures highlights the inability of area concerns to influence LSP decisions in any meaningful way given the reluctance of local government to relinquish control and decentralize power and resources to sub-locality partnerships (Coaffee and Johnston 2005).

Bailey (2003) has also highlighted many issues of accountability and control which LSPs have failed to learn – in particular around the construction of equal partnerships – as they attempt to search for collaborative advantage in partnership organization. He argues that they have become, in most cases, local authority-dominated funding bodies with local communities feeling undervalued and by-passed by 'more powerful stake-holders' (Bailey 2003: 455). Indeed, preliminary research conducted in the north west of England on 40 LSPs highlighted the reluctance of the local authority to relinquish control and that this risked sending out an 'exclusive message to local communities' (de Castella 2001). As Coulson (2005a: 160) also noted community representatives (often backbench councillors) from these partnerships often feel frustrated because, from their point of view, very little happens – the main decision appears to have already been taken elsewhere. However, other examples highlight how in some cases community representatives are fully engaged and indeed financially remunerated for attending LSP partnership board meetings (see for example Johnston C. 2005).

Some academic commentators are now questioning whether LSPs actually add value and contribute to the creation of collaborative advantage or whether they operate in parallel to, instead of in conjunction with, existing local partnerships and become another layer of bureaucracy in an already over-bureaucratized system (Bailey 2003). More recent evaluation reports commissioned by central government argue that a lack of appropriate funding is severely restricting the ability of LSPs to deliver and achieve local priorities and that the complexity of the governance system they operate in is impeding community and voluntary sector involvement (ODPM 2005b).

What has however become clear is that LSP have begun to shake-up and *destabilize* embedded governance systems leading to potential new opportunities, and facilitating

81

new ways of working and new participants in local decision-making processes, albeit under the shadow of a reluctance to cede control and influence from the local authority level.

In many cases local authorities, often in conjunction with LSPs, developed neighbourhood governance structures or area committees, 'managed' by backbench councillors in an attempt to provide functional linkage between city-wide and area concerns. It is to the development of these types of governance structure that this chapter now turns.

AREA DEVOLUTION AND THE SEARCH FOR COMMUNITY VOICE

Post-1997, New Labour embraced a host of complex policies linked to the need for change aimed at reshaping the relationships between different nested territorial scales of government and governance. Such change was particularly pronounced after the Local Government Act (2000) that focused on 'what devolution to neighbourhoods' means in practice and how local authorities can define a fresh and innovative approach that responds to the needs of local communities (Corrigan 2000). This Act articulated a need for, and the development possibilities of, sub-local structures within local government areas in order to streamline decision-making processes (Coaffee and Healey 2003; Sullivan *et al*. 2001).

The Local Government Act (2000) guidance made clear that area committees would allow for decentralization of limited power and responsibility from the executive of the local authority to area structures in order to carry out a range of functions. This would effectively allow local people, and in particular local councillors, the opportunity to manage specified local government functions and budgets. It was intended that area committees comprise all, or some of, the elected members, which the area covered. The committees main roles were to provide a role for non-executive (backbench) councillors especially in relation to community leadership and the scrutiny of local services, and provide a vehicle for public involvement in council matters. These roles were intended to allow such committees to strategically link city-wide and area-based concerns, facilitate partnership working amongst key stakeholders, complement LSP structures and the development of community strategies, work with other regeneration partnerships or service delivery structures, and to help with overall local government modernization.

Area committees were also seen as an attempt at coordinating wider corporate structures with decentralized service delivery, highlighting the rhetoric of joined-up thinking and transformation from clientelistic government to community-led governance (Coaffee and Healey 2003; Taylor and Gaster 2001). Figure 6.1 shows the imagined relationship between corporate structures and area concerns which were, at the time of the Local Government Act (2000), already operating through area-based initiatives but which, in the future, it was hoped would increasingly link to area committees.

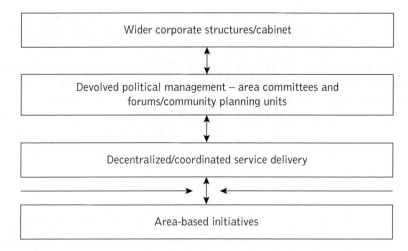

Figure 6.1 *Linkages between corporate and devolved areas structures*
Adapted from DETR 2000.

Area committees were seen to have a huge potential in terms of decentralization – to determine local priorities within a strategic framework, to set annual targets to achieve measurable and positive outcomes, and to promote best practice. No prescriptive prototype of the way area committees should operate was given by central government. Instead, local government was advised to use flexibility in interpreting and adopting guidance in order to fit local agendas and policies. In practice however, a number of local authorities interpreted area committee policies in a straightforward and prescriptive way, whilst some authorities took their time implementing area committees in order to learn lessons from others.

GOING LOCAL

Adopted structures for area committees across the UK have varied in terms of size, representation, function, degree of power devolved, and linkages to the LSP and service providers. Some area committee-style structures can be seen as radical with large-scale funding and power devolved to the area level. For example, Birmingham City Council in 2003/4 adopted area structures or mini councils as a 'revolutionary effort at localisation' aimed at replacing 'the bureaucracy of centralisation' in order to better link civic renewal and improvements in public services (Bore 2004). Under this reform eleven area/district structures replaced the previous 39 wards, and were managed by constituency directors, and run by area councillors. According to the council's strategic director these constituency councils will 'provide a structure through which all sections of the city's community can participate in decision-making' with measures in place to prevent constituencies creating mini empires. However,

83

the envisioned pace of change is slow with the devolution of wide-ranging responsibilities to the local committees taking up to ten years (see also Randle 2005; ODPM 2005a).

By contrast, Newcastle upon Tyne has provided an example of more advanced attempts to set up area committees more prescriptively following government guidance. In Newcastle, area committees were introduced with three key ideas in mind – to attract Neighbourhood Renewal Funding (and associated community empowerment funds), to transform entrenched council working practices, and to involve the community in local government processes. Pressure also came from citizens' concerns about appropriate levels of involvement in policy discourses (Coaffee 2004).

In Newcastle, the structure and function of the area committees were first developed in 2000 alongside the City Council's commitment to community planning and focused upon identifying and representing local priorities with an aim to improve service provision and mechanisms for community consultation. Newcastle's seven area committees were formally launched in April 2001 with each area committee consisting of a group of pre-existing wards and overseen by local councillors. With the introduction of cabinet-style government, the area committees thus gave a strategic role to all councillors, above the ward scale.

Area committees were presented as the interface between local and city-wide issues. In particular, strong links were envisioned with the emerging LSP, the community strategy and the city-wide regeneration policy. However, these ambitious assumptions were not supported with sufficient training for councillors or community and voluntary sector representatives, or strong leadership, and hence the seven area committees developed unevenly and in very different ways with little or no overarching coordination, leadership or strategic focus. There was also much confusion and misunderstanding about where area committees fitted into the city's governance structure. As they developed a number of committees were also perceived to be little more than 'councillor committees' – controlled by, and for, locally elected representatives (Johnston L. 2005).

The danger of old-style council committees being reconstituted in sub-localities as 'mini-town halls' (Sullivan et al. 2001) had not been entirely unexpected but reflects the difficulties local councillors have faced in the transition from their old roles to that of community leaders. In particular the reluctance of many councillors to think 'outside the box' and attempt to facilitate the development of community voice in creative or innovative ways has been sadly lacking.

Most of the area committees in Newcastle were plagued with poor or non-existent attendance from local citizens, many of whom were unaware of the committees' existence. There were also complaints made that all area committees in Newcastle lacked suitable funding mechanisms, and service directorate support. Initial evaluation highlighted the need for area committees to be less ambitious in their early stages of development. However, such evaluation did highlight the unsettling role such committees were having on existing governance and political structures in the city (Coaffee and Healey 2003; Johnston L. 2005).

In 2003, a process to restructure area committees began which aimed to encourage greater strategic management and more coherent linkages to the LSP. This however led to proposals for three or four area networks which once again were aligned to ward boundaries but reduced the role for local councillor's involvement – the idea was to allow one out of the three members from each ward to sit on the area network. The idea behind this was to reduce the number of committees and roles for councillors – in short to reduce democratic burden. This led to much displeasure amongst locally elected members who saw the influence of their representative role further diluted. In 2005–6 this strategic network idea was superseded by a different approach which increasingly localized governance decisions and increased the power and resources given toward committees and their elected members.

Whereas Birmingham's 'Going Local' initiative provides a radical example of how area devolution and organizational cultural change might, in the long term develop, and decentralize real power, resources and responsibility to the local level, the Newcastle example highlights the many complex issues surrounding the minutiae of establishing area committees linked to changing governance practices and expected roles for local councillors – around different decision-making powers, budgets, membership, community participation and links to strategic bodies, particularly the LSP.

The decentralizing and devolutionary rhetoric behind area committees has proved controversial, partly because opposition political parties, especially the Liberal Democrats, have supported it, at least conceptually. However, in many localities they remain an ill-defined part of the local governance network. Myerson (2005), writing in the *Guardian* newspaper, argued that the area committee was one of the best ways to waste a councillor's time without succeeding in engaging the community as intended:

> Through the brainchild of the Office of the Deputy Prime Minister, these have been embraced enthusiastically by the Lib Dems. 'Give power back to the people!' they shout. Unfortunately, they do not give power to the committees let alone a genuine budget. No administration is ever going to grant them this kind of power, so all area committee decisions have to be referred back to the executive. I use the time to do my paperwork and catch up with old friends. There are never any new faces to be seen.

SUMMARY

This chapter has highlighted the current complexity involved in managing the regeneration process and in particular the tensions that emerge within new partnership structures – seen as a panacea in developing effective and efficient local governance. Many of these new tensions are connected to the changing role of the local councillor, who, on one hand, appear to have been marginalized from the central decision-making processes in local government but, on the other hand, are tasked with providing a community leadership role in their electoral area and then feeding back community priorities to higher levels of governance. This change in traditional councillor roles has, however, been problematic. There has been insufficient training and skill development and an inability in many cases to transform embedded councillor cultures. This has meant that new, innovative and creative forms of local or area-based partnership working have not been as successful as predicted and in many cases have become mini town halls or councillor committees. In part, this is a reflection of the overall New Labour subsidiarity project. There appears to be a decentralization of responsibility occurring but not the devolution of power. This is related to an inability or unwillingness to let go from central to local levels of government and from local government to sub-local partnerships or committees. However, there is some evidence that things might be changing, at least at a local level as there are an increasing number of new councillors who have not experienced this old and outdated committee system way of doing governance. That said, the increased and active participation within local and sub-local partnership by un-elected actors (especially local citizens or the business sector) is also causing a growing tension between the roles of representative versus participative democracy.

ACKNOWLEDGEMENTS

Lorraine Johnston is a Research Associate in the Institute for Political and Economic Governance and Dr Jon Coaffee is a Lecturer in Spatial Planning and Urban Regeneration, both at the University of Manchester, UK. This work has been funded in part by the UK's Economic and Social Research Council (ESRC) (PTA-033-2002-00003).

NOTES

1   A small number of councils adopted a Mayoral system.
2   In particular, the Maud report (1969) and Bains report (1972).

Chapter 7

Managing inclusion

Ruth McAlister

The idea of citizen participation is a little like eating spinach; no one is against it in principle because it is good for you.

(Arnstein 1969: 216)

INTRODUCTION

The last twenty years or so have seen a major growth in the phenomenon of place marketing or 'selling the city' which has shaped urban regeneration on both sides of the Atlantic (Neill 1995). The need for constant renewal and change of the fabric of cities is a manifestation of their response to the economic and social pressures placed on them. However regeneration is not a fast process and cannot be simply left alone to conventional property developers, planners and urban regeneration agencies to go it alone like lemmings in a regeneration game. The general belief that imposed solutions to complex long-term problems do not work is evidenced in the failure of property-led regeneration, a method favoured in the recent past to quickly turn around disadvantaged areas without showing any real concern for how it would impact on local residents. In other words, city centre planning and regeneration processes have been leaving inner city neighbourhoods behind made up of alienated, marginalized and disempowered residents. As Hastings *et al.* (1996) acknowledge 'although the property led approach to regeneration was responsible for a great deal of physical development and improvement of urban areas, it was weak in meeting the needs of residents living in disadvantaged communities'. It has been realized that for urban regeneration policies to become effective it is necessary to consult with local people, to facilitate a more open approach to decision-making (Short 1996). This is not a new phenomenon however despite the rhetoric of inclusive planning, with consultation and participation becoming the buzz words of the 1990s and beyond, the reality is that the participatory debate has been long running (Davidoff 1965).

Public participation in planning was officially enshrined in UK law in 1960s following the Skeffington and Seebohm Reports which argued that for planning to be effective it was necessary to consult with local people (De Castella 2000). There was however a change in the attitude towards public participation in the 1990s: Duffy and Hutchinson (1997) noted that there has been 'a new turn to community'. Indeed, wherever one turns within the urban policy arena the terms 'community' and 'participation' are used with great frequency and aplomb. It is suggested that when communities 'own' the solutions, the results are more sustainable than those that have been imposed from the outside.

The actual process of public consultation can be divided into two general types – one-way and interactive. One-way methods include information-giving, fact-finding and campaigning methods. Interactive methods seek to foster debate and include techniques such as focus groups, design workshops and preparation methods which seek to educate local people so as to better equip them to participate actively. At the centre of methods involving citizens is the belief that participation needs to be open to everyone, not just the articulate and those with time and experience (Colenutt and Cutten 1994). However, while participation may be agreed with in principle, the practice is much more problematic. There will always be questions of just how inclusive planning should be and how much the concerns of a particular individual or community should influence policy.

This chapter will first examine the concepts of community and social exclusion, both of which are vital when discussing how best to manage inclusion. Indeed, the contradictory and conflicting ways these two terms have been employed will be explored before looking at what further barriers are in place that may prevent local residents engaging in consultation processes: this discussion will reflect some data taken from my own study into how Belfast plans its regeneration. Advice will also be offered to those charged with regeneration practice, as the evidence clearly suggests that if communities and community leaders are involved in the decision-making process they are more likely to feel a sense of ownership of new developments (Joseph Rowntree Foundation [JRF] 1999).

THE COMMUNITY AND SOCIAL EXCLUSION IN THE PLANNING PROCESS

The constitution of the 'local community' out of groups of people living in a local area has been at the core of debates surrounding communication in planning and urban regeneration policy for some time (Hill 1994). In recent years too there has been an increasing emphasis upon the local scale in spatial planning, such as community planning and other bottom-up approaches (Boland 2000). One of the central problems with any approach to local development in spatial planning lies in the defining of community. Historically, the term has been used to distinguish between 'common people' and those of rank, and today it is possible to uncover some one hundred competing definitions (Blackman 1991). It is not surprising therefore to discover that the concept 'has been used in inherently ambiguous and contradictory ways' (Mayo 1994: 37). The concept of community as used and interpreted by policy makers is, however, in danger of losing its meaning and sense of complexity (Cohen 1985). This is a consequence of two key interrelated features. First, the term community is at risk of becoming a meaningless hollow concept due to its overuse within policy documents and public statements by politicians and policy makers. Second, and perhaps more importantly, policy makers and others have a tendency to construct a narrowly defined perception of who or what constitutes the local community. In simple terms, policy makers seem to have constructed an image of the local community with the following characteristics: monolithic in structure, static in profile and nature and bounded and attached to a particular spatial locale (Maginn 2004: 44).

The notion of community therefore is highly contested both conceptually and in urban regeneration practice (Hill 1994). This contestability has major implications for regeneration policy, where community and participation are now fundamental issues. It is necessary for policy makers to be more aware of and informed about the profile, relations and dynamics that exist within and between the various communities that coexist within urban regeneration areas.

As well as increased emphasis on the term community and the exploration of different concepts of community there has also been a move amongst policy makers (and academics) towards studying social exclusion, a term made popular by European policy documents in the 1990s. Although this is a popular term, Levitas (1998: 2) cautions 'there is no monolithic, pan European definition of social exclusion; rather there is a range of national discourses which use the idea of social exclusion in different ways'. Furthermore, as some argue 'definitions belong to the definer and not to the defined' (McClean 2003: 68). That said, the approach taken in this chapter is to focus on the process rather than the state of social exclusion, and explore the dynamics of how the process of urban regeneration relates to people living in economically disadvantaged communities. The line between inclusion and exclusion is not viewed as a simple dichotomy but as a continuum through which individuals and communities move. Individuals for example may feel included in their own community while feeling excluded from wider society. Urban regeneration is seen as one aspect of how this process works in practice. Issues surrounding participation in planning and decision-making are crucial in understanding how communities actually become involved in the process of development. Although the lack of participation in education and the labour market can be some of the most fundamental forms of exclusion, a lack of access to decision-making within other areas of public life such as land use planning can be seen as a broader denial of citizenship rights (Berghman 1995). These collectively combine to form an important element of the processes that contribute to social exclusion.

Planning does have the potential to include those who are generally considered to be on the periphery of society and so allow them greater access to the benefits of citizenship as well as creating a greater sense of inclusion in wider society. As Community Technical Aid (CTA) noted in 1995 'community participation is inextricably linked to effective social and economic regeneration in cities throughout the world. It's valued and embedded in the policies and programmes of national bodies, European programmes and international strategies' (cited in Acheson 1998: 11). Furthermore, research and evaluation in Britain and the Republic of Ireland confirm the view held by community groups in Northern Ireland that participation is intrinsic to the sustainable development of disadvantaged communities. This is because involvement in regeneration is not simply limited to land use planning, but can also include training and employment opportunities, education, increased access to public space and public events. Participation is therefore explored as one way in which decision makers can attempt to tackle social exclusion by involving economically disadvantaged communities in decision-making.

BARRIERS TO PARTICIPATION

There has been widespread recognition in recent years of the problems of top-down development and the resulting distance between those who plan the urban environment and those who have to live and work in it. The paradox, as Short (1989) observes, is that those who have the greatest power in planning decisions are those with whom the public have least contact, while those decision makers with whom they are likely to have the most contact are those with the least influence.

The realm of planning too over recent years has become increasingly complex and bureaucratic, creating a system in which the individual may feel insignificant and power-less, resulting in a distancing between those who make the decisions and those they will affect. There is a realization that planners and others have been and in many cases continue to be part of a political and cultural system which has actively excluded certain sections of the population from the planning of the city. It is evident that pressure is growing for a new form of planning which takes into account the need for public involvement in the planning of cities in which they live. One problem identified by a planning consultant in Belfast is:

> How do you actually engage with the community and not run the risk of either, on the one hand consulting people to death where they don't feel there is any value in it, or where you actually do it as a token gesture?
>
> (Interview 7 February 2005)

The World Summit for Social Development in Copenhagen in 1995 (cited in Acheson 1998: 3) observed that essential actions for community participation in redevelopment issues include:

> strengthening opportunities for all people especially those who are disadvantaged and vulnerable, to enhance their own economic and social development, to estab-lish and maintain organizations representing their needs and to be involved in the planning and implementation of government policies and programmes by which they will be directly affected.

90

Frazer (1991) further states that their active participation in the planning, management and implementation of development is seen as essential for success. Therefore the development of people's skills, the encouragement of self-help and the creation of structures that maximize community involvement and control are key elements in the process. Local people drawing on their own experiences of life are best placed to identify the issues that need to be addressed. This means that needs can be targeted accurately and more relevant initiatives developed. If communities are excluded at the beginning of regeneration programmes then there is serious danger that the wrong issues will be prioritized and resources misdirected or wasted (JRF 1995: 14). Community involvement is not a 'bolt-on' activity (JRF 1999). Successful area regeneration can *only* occur when local people are involved in the process and are equipped with the skills they need in order to have an impact. Few people (if any) appear to disagree with these sentiments, unfortunately, however, interpretation and implementation can often leave a lot to be desired. All too often 'regeneration professionals' wish to decide what role the community should play, who should play it and how they should play it.

This can have a huge impact on the number of those from the community taking part in consultation exercises. Community participation in the recent past has been modest at best. When challenged about the lack of involvement in consultation exercises from the local community regeneration professionals will often argue that local people are apathetic, they do not attend consultation meetings, and if they do they have little or nothing to contribute. There are a number of factors that are invariably overlooked here; the first is the life experiences that cause dissatisfaction, including previous examples of inadequate consultation, where consultation did occur but had no real impact or influence on how plans and policy were developed: 'we sit through consultations many times, we express views, and they never appear, why do we waste our breath saying things again and again' (West Belfast community worker). Similarly a South Belfast community worker stated 'to be honest sometimes people feel that consultation is the time between when an organization decides to do something and then goes and does it'. Connected to this are the barriers which prevent those who are relatively inexperienced from communicating with professionals, as the language and terminology used by planners can prevent some members of the public understanding the discussion relating to decision-making.

These barriers, along with more practical considerations, such as limitations of time and problems of access, work to limit the extent to which communities become involved. One suggestion to encourage those to become involved and overcome these barriers is to 'bring it to the people, depending on what the policy or issue is you can go and set up a small stall in a shopping centre and people will go, there are ways to do it and get people interested' (West Belfast community worker). Even where regeneration agencies and local authorities have a strong commitment to community involvement the short-term nature of many of the initiatives militate against genuine inclusion because the timescales of projects mean that lead partners must quickly gear up to deliver their contracted outputs, rather than have time to study the area in detail or consult widely on priorities (Brownhill and Darke 1998). A similar point has been noted by Taylor (2000: 9) 'if adequate time is not allowed, commitment only runs skin deep in statutory authorities, meanwhile community involvement is confined to those already known to public bodies – the "usual suspects" who can hit the ground running'. This tendency to recruit the same faces can lead to serious tensions within a neighbourhood. One study suggested that those who are involved may feel the burden, 'it's always left to the committed few' while those who are not included may feel debarred from involvement by an unrepresentative clique (Carley *et al.* 2000: 16). Meanwhile Frazer (1994) cites among his barriers to community involvement attracting area representatives, intra-community rivalry and competition. In Northern Ireland the problem is further accentuated by the existence of paramilitary representation during a number of consultations. One community worker from East Belfast commented:

> They [statutory bodies] think all consultation is good, however, they don't realize that if there are paramilitaries around the table they tend not to represent the majority viewpoint in the east. So the political and statutory bodies need to realize the reality of who they are talking to and who they are targeting rather than just listening to the one political or religious viewpoint.

> A local government worker in Belfast expressed a different view. You can talk about this until you're blue in the face – consultation, what does it mean? Does it influence outcome? We ourselves have been wrestling with that for a long time, in terms of whether it does make a difference and you know trying to find a way to demonstrate to a sometimes very sceptical public or publics that their input can make a difference is very tricky.

A further difficulty in attracting local people to participate in consultation exercises was raised with reference to the particular complex system of governance that exists in Northern Ireland and the statutory provisions that emulate from this.

> I think if you could establish some kind of institutional map of who is out there in terms of land use planning or impact on territory and how it is planned or developed, it would be a useful starting point to illustrate the difficulty the public have in getting access to the planning machinery.
>
> (Public sector employee)

With all the competing views of the role of the planner even the most well-intentioned planner could be caught out trying to balance conflicting loyalties and whose interests they should prioritize. Within the current planning system planners are often forced to choose between the community and the statutory authorities, 'choose the community and you are choosing professional death, choose to work for the state and retain your professional identity, but don't delude yourself about whose interests you are serving' (Sandercock 1998: 99).

92

LIFTING BARRIERS TO PARTICIPATION

Atkinson (1999) notes that in relation to engendering community consultation and involvement, progress needs to be made in recognizing that targeted areas contain a plethora of dynamic communities. Put simply, policy makers need to be more aware and informed about the profile, relations and dynamics within and between the various communities that coexist within urban regeneration areas. A failure to map and take account of the diversity and dynamism within the communities may produce serious negative reactions. A community backlash to regeneration proposals may result in at best a short delay in the programme, or at worst an abandonment of parts or all of a regeneration scheme. However, with recognition of the potential barriers, to participation solutions can be created and consultation processes can be made more inclusive. As Forester (1993: 34) observes, 'at every level, we find dynamics of power and distortion that jeopardize democratic participation and autonomy, and we can identify, anticipate and work to counteract such influences'.

Short (1989: 2) offers the ideal model of 'cities as if people matter' – the starting point for which might be 'to see citizens as part of the solution to, and not the cause of urban problems'. If this is to be the case individuals must be able to become actively involved in the planning and development of the urban landscape. Currently while most Western states accept the idea of public involvement in the planning of cities, in reality the extent of consultation and the distribution of power between social groups varies markedly, with the interests of the economically and socially elite tending to dominate in the planning of the city. It is the nature of the capitalist city that power tends to be concentrated in the hands of business interests because of the importance of the economy and commercialism within its life. In competition with these two interests it is questionable how much influence the average citizen can have with the decision-making system. That said, capacity-building is increasingly considered to be an important precursor to effective involvement and refers to the process of developing the abilities of local people to organize themselves so that they may have more influence over the process and involvement of outcomes. It stems from a recognition that the pace and nature of regeneration initiatives can continue to exclude local output. However the term capacity-building needs to be used carefully as all too often there is an assumption that local people lack the wherewithal to deal with the complexities of the urban regeneration and planning process. Henderson and Mayo (1998: v) comment 'to imply that local people are empty vessels simply waiting to be filled via training and capacity building ignores the wealth of existing knowledge and skills within communities'. Yet, on the other hand, the term acknowledges the very real power relationships that exist between professionals and residents and the need to ensure that local people are in a position to take as much control as they wish and are equipped with the knowledge and skills which to do so. As McClean (2003: 68) notes 'by playing an active part in planning their communities, skills and confidence are developed which contribute to the communities long-term sustainability'. Capacity-building, however, is not a quick process: some

93

residents may have had years of experience of community action, while others could be entirely new to the experience. Unless capacity-building actually begins to challenge these power relationships exclusion from consultation processes will continue. It should also be borne in mind that the process of capacity-building is futile without the associated cultural changes that are required within regeneration agencies, local authorities, planners and those otherwise associated with regeneration, including various funding bodies (Taylor 2000). Therefore those charged with regeneration must keep communities informed of the developments taking place: although awareness will not necessarily result in inclusion it may prevent people from feeling excluded. Communities also need to feel that consultation is genuine, simply 'consulting' residents in as narrow a definition as possible is a long way removed from genuine community involvement. Thus communities should be supplied with the resources to participate, believe their views are taken seriously and be involved in feedback from meetings, particularly those involving schemes which have a meaningful impact upon their lives. A failure on the part of organizations to take heed of this can lead to great frustration in the local area, a view that was strongly expressed by a community worker in West Belfast regarding one particular regeneration policy:

> We have never seen on the web site or anywhere else what people's comments were and that made people really disillusioned because people were really engaging in the nuts and bolts of that strategy, of what it would mean and how it would be rolled out and it all seems to have been completely ignored.

PARTNERSHIP

Partnership has been one-way, in which local authorities, statutory agencies and others have attempted to include people in regeneration and planning strategies. This is evident particularly in the last decade or so with 'partnership arrangements' becoming more common place. Taussik and Smalley (1998) claim that partnership is fast becoming the orthodoxy of policy of the twenty-first century. Similarly, Hastings et al. (1996) have commented that it would be unthinkable to discuss regeneration without referring to partnership. This new emphasis on partnership is due to a number of reasons, primarily that there is now an emerging consensus within urban regeneration and other area policy fields on the need for a multi-agency approach to tackle the problems associated with socially excluded neighbourhoods (Bailey et al. 1995). Second, the partnership approach has also helped to integrate voluntary and community sectors with the private sector to give the perception that policy is locally driven. This is particularly important given the strength of the community sector in Belfast, which emerged from the 1970s onwards as state legitimacy broke down in many areas of the city and residents organized many of the local services for themselves. However, even working and being established in a partnership is not a guarantee that the voices of local people are reflected in the decision-making: essentially power struggles may continue, with influential voices vying for the majority of the power while those less articulate can be left floundering from the sidelines (Hastings *et al.* 1996). One community worker from South Belfast said:

> Those who are discriminated against by dint of their gender, socio-economic status, disability or ethnic origin must find a space within a partnership to articulate and have validated the relevance of their experiences for the policy making processes. The extent to which the partnership can accommodate or reflect these interests and foster respect for such diverse experiences and points of view in its decision taking arena will be an index of its maturity . . . this kind of agreement threatens everyone precisely because it necessitates compromise on the part of those who hold power and authority in favour of those who do not.

However, even working in a partnership arrangement requires time and commitment from participants, which may deter some. There are also issues regarding how people are selected from the local community to sit in a regeneration partnership. For example, are these people representative and will they express the view of the collective majority in the area? If not this could raise crucial questions regarding the viability and validity of the partnership. That said, commentators do favour the partnership arrangement in tackling exclusion from consultation processes. Acheson (1998: 14) comments 'tackling the problems of the most marginalized communities through new partnership structures, with a strong emphasis on the involvement of local communities should be a core element in the struggle to build a fairer and more inclusive society'. What inclusive regeneration requires is clear lines of communication, as each of the bodies involved in the partnership needs to be aware of the responsibilities and powers of individual members and other organizations. This helps to create an environment of openness between organizations and a realistic sense of the possibilities of developments which will result in the creation of more trusting relationships and ideally more confident, skilled and empowered local residents.

CONCLUSION

Our cities are hugely important in how we as people identify ourselves and how we represent ourselves to the world. Urban regeneration is a concrete and ideological representation of our society. If the identities, needs and concerns of marginalized communities are not included, urban regeneration will reflect only one aspect of our identity, and our cities as a consequence will be deprived and not reach their full potential. However, this chapter has shown that regardless of debate, policy documents and government initiatives concerning social exclusion and despite some innovative and some not so innovative methods of engagement in planning and regeneration, decision makers continue to struggle with involving those from disadvantaged communities. As

Paddison (2001: 202) notes 'bringing the community into the practice of urban regeneration is a demonstrably more fraught exercise than governments had assumed it to be'. One key issue identified earlier was how do you conceptualize community? Unfortunately what constitutes a community is still being debated and as such the term is used and applied in interchangeable ways. What has been established is that who and what comprises a community is not easy to identify. Local communities are a highly complex and dynamic phenomena and individuals may be members of many communities at any given time (Hill 1994).

The evidence presented throughout this chapter calls for communities to be better equipped to take advantage of opportunities, while those working with disadvantaged communities need to be aware of the history of that community's experience with consultation and the barriers which exist to participation. Finally, regeneration bodies need to be honest with communities and respect the knowledge and experience held within them.

The basic principles of respect for individuals and communities, culture and heritage and recognition of the rights and responsibilities of citizenship and adequate support for economically disadvantaged individuals and communities emerge as key factors in ensuring inclusive regeneration. The ideal solution as identified by those working in communities is a greater openness on the part of decision makers so that the community are made aware of the hard facts and decision-making, allowing them to act as equal partners so that consultation becomes real participation. 'Communities are intelligent and understand the realities of life and business and they would like to be treated as equals, we want to be listened to and discussed with, not talked at' (North Belfast community worker). Similarly, Frazer (1994) concurs that tackling the problems of the most marginalized communities through new partnership structures should be a core element in the struggle to build a fairer and more inclusive society. Of course, there is a balance to be reached on the extent to which public views are taken into account, and Sandercock (1998) warns against current trends towards romanticizing the community voice. Meanwhile Castells (1972) cautions that there is a danger of over-simplifying the issue of public participation and consultation. People do not act purely as individuals but also as a social group or class section: citizens will therefore not always act in the interests of other excluded groups. Therefore while the general trend towards empowerment of individuals and communities is welcomed, this is by no means an unproblematic issue, as 'participation means more than having people express their opinions. The right to participate in the decision-making process brings with it responsibility to act for the common good' (Wilson 1997: 746).

There is no universal panacea to involving citizens – methods and approaches need to be adapted to suit the context in which they are applied. The rewards for creating inclusive consultation and participation are many, including making plans and policies more successful and creating a greater sense of empowerment for those involved. What this chapter has revealed is that although many of our regeneration professionals recognize the importance of including those residents from the locale in decision-making processes, much more needs to be done to encourage citizens to participate. One key issue identified from this study is how you actually engage people who do not understand the processes involved in planning and regeneration. A planning consultant in Belfast offered some assistance with regard to this:

> In every consultation process the very first thing communities should ask, and indeed the very first thing the person conducting the conversation should ask is what is this conversation about . . . and unless the two parties know what it's absolutely about, it's probably going to end up worthless with one or the other being grossly disappointed.

Part Three

Accountability

KEY THEMES

■ Developing models and systems of local accountability.
■ Enhancing the status and role of evaluation and monitoring.
■ Strengthening the capacity of local regeneration partnerships to understand and learn from evaluation.

LEARNING POINTS

By the end of Part Three we hope that you will be able to:

■ Identify different models of accountability.
■ Reflect upon how local regeneration partnerships currently use the lessons of evaluation.
■ Develop strategies of capacity building to promote evaluation and to involve local residents and practitioners in the process.

CONTEXT SETTING

A recurrent theme both in this edited collection and in the regeneration management literature is the extent to which regeneration partnerships are accountable to the diverse set of interests present in local partnership boards. Andrew Coulson provides a useful and informative commentary on the different models currently in place and identifies ways in which local trusts can provide alternative models of management and representation for local interest groups. In his essay Coulson argues that it is possible to reconcile legal and managerial requirements with local (and political) needs. This overview of different systems and his analysis of potential solutions illustrates the need to examine ways in which local interests can secure their voice as well as meeting the legal and financial expectations of agencies.

Joyce Liddle and Stuart Smith explore the different ways in which evaluation processes have come to be used in regeneration initiatives. They examine some of the underlying assumptions of evaluation systems/processes and, at the same time, point to ways in which evaluation methodologies can draw upon the experiences of a range of participants who have an interest in understanding what has worked and who themselves represent interests broader than those of regeneration professionals or policy makers.

Chapter 8

Regeneration initiatives

Governance and accountability

Andrew Coulson

Previous chapters described the roles played in regeneration by many different types of people: community leaders and those they endeavour to lead, councillors, civil servants and administrators from government offices or departments, professionals from many different backgrounds including those who work for local government, the health service and the police; also those who lead, or are employed by, independent organizations in what is often no longer accurately described as the voluntary sector. Relatively little has been written about how these players, either individually or as members of boards or partnerships, spend public money, and account for their actions, both to the people who live in local areas and to the tax-paying public at large.

This chapter begins by identifying the basic types of *network*, or *partnership structure*. Most partnerships have some kind of *administrative centre*, or *hub*; so often the best way to understand a network is to study the hub, and ask who controls or manages the activities of the network, and who holds the power. The next section of the chapter discusses the many potential benefits from working together, but these are not inevitable: there are many pitfalls and the potential benefits may not be realized. Different types of hub or administration can be associated with different *legal forms*, and these have various advantages and disadvantages, which make them more or less appropriate in different circumstances. A similar range of governance arrangements is available to organizations in the voluntary sector. The final part of the chapter looks in more detail at the issues of *accountability*, and the challenges and *ethical dilemmas* that arise through being a board member of a regeneration initiative.

NETWORKS AND PARTNERSHIPS

The simplest cooperation is between just two organizations. They may work together on an activity of common interest – as in the top half of Figure 8.1. Or they may set up a separate structure or organization, a joint venture, to develop a particular piece of work, as shown in the bottom half of Figure 8.1. If so, the joint venture must have some understanding of how it will work – a *memorandum of understanding* (which may be no more

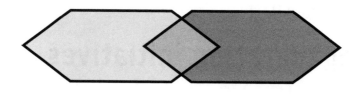

Strategic alliance

Joint venture

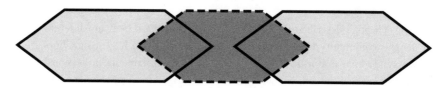

Figure 8.1 *Joint work with two partners*

than an exchange of letters or emails), or a *constitution* of some sort, or, if the work is likely to go far and lead to identifiable costs and income streams, a more complicated structure such as a company.

A *network* is similar, involving several organizations in different relationships. There is only a weak centre or administration – perhaps membership of a local chamber of commerce or trade association, or possibly the administrative support for a local strategic partnership provided by its local authority. In a *federation*, illustrated in Figure 8.2, the actions of the centre are not binding on the participants.

The relationships are matters of convenience, some fleeting, some more permanent. They occur because there is mutual benefit between pairs, or larger groupings. Table 8.1 lists a set of circumstances in which it might benefit organizations in the private sector to cooperate with someone else.

Other networks are created from the start with a definite structure and the purpose of achieving very clear objectives. These are *hub networks*. The individual or organization at the hub controls the other members.

This could, for example, be a main contractor, hiring a set of subcontractors to complete a complicated building project, or the producer of a film, hiring a series of specialists to make the production, or a group of companies developing a complex new product, such as an aircraft, and needing a wide range of skills and expertise, all working together to bring the product to fruition, yet ultimately controlled by and dependent on a main contractor.

Hub networks may also emerge over time – as when a group of individuals or organizations meeting together decide that they need to create a central coordinating

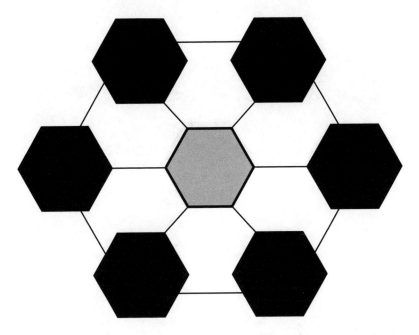

Figure 8.2 *A network of organizations or federations*

Table 8.1 *Collaborative advantages in the private sector*

Direct activities with competitors	Direct activities with non-competitors
Using competitors' workers when one has work and the other not	Using suppliers' or buyers' workers
Exchanging information with competitors	Sharing information with suppliers or customers
Engaging in joint research	Joint research with suppliers or customers
Developing a new product or venture	Developing a new product or venture
Engaging in joint advertising	Joint advertising with suppliers or customers
Joint training	Joint training
Engaged in licensing agreements	Engaged in licensing agreements
Sharing transportation costs	Sharing transportation costs
Joint purchase or sales agreements	

Source: Darwin (2002) from a study of 677 alliances researched by Marc Dollinger.

103

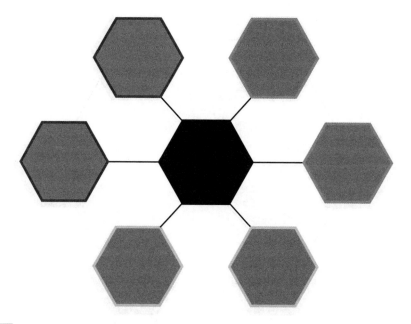

Figure 8.3 *A hub network or partnership*

organization. Even then there can be problems – witness the history of conflict and disagreement between the Football Association, representing the game as a whole and needing a strong centre, and the Premier League, a much looser organization representing the interests of the elite clubs, whose direct interests frequently conflict with those of the FA.

Most regeneration partnerships are hub networks – a hub is formed when a dedicated organization is created and staffed, and achieves a level of independence from individual partners. But who controls and governs the hub, and to whom is it accountable? These are key questions for this chapter. First, to get a better understanding of why we are dealing with hub partnerships, we look again at some of the reasons why public sector bodies might work in partnership.

WHY WORK IN PARTNERSHIPS?

Maureen Mackintosh (1992) identified three categories of benefits which may arise from working together in partnerships: first, there may be *synergy*, where a joint venture can achieve outputs which its partners on their own could not achieve; second, benefits may come from *transformation*, or *culture change*, where working in partnership transfers the benefits of the culture of one partner to another, for example when public sector partners adopt methods from the private sector; and finally there may be benefits from *budget enlargement*, where the partnership has access to more resources than otherwise would be available (this may be because the government makes the existence of a partnership a condition of financial support, or because, with several partnerships contributing, capital sums may be raised which no individual member could find alone).

Christine Huxham made similar points. She identified a *financial or efficiency* motivation: the funding of a project, or its delivery, may require a number of partners. Or collaboration may be desirable to avoid overlaps ('it is *ceteris paribus* not sensible for two public agencies to provide a housing placement service in the same area') (Huxham 1996). But, she argued, partnerships may also be imposed for political (but others might describe as *cultural*) reasons: for example in the hope that 'what is seen as private sector managerial "good practice" may rub off on what are seen as the more inefficient public agencies' (Huxham 1996). Finally, Huxham identified what she calls *moral* arguments for collaboration, based on:

> the belief that the really important problem issues facing society — poverty, conflict, crime and so on — cannot be tackled by any single organization acting alone . . . they are inherently multi-organizational. Collaboration is therefore essential if there is to be any hope of alleviating these problems.
>
> (Huxham 1996: 3–4)

The UK government has argued strongly for working in partnership. Here are some of the arguments it uses to make the case (clearly reflecting thinking such as that of Mackintosh and Huxham above):

- Bring in new ideas: not just how things were done in the past
- Especially bring in new ideas from the private sector
- Bring in extra money
- Enable existing money to be better used
- Make different agencies work and think together
- Avoid duplication
- Involve service users and local communities
- Save costs of duplication
- Avoid disputes in public
- Move resources to where they are most needed
- Confront vested interests.

As noted earlier, the literature about the benefits of partnership working in the private sector distinguishes between benefits from working with partners who do more or less similar things — from economies of scale and sharing of key or expensive resources such as research or marketing — and benefits which come from working with suppliers or contractors, where the gains accrue to the supply chain as a whole (Kanter 1989; Porter 1990; Coulson 2005b).

105

As for regeneration, we can cut through the rhetoric and find three very basic reasons why organizations locally are working in partnership:

- There are many different funding regimes, sponsored by different government departments, so organizations and agencies on the ground have to work together to prevent overlap and get the best results;
- Central government makes partnerships a condition of its funding;
- It does so as a means of forcing the different agencies to work together.

The benefits of working in partnership are by no means inevitable. The literature summarized above also recognizes that partnerships may break down or disappoint. Most partnerships in the private sector depend on trust – a willingness to share information on the assumption that partners will share with you some time in the future (Kanter 1994). In the public sector, there may be elements of coercion (for example where legislation requires a partnership to be created), or the exercise of power (when the only way to access resources is to form a partnership).[1] Partnerships can be problematic if the partnership members are unequal: if they are perceived as a mechanism for the strong to co-opt the weak (Mayo and Taylor 2001), as with some partnerships formed to access government money and required to include representatives from the local communities they are attempting to serve. Rowe (2005) compares partnerships between organizations with partnerships between individuals, where there are many possible causes of breakdown. He goes as far as to describe many regeneration partnerships as 'abusive partnerships'. Marilyn Taylor (2003), who has also been very critical of such arrangements, recognizes that they offer unprecedented openings to local communities, but also require recognition from the public sector partners of their complexity and the conflicts they may create for community representatives.

There are choices in how partnerships are governed. A partnership may be little more than a talking shop which coordinates the activities of the other agencies; though even then complications can arise if a partnership (such as a Local Strategic Partnership) employs staff or controls funds. It is once a partnership has access to significant stand-alone resources, and especially if it sets itself up as a limited company, that complex issues arise. They concern the accountability of the boards, the probity of their decisions, and whether they provide value for money given other partnerships and the additional costs of accountants, legal advisers, etc., and the tax disadvantages of the private sector when compared with the public. They are key issues for both practice and theory; they feature surprisingly little in most of the partnership literature. However, Skelcher, Navdeep and Smith (2004, 2005) identify three types of partnership, and suggest that different governance regimes may be appropriate for each type:

1 *Club partnerships*: meet to coordinate the activities or services which take place in a defined geographical area, or share information or resources. Examples are Local Strategic Partnerships, which involve the leading players from the public, private

and voluntary sectors in a local council area and which exist to coordinate policies and spending plans; or Councils for Voluntary Services which exist to provide services to, and if possible coordinate the activities of, the wide range of voluntary sector organizations within an area.

2   *Polity partnerships*: These are the governance structures for government funding streams which are provided for geographical areas, usually areas with special problems, such as concentrations of poverty. Examples are projects funded through the Single Regeneration Budget, or New Deals for Communities.

3   *Agency partnerships*: These are created to advise government agencies which operate at local or subregional level. Examples are Local Learning and Skills Councils (which provides the funding for further education), or Connexions partnerships (careers advice and related services). The money for these comes from central government, but how they spend it is agreed locally, on the basis of decisions of a partnership board of local representatives of relevant organizations.

THE RANGE OF LEGAL FORMS FOR PARTNERSHIPS

Partnerships come in different shapes and sizes – and are governed in different ways. Possible forms of governance include:

1   Unincorporated partnership
2   Incorporated partnership
3   Company limited by shares
4   Company limited by guarantee
5   Company limited by guarantee with charitable status
6   Trust or 'Community Benefit Society'.

UNINCORPORATED PARTNERSHIPS

This is the legal position of many public–private partnerships – including most local strategic partnerships and regeneration partnerships which do not have company structures. They may have constitutions, or funding agreements with external agencies, but these are essentially private arrangements, and they do not protect those who take decisions on behalf of the partnership from financial risk. If the members of a management committee or board take decisions which commit money or staff, then they may be personally liable and, in the worst case scenario, lose their savings and assets.

The board meetings of Local Strategic Partnerships, Crime and Disorder Partnerships, Health Partnerships, and similar bodies, largely involve discussions which coordinate activities. Most of their decisions are of the nature of recommendations to their partner organizations as to how they should act. When they do spend money, it is usually *the partner organizations which take the risks*, and carry the responsibility if anything goes wrong.

Where non-incorporated partnerships are responsible for spending programmes, the board may take decisions which only come into effect when they are approved by an *accountable body*. The British government has made this a requirement of many of its funding regimes, with slightly different detailed guidance for each regime, and differences of interpretation of the role by different accountable bodies: some are very hands-off, little more than postboxes, while others are hands-on, requiring detailed information about spending plans and proposals and virtually reappraising projects. The accountable body carries most of the risks. It may also employ staff and second them to the partnership, deal with payroll, pension, PAYE and national insurance, equal opportunities policies and any personal grievance issues – all potentially onerous areas of responsibility for a small new organization.

As a working example, Aston Pride, a New Deal for Communities in Birmingham, was created as an unincorporated partnership, but the members of its management board chose to create a company limited by guarantee, which had many problems. One of the conditions for the Neighbourhood Renewal Unit continuing to support the programme was that this company be wound up, and the NDC run as an unincorporated partnership with Birmingham City Council as an accountable body.

INCORPORATED PARTNERSHIPS

This is the legal form used by many professionals – for example firms of accountants or practices of medical doctors. They have a legal arrangement which defines their responsibilities. Thus each partner may earn money on his or her own account; but certain overhead costs are shared, as are some responsibilities. Staff may be employed either at the cost of the account of one of the partners, or of the practice as a whole. There is no limited liability, which means that individual members of the partnership, or the partnership as a collective organization, may be sued; however, insurance policies are used to cover the partners against the most obvious risks, for example being sued for medical or professional negligence.

This legal form is not commonly used in regeneration. The balance between individual and collective responsibilities would not be appropriate for most regeneration partnerships. It is needlessly complicated for informal partnerships, and does not give sufficient protection where there is a high level of risk.

Another relatively new legal form, *limited liability partnerships*, do give protection to partners and employees, and this could, in time, be a valuable legal form for some partnerships.

108

COMPANIES LIMITED BY SHARES

A *private company*, with shares, is the form chosen by the great majority of trading businesses and a few partnerships. Under the Companies Act 1985, this must have 'two or more individuals who, for a lawful purpose, subscribe their names to the Memorandum [which includes a statement of the objectives of the company], and Articles [which define how the company is constituted and how it will work]'. A company must have at least one director, a registered office, a company secretary, auditors, and must file its accounts every year at Companies House. There are many different types of shares and financial instruments – with different voting rights. There must be an Annual General Meeting of shareholders which will approve the accounts and elect directors – and agree any dividends. The directors appoint executives to run the company. It can then: buy and sell property, employ people, take legal actions, borrow money, take out insurances to protect board members, and so on.

The company is a separate entity in law from its directors, who are not personally liable if the company is put into receivership by one or more of its creditors – that is unless as individuals they have guaranteed certain borrowings, ignored health and safety issues, racially discriminated, or otherwise acted recklessly, for example by knowingly letting the company trade while insolvent. They are responsible for important aspects of Health and Safety, for certain aspects of employment law (which may mean that they are named in appeals to employment tribunals), and some aspects of child protection. The company pays corporation tax, VAT (unless its turnover is below the threshold), and non-domestic rates on any property it owns.

Company directors must take their duties seriously. They must understand the business and the activities in which the company is involved. They must act in the interests of the company or trust, and with reasonable 'care, diligence and skill'. They must be on the lookout for, and where appropriate declare, conflicts of interest.

COMPANIES LIMITED BY GUARANTEE

Most partnerships are not set up to make profits, and certainly not to distribute them to shareholders. They may then choose to register as *companies limited by guarantee*. These are also constituted under the 1985 Companies Act. They do not have shares, but they have *members* – whose liability is limited, usually to £1, and who play a role similar to that of shareholders in a company with shares: they can attend and vote at the Annual General Meeting, which must include approving the annual accounts, and will elect or confirm the appointment of directors in line with the articles of the company. The directors will employ a chief executive, who may be one of themselves, i.e. a managing director. Staff will be employed by the company. If profits are made, these are ploughed back into the company, or covenanted to some external source which fits criteria set out in the articles. The company is liable for corporation tax and VAT, and must file its accounts at Companies House, just like a company with shares.

109

If a company is new, or weak, it may still have a formal accountable body, or informal arrangements with a parent body which enable that body to take some of the risk. For example, staff may be reluctant to give up careers to work for a small independent company, but prepared to do so if they are employed by an established body and seconded to work in the company.

TRUSTS AND PROVIDENT SOCIETIES

These are not the only possible legal forms. Partnerships that want to limit the liability of individual employees or board members can also be legally constituted under the Industrial and Provident Societies Act – the legislation used by many cooperatives. This form is used, for example, by several of the leisure trusts which run swimming pools or sports facilities – it provides a means whereby these can be owned, or part-owned, by the people who work in them.

COMMUNITY INTEREST COMPANIES

The Companies (Audit, Investigations and Community Enterprise) Act 2004 created a new form of limited company, called a *community interest company*. These are designed to appeal to community businesses that want 'to trade with a social purpose' in a framework of limited liability, with some restricted forms of share capital, but without charitable status.

Charitable status

Some partnerships that are companies limited by guarantee, a few provident societies, and some non-incorporated partnerships become charities. To achieve charitable status, i.e. be approved by the Charity Commission, the Charities Act, expected to become law in 2007, will require them to demonstrate 'public benefit' (which will not include making money for shareholders – so they will not normally include companies with shares). They then qualify for certain tax advantages: exemption from corporation tax, capital gains tax and stamp duty on private gifts, and concessions on non-domestic rates. Charitable status is an aid to fundraising. If there are activities outside the charitable objectives – e.g. trading activities or political activities – these can be conducted by a separate company which covenants its profits to the charity. Accounts must be submitted both to Companies House and to the Charity Commission. Directors cannot normally be paid (other than 'reasonable expenses') or gain personal benefit (these provisions will be relaxed somewhat when the Charities Act becomes effective).

The new legislation is also expected to create a legal framework for *charitable incorporated organizations* which can have both commercial objectives and charitable status. The main advantage is that each CIO will have a single regulator – either Companies House or the Charity Commission. It is likely that this form, and the *community interest companies* already mentioned, will be widely used by the voluntary sector, and they may also provide a valuable legal form for partnerships.

ADVANTAGES AND DISADVANTAGES OF COMPANY STRUCTURES

There are important advantages to be gained from company or provident society structures:

- It is easier to trade (in comparison to unincorporated partnerships, but also to local authorities where there are restrictions on trading activity).
- They can borrow money – by comparison public sector borrowing is tightly controlled.
- They can more easily protect commercial confidentiality – the public sector can do this too, but it is often difficult to keep secrets in a large organization, quite apart from obligations under the Freedom of Information Act which are more likely to be used to gain information from public bodies than from private companies.
- They can offer more flexible terms of employment – whereas the public sector is subject to national negotiations.
- They are more easily understood by other parts of the private sector, and therefore find it easier to develop collaborative relationships.
- They may find it easier to fundraise.
- Last but not least, from the point of view of their directors, especially some from local community organizations which may have a majority or significant influence on the boards, they become independent bodies, able to own their own property and make their own decisions – out of the public sector and into the voluntary sector.

There are also possible downsides to arm's-length structures:

- They require separate accounts and more complex accounting conventions.
- They have different tax regimes – and generally pay more taxes.
- Bodies deemed to be in the private sector may not be eligible for European or some other grant regimes – e.g. problems with state aid.
- There are greater risks – and it can be time-consuming and expensive to sort out the affairs of an arm's-length body if it gets into difficulties.
- Above all, if control passes to an arm's-length body it passes away from its parent; so if a parent is not sure of a partnership, it should not permit it to set up as an independent entity.

111

THE COMPOSITION OF PARTNERSHIP BOARDS

The board of a company or partnership body is responsible for its strategic direction, for its finances, and for its probity. Some boards are purely *advisory*, or treated that way by their parent organizations. Examples are the agency partnerships, or advisory boards, of the Business Links or Local Learning and Skills Councils: their funding, and hence the accountability in the last resort, lies somewhere else. Others are at the heart of executive management. An increasingly common arrangement is to have a large *supervisory board* which meets from time to time, perhaps quarterly, and takes strategic decisions, and a smaller *main board* which meets monthly and approves more routine decisions. This, for example, is the structure of Birmingham International Airport, a partnership between seven district councils together owning 49 per cent of the shares and two private companies owning the remainder.

By definition, the board members of a partnership come from its different partner sources. For regeneration partnerships, these may be considered in six groups, or types of directors or board members:

1   Nominees of local authorities (councillors or council officials)
2   Representatives of local communities or neighbourhoods
3   Representatives of the voluntary sector active in the area
4   Representatives of statutory agencies, such as Local Learning and Skills Councils or Primary Care Trusts
5   Business representatives
6   Individuals chosen for their competence, connections or experience.

Precisely how the board of a company is constituted is a matter for its *Articles of Association*. The Articles may allow a local authority, or an agency representing a type of businesses in an area (e.g. an Asian Business Forum), to nominate one or more directors. Or they may specify how directors may be chosen to represent local communities. The *members* of a company limited by guarantee (as distinct from its *directors*) may find that their rights are quite limited – to attend the AGM and approve the accounts, to note the various nominations as directors from other bodies, to elect individuals in the sixth category above, or to vote to change the Articles (a complex matter, not to be undertaken lightly).

One of the key questions to ask of any partnership is who appoints the staff – especially the senior staff. If the chief executive is appointed by the board, as is likely if it is constituted as a company, then this is one of the most important tasks the board performs (along with the annual review of the remuneration packages of the senior executives).

Employees of a company, such as the chief executive, may also be directors. This is common practice in companies limited by shares, where non-executive directors are usually a minority, but until recently has not been possible for a charity. With partnership boards, the most common arrangement is for all the directors to be non-executive, with the senior staff present as observers or advisers. It is also common practice for officials from some sponsoring authorities, such as a local authority, the Regional Development Agency, or the local Government Office to be 'in attendance' to answer questions and advise on procedures, especially if one of these is also the accountable body.

GOVERNANCE IN THE VOLUNTARY SECTOR

The voluntary sector, or third sector, or non-government organizations (NGOs), or not-for-profit organizations, are key components of what is sometimes called *civil society* (Putnam 2000). They are delivery agents – that is they do the real work – in most regeneration programmes. They may use volunteers, and raise funds in many ways, and the larger and more professional organizations bid for and often win contracts from the public sector. Others receive grants, in return for which they are expected to deliver services (which may be defined in *Service Level Agreements*).

ETHICAL ISSUES, PROBITY AND ACCOUNTABILITY

Directors of a company are required to act in the interests of the company and to respect its confidences. This can produce conflicts of interest. These can be commercial conflicts – as when a director gains information which is valuable to another company with which he or she is involved. They can also be geographical conflicts, when a decision has to be taken about the location of a particular investment, which may favour the interests of one director rather than another. A director, however elected to that position, is required to act in the best interests of the company. A director placed on the board by another agency, or by a parent company, has two loyalties – to the company and to the body that nominated him or her – and may need to use their judgement to balance these loyalties. Or there may be conflicts between organizations – for example the role to be played by the local authority, or college, which may have a director on the board. A well-run board will have formal *codes of conduct* whereby directors are required to declare conflicts of interest, and if these are extreme take no part in the relevant decision. The private sector deals with such conflicts all the time – for example when the interests of a subsidiary company conflict with those of its parent. It also recognizes that boards will not always be unanimous – and that those outvoted may have reasonable arguments even if they cannot win majority support for them. Issues like this can put community-nominated directors of regeneration organizations in a difficult position if they are asked to take decisions which their parent community organization disagrees with.

Organizations spending public money need to have clear procedures in place so that they can demonstrate that it is spent fairly and well. Thus salaried posts should be publicly advertised, and if applicants are known to members of an appointments committee (as may often be the case), this needs to be recorded and known – if the relationship is close,

113

it may be advisable for the appointments committee to be reformed. It is desirable to spend money locally, but not at the expense of value for money: hence the need for formal tendering processes (which may give weight to local suppliers, up to a point) or, for small purchases, three or four quotations. If there are doubts about the quality of work, then those suppliers should not be used in future. One of the benefits of an accountable body is that it can provide oversight of these matters, and bring in financial specialists if there are suspicions of impropriety.

Above all, regeneration organizations need to be accountable to their local communities, in so far as this is possible. It is good practice to produce an annual report, and to have an open meeting, widely advertised, at which this is presented to the public. Roadshows, demonstration evenings, newsletters, speakers sent to community meetings who can answer questions, and stands at carnivals or fairs, are all ways of being seen, but also being accountable. Good practice would allow the public to attend board meetings, for at least part of the time, and perhaps to have the right to ask questions or put items on the agenda: but in practice it often proves hard to get many people to come.

CONCLUSIONS AND SUMMARY

The governance arrangements of partnerships are complex. They involve costs, risks, inflexibility and potentially conflicts, and it takes time for trust to be created.

On the other hand they bring into a relationship a wide range of interests, and a great variety of skills. When they work well they are hugely rewarding.

Public–private partnerships will be with us for years to come, even though the government is committed to rationalizing them, and realizes the problems of too many partnerships which cross each other's territories, and drain the scarce resources of talent (Peck and Tickell 1994; Audit Commission 2005; Coulson 2005c).

Regeneration partnerships are examples of hub networks, where a number of bodies are working together, but the partnership has its own administration – which may be very low-key, or, in some cases, become a major player in its own right.

They can be governed through a variety of legal forms. A key decision is often whether to create a company limited by guarantee. This has the advantage of independence – but the costs and inflexibilities of being involved with company law. There are many cases where company structures have not proved necessary, and some where they have become an expensive problem. A partnership body often works well as an unincorporated partnership with a constitution of some kind, backed by an accountable body, usually the local council, which can ensure that decisions are taken properly, staff employed on local authority terms and conditions, and audit arrangements are in place.

In summary (following Skelcher *et al*. 2004), the key issues about the governance of a partnership or arm's-length agency relate to:

- Internal governance (who appoints the board and what powers do they have?)
- Accountability (how do they account for their decisions?)
- Member conduct (are there codes of conduct for the board?)
- Public accessibility (who can attend their meetings?)
- Board members and staff (who appoints the chief executive?)
- Accountable body responsibilities (how does the accountable body – usually a local authority – function?)

Explicitly, the analysis above suggests that:

- Partnerships should not turn themselves into limited companies unless a clear case can be made that the advantages will outweigh the disadvantages.
- However, non-incorporated partnerships should act with care, and if they employ staff or take responsibility for spending programmes, be prepared to work through a properly appointed accountable body.
- Company directors should be made aware of their responsibilities, through appropriate training.
- Induction training should also be available for newly appointed directors of public–private partnerships from the private sector.
- Directors appointed from local community organizations, and from some of the smaller voluntary sector, may have special problems with their roles and responsibilities, and dealing with possible conflicts of interest. They may also have problems with getting time off work to attend board meetings. There is increasing pressure for them to be paid some kind of allowance or remuneration, and in principle this is not unreasonable.
- Partnership boards should be kept to manageable size.
- The Local Strategic Partnerships should be required to review all public–private partnerships in their area on a regular basis (annually or twice a year) to ensure that opportunities for coordination are being taken, and that companies are not kept alive unnecessarily.
- Regular checks should be made on the accountability and openness of all local partnerships.

ACKNOWLEDGEMENT

I would like to acknowledge very helpful comments from Chris Skelcher.

NOTE

1. I am indebted to Chris Skelcher for this.

Chapter 9

Evaluation approaches

Joyce Liddle and Stuart Smith

INTRODUCTION

Evaluation is a fundamental part of the regeneration space as we seek to examine some of the most common mechanisms used to evaluate regeneration projects. We will see that very often, the techniques employed are too simplistic and reductionist to ever fully understand the complex motivations and success factors in regeneration. Nor do they ever really stand a chance of transferring knowledge and learning onto other projects.

Critically, the delivery and therefore evaluation of many regeneration projects focus on tangible (i.e. measurable) outputs, which may be at odds with the reality of what *actually* helps regeneration and renewal to occur, the intangible and non-measurable.

This chapter demonstrates how the evaluation of regeneration initiatives can be more effective by:

- Adopting appropriate tools and language for the complex physical and social space that regeneration occurs in – such as complexity theory, action research, anthropology, narrative, social network analysis or other cultural evaluation techniques. These are proven and well used in other domains.
- Using evaluation to attempt to understand the linkages between regeneration success, local cultures and the cultures of the regenerating authority.
- Recognizing that organizational behaviours will have a key impact on the success of regeneration and that money (although important) is not the sole determinant of regeneration success. Therefore, anybody tasked with carrying out an evaluation should understand the context.

THE PURPOSE OF EVALUATION

Evaluation is not an audit process, although some audit skills may help. Nor is evaluation a simple consumer poll which asks whether or not participants, recipients and others received benefits from a particular programme, although again elements of this will be incorporated. Instead evaluation is designed to be a *holistic* assessment of how a particular programme succeeded or failed, and it should be carried out in such a way that all participants wherever possible have learnt something about and from the programme.

At the very least the evaluation of a regeneration programme should aim to touch upon some (or all) of the following aspects:

1 *Accountability* Evaluation should support accountability for programme performance and spending. It does this through providing information for stakeholders and through examining whether projects met the requirements of funders. This is the audit part of the process.
2 *Decision-making* Evaluation can help organizations and individuals to make better decisions about programme direction. It can assist in helping set goals and priorities as well as reviewing these at points throughout the programme.
3 *Resource allocation* An evaluation can help in determining what the 'value' of a programme might be and help allocate resources within or to a particular aspect.
4 *Programme improvement* Improving programme design, implementation and cost-effectiveness are all within the evaluation remit. As is supporting effective management practices, which will include making more effective use of evaluation.
5 *Enhancing knowledge and skills* A good evaluation can increase understanding of the programme being evaluated and can build knowledge about existing/potential needs and about programming that can address those needs.
6 *Capacity-building* An evaluation which closely involves programme stakeholders can help to develop capacity for effective programme design, assessment and improvement. It can help with learning to think more critically about programmes.
7 *Social change* Evaluation can be used to promote, defend, or oppose specific methods, approaches, or programmes. In this way it can be used to shape public opinion. A good evaluation will allow us explore diverse perspectives on a programme.
8 *Cohesion and collaboration* Evaluations can potentially increase consistency and communication between departments or organizations. They can also build pride and confidence within a programme team.

Despite all of the potential benefits of good evaluation and the fact that most programmes require some form of mandatory evaluation all too often we see that the evaluation process is badly designed, and frequently dismissed as a tick in the box 'compliance' exercise.

Common problems with evaluation are:

1 *Lack of budget or resource allocation* Very often the evaluation of a programme will come towards the end of the programme life cycle and is allocated a small amount

from the wider programme budget. It is natural for those running projects to use programme monies to deliver the programme rather than keep money aside for evaluation.

2 *Lack of engagement in key stakeholders* So many evaluations are approached as 'tick in the box' exercises by those responsible for regeneration programmes. It is often apparent from the outset that the findings of the evaluation will go no further than the small programme team and that mechanisms to pass that learning or knowledge on to future programmes is certainly not in place.

It is also around this stage that evaluations can run into 'political' problems. These are manifest if the evaluation is going to be used as evidence to justify further spending or programme extension. They will also surface if the evaluation is critical or highlights shortcomings in the programme and stakeholders respond defensively to this.

3 *Lack of methodological innovation* Lack of budget is a very real problem when we examine the list of ideal deliverables that an evaluation may touch upon. Many programme managers fail to allow sufficient time or money to carry out proper evaluations. Many evaluations are carried out by third parties (independent) and these are drawn from the private, academic or social enterprise sectors.

The approaches used by these evaluators will depend on several factors including the time, budget, the requirements of the programme and their own internal dynamics. Time and again the evaluation ends up being a small social survey tagged onto the end of a larger programme when, with a little foresight and creativity, it could have achieved so much more.

These problems are not easily addressed and all regeneration managers who commission evaluation or wish to carry out evaluation need to be cogniscent of these. In the following sections we examine how some innovative evaluation techniques can be adopted which can possibly achieve greater success.

BASIC EVALUATION APPROACHES

Most evaluation approaches have at their core a combination of quantitative and qualitative primary research. This is often combined with secondary research generated by the programme itself or drawn from existing sources.

ALTERNATIVE EVALUATION APPROACHES

Many of the approaches to the evaluation of regeneration described above have their roots in a reductionist/mechanistic/'top-down' model of the world which, although prevalent in Western thinking, is not applicable in complex domains such as human social systems, or those typical within regeneration.

Complexity theory, and some of its associated tools and metaphors, we argue, can provide an alternative perspective to planning and evaluating regeneration because it moves us away from reductionist and deterministic perspectives that reduce holistic systems and isolate observable phenomena. Instead, complexity theories offer a way of seeing organizational forms as complex adaptive systems composed of a diversity of agents, interacting with each other, generating novel, innovative and often unexpected benefits for the whole system (Marion and Uhl-Bien 2001).

Mechanistic views of a system often assume a linear rational worldview. The problem with linearity (and therefore linear approaches) however, is that it fails to take account of the dynamic and continuous interactions between and within organizations over time. Surviving organizations change structures and directions, and in doing so threaten or provide opportunities for other organizations. Paradoxically these interactions over time create stability and instability, predictability and unpredictability and creation and destruction at the same time (Stacey 1996: 5–8).

This statement will not be surprising to most people and certainly many people involved in regeneration will recognize it. Indeed, regeneration takes place in fuzzy and complex worlds where we attempt to seek order and clarity. Unfortunately we cannot rationalize away paradoxes, chance, luck, errors, subjectivities, accidents and sheer indeterminacy of life through a prism of apparent control and rationality (Grint 1997b: introduction).

One of the key features of current regeneration is the growth in the use of specialist consultancy firms and a wholly new cadre of regeneration managers and 'experts'. Whilst in many instances these organizations and individuals add substantial value to the regeneration mix, their emergence has the effect of maintaining power structures within regeneration, but can also have the effect of continuing the top-down technocratic application of solutions to community problems and as well as adding another layer of disconnection between the democratically elected and accountable agency (local authority, Central Government) and communities.

Lovering (2001) has referred to the new 'service class' created within Wales at the height of the period when Wales successfully attracted some significant foreign investors, and it is undoubtedly true that local and regional regeneration has had a similar effect. Moreover, those technocrats who work within regeneration may be reluctant to reduce their own roles, so are more than happy to maximize their bureaucratic input at the expense of *real working* with communities to solve some of the fundamental problems. This is a serious issue if we genuinely believe in involving all stakeholders in programme evaluation. It also means that if we wish our evaluations to be genuine learning and knowledge-sharing vehicles we need to understand these structures as well.

For example, many regeneration consulting firms have developed standard methodologies for evaluating regeneration projects. This in itself is no bad thing, although the application of the 'one size fits all' approach to project evaluation would cause problems. The assumption here is of course that the approach taken in one domain can be repeated successfully in other spaces because the world is linear, known and predictable.

119

Regeneration organizations are culpable in this in that they inevitably require long track records of evaluating certain programmes.

The culture of communities is essentially different from the bureaucratic cultures that technocrats work within, and this makes conflicts inevitable.

Skilled regeneration 'artists' are able to play both the formal and informal 'game', but instinctively know that it is the informal that works – especially in connecting with communities. Experience from around the world suggests there are champions who are willing to give up traditional forms of control and share power, but more significantly 'some public servants (and *professionals*) are good at doing what they've always done in a different wrapping' (Taylor 2000: 197). Too much top-down managerialism can displace the social and political dynamics that operate locally and because regeneration is fertile ground for contestation and conflict as well as consensus building, regeneration managers must serve as enablers who assist in developing the understanding of the causes of deprivation and increase the social capital of communities (Southern 2003). In developing this understanding they will clarify the mechanisms needed to evaluate initiatives.

Some of the key policy issues facing both EU and national governments are: how to involve the private sector in regeneration, how to ensure that European and national funding sources are used efficiently and effectively, also to realize that there is a fundamental difference between these two concepts, and how to involve the correct stakeholders to ensure social inclusion. Moreover, the tools and instruments for evaluating all funding, including European funding, are part of a complex framework to ensure that all stakeholders are now intimately involved in balancing economic and social regeneration.

Changes were introduced to improve both formative and summative evaluation processes. This was to enable regional partners to reflect upon how their own objectives were being met (Schedler 2002). In the new European framework regions must link European policies and national policies to achieve overall objectives. Measurement and evaluation of funding are based on objective indicators such as numbers of jobs created and other output and impact indicators. However, greater importance is now attached to context indicators; those indicating the value-added activities created by trans-boundary linkages.

Under Neighbourhood Renewal local strategic partnerships (LSPs) were created in 88 deprived areas of the UK as the forums for fusing existing mainstream UK local and neighbourhood initiatives, and other national and European polices, plans and programmes to satisfy community needs. The Index of Multiple Deprivation (IMD), consisting of 33 indicators of need was used to determine eligibility for funding (IMD was revised in 2004), and NRF was aimed at kick-starting mainstream programmes (DTLR 2001).

Despite Neighbourhood Renewal being focused on affecting change at neighbourhood level, there is still a hierarchy of interventions, and in the north east in particular, four subregional partnerships (Northumberland, Tyne and Wear, County Durham and Tees Valley) were established as key delivery mechanisms to implement the six key objectives reflected in the Regional Economic Strategy by One North East (ONE) (Liddle 2001).

120

Each SRP signed up to an action plan with ONE to achieve certain objectives, and each LSP was formally accredited by Government Office on six key criteria, determined by a combination of self-assessment and stakeholder views. LSPs were initially assessed on the six criteria: (i) effectiveness and representation, (ii) developing common priorities, (iii) aligning management systems, (iv) reduction in bureaucracy, (v) building good practice, and finally (vi) drawing in a broad range of agencies and other stakeholders to identify community need. Furthermore, recent (November 2005) changes in how HM Treasury measures regional funding, PSAs (Public Service Agreements) and Local Area Agreements have all impacted on regeneration activities at local and subregional levels. Myriad targets for measuring regional funding and PSAs have been jointly developed by three government departments (DTI, ODPM and HM Treasury). LAAs, on the other hand, are the new mechanisms for delivering better local services outcomes through coordinated effort between central government, local government and various partners. LAAs are an attempt to mainstream key funding streams and help people and agencies in local areas to identify and measure their own priorities and local needs in services for children and young people, healthier communities and older people, safer and stronger communities, and economic development and enterprise. They will be assessed on how well targets are met, and each LAA will last for three years, from an initial framework to be established during March 2006. Successful LAAs will receive a series of LAA Reward Grants, as well as certain flexibilities on utilizing future funding.

The inherently complex nature of the world means that the chances of repeating a regeneration success in an identical way are unlikely if not impossible. Whilst different regeneration scenarios may appear to be the same at first glance there will be subtle differences and nuances which make it individual. Generic approaches which draw on experience from elsewhere are fine as long as those using them understand the limitations of their model. Sensitivity to initial conditions, which is a key feature of complex adaptive systems, means that a fixed, model-driven approach to regeneration is both impractical and dangerous.

Measuring success in neighbourhood renewal and regeneration initiatives has been an issue of concern and the 'obsession with targets, outputs, outcomes and indicators mainly handed down by DETR' were regarded as flawed because they were either imprecise, unobtainable, did not measure what they were supposed to measure or were unrelated to the prime concerns of residents. Furthermore it is argued that indicators such as PSAs, benchmarking exercises (*and latterly LAAs, authors' own italics*) are equally poorly related to residents priorities (Ambrose 2001: 15). More creative indicators need to be established, and as one Government Office spokesperson said at an LSP meeting *'This is a good opportunity for you (LSP members) to customize your own quality of life measures and use them to lobby the higher levels of governance on behalf of communities.'*

Clearly, qualitative and quantitative measures for performance review are not very well developed. Indeed there is a real concern that most LSPs have under-spent, and central government has said it will clawback unspent funds. LSP representatives have prioritized programmes, but have experienced difficulties in setting their own criteria to show how

121

targets are being met, milestones reached, or timescales developed. At one LSP meeting, after a lengthy discussion on criteria setting, the following suggestions were made:

- Identify activities where 'early wins' could constitute best practice
- Identify how each activity contributes to Treasury floor targets
- Assess outcomes and impacts of each activity
- Evaluate the learning obtained from each activity
- Identify those activities that were contributing to regional, subregional and local priorities
- Identify those activities that could be seen to contribute to sustainability.

Some LSPs have used the European Foundation for Quality Management (EFQM) model to measure performance whereas others have taken guidance from the ODPM and adopted the 'Green-Amber-Red Traffic Light' system of auditing their activities. As most Local Authorities are beginning to recognize that as the Responsible Authority for delegating finance to LSPs, they should perhaps use their own internal scrutiny panels of members to check on activities, early problems are beginning to surface about who has responsibility or accountability to whom, and for what. One of the authors was an expert witness to a scrutiny panel measuring the activities of an LSP, and it became evident that numerous conflicts and differences between the elected local authority and the unelected LSPs have yet to be resolved.

Clearly the move from representative forms of democracy to more deliberative and participatory arrangements will exacerbate some of the problems already apparent in measuring effectiveness. Pratchett (2000) argues that representative democracy has been replaced by consultative and deliberative forms of democracy involving broader groups of interests and views. However, broadening decision-making to multi-stakeholder groups is not without difficulties, not least the capacity to develop effective decisions, based on appropriate evidence, data and information to measure effectiveness.

Goverment Offices have recognized that there is an issue of developing competences and capacities within communities and especially those officers from mainstream agencies represented on LSPs. Not least of these the importance of monitoring and evaluating performance and transferring good practice. Indeed the ODPM has recently made £250 million available to build up the capacities of local government officers within neighbourhood renewal. The key skills areas where deficiencies have been identified are:

- Leadership
- Performance management
- Evaluation.

The latter two are of crucial importance here, as evaluation and managing performance are key areas for development, but we contend that continuing to foster the belief that unsuitable interventions, designed by technocrats and based on flawed assumptions, will not bring about the necessary changes. Rather we suggest that it is imperative to develop new metrics, ones that have community consent, as the following discussion articulates.

INTRODUCING AN ALTERNATIVE APPROACH

The authors' practical experience of evaluating and delivering regeneration projects indicates that from the outset many projects, although well-meaning, are planned and delivered on flawed assumptions which are either never challenged or more importantly never seen. Of course this statement comes from the wonderful position of hindsight where everything makes sense. One of the key characteristics of a complex space is that cause and effect are only ever revealed in hindsight (Snowden and Kurtz 2003). In fairness many regeneration initiatives are probably well-designed at the outset (or at least appear to be) but only in hindsight do we see the flaws.

One of the key things that we can gain from a complex perspective is that many initiatives have at their core a set of flawed assumptions based on a worldview which is incorrect. Foremost amongst these is the belief that cause and effect holds true and that the linear and structured delivery and evaluation of regeneration initiatives will provide us with the results and insights that we require.

By understanding that a social system is complex at the outset we can then design regeneration initiatives and evaluations with more subtlety and with a greater chance of sustainable success.

ADOPTING APPROPRIATE EVALUATION TOOLS FOR THE COMPLEX REGENERATION SPACE

As we have discussed, regeneration initiatives are often designed by a well-meaning technocratic elite, with the imposition of value systems and beliefs that are disconnected from the value sets and beliefs of the recipients. This is not to apportion blame on any side, but rather to make clear a genuine state of affairs.

So how do we truly involve the community in evaluation, how do we engage to get genuine community involvement? This is an extremely difficult task, as anyone who has attempted community engagement will attest. However, there are simple steps that can improve the situation.

Often evaluation involved inviting the community to view the plans for a development once they were almost finished a tick in the box exercise carried out at the end of the process. We will call this 'end of pipe' consultation.

As the model shown in Table 9.1 demonstrates, on a continuum of community engagement, most regeneration programmes remain at the consultation or involvement stage, without ever moving across to the delegation stage where people are given direct control. This is in line with the top-down bureaucratic and technocratic fixes in which

Table 9.1   Community engagement spectrum

Information provision	Consultation	Involvement	Delegation
Telling people what to do	Asking people what they think of what you do	Asking people about your priorities	Giving people direct control

Source: Warwick Best Value Series (December 1998).

community engagement is seen as confirming or verifying existing practice, rather than challenging the whole basis of service provision.

The alternative is to ask the community views and engage at the outset and throughout the regeneration process. This allows the community, from a process point of view at least, to input their views into the project at an appropriate point, one at which they can genuinely make a difference.

This approach requires a rethink on behalf of regeneration organization, because doing this properly requires an apparent loss of control by the organization concerned and a humility which many organizations lack.

However, as practitioners will testify, engaging with the community is a very difficult task. Within regeneration, greater citizen participation and broader stakeholder engagement in decision-making and problem-solving is seen as a good thing, and indeed many recent public sector reforms have at heart the need for increased involvement. Demands for more, better or enhanced citizen participation have arisen due to the apparent limitations of representative democracy and the role of the state as a moderator between social actors and a promoter of societal self-regulation, rather than a Leviathan intervening in society from above (Abels 2005: 15). By involving the views and interests of groups usually excluded from the political process, recent reforms (such as those evident in regeneration) have sought to broaden the cognitive and normative basis, initiate social learning, reduce social conflict, promote public interest and increase the legitimacy of political decisions. Martin (2003) developed a model of co-planning and co-production of service delivery, which could be utilized within regeneration programmes, and Figure 9.1 shows how the public and users of services can achieve active involvement in policy design and delivery of services or programmes, which is superior to the traditional one-way flow of information to stakeholder or service users. However, to achieve this co-production and co-planning requires greater use of evidence, data and information than in past practice.

We would also argue that a large proportion of evaluation is sanitized either by the arm's length approach taken (surveys, focus groups) or by pseudo-scientific attempts to convert qualitative data into meaningful statistics. This is probably because the statistics are seen to give more weight to any argument that may emerge, and they can also provide the tangible measures initiatives desperately crave.

Communication	Consultation	Co-planning and Co-production
One-way flow of information from service/ programme providers to users	Two-way dialogue between service/ programme providers and users	Active involvement of public/users in design and delivery of services/ programmes
⟶	⟶	⟶

Figure 9.1 *Processes of communication*

So what are the alternative approaches that we might use for evaluation? None of the methods we suggest here are too removed from mainstream approaches – but they may be more suitable for achieving the desired consultation or research outcome.

ACTION RESEARCH

Action research has a long history, going back to social scientists' attempts to help solve practical problems in wartime situations in both Europe and America. Greenwood and Levin (1998) trace its origins to the work of Kurt Lewin in the 1940s to design social experiments that could take place in natural settings.

These early action research experiments strongly influenced the links between action research and social democracy in Scandinavia. Pioneering work with Volvo, Saab-Scania and Alfa Laval helped begin to change our understanding of industrial organization away from rigid Taylorist approaches to work design, and toward the more flexible forms of semi-autonomous work organization. This view of the organization is in line with a complex adaptive systems perspective.

Action research has a double objective. One aim is to produce knowledge and action directly useful to a group of people – through research, education and direct action. The second aim is to empower people at a second and deeper level through the process of constructing and using their own knowledge: they 'see through' the ways in which the establishment monopolizes the production and use of knowledge for the benefit of its members. Other important influences on action research have been the experiential learning movement, action learning, humanistic psychology, popular education, organization development and feminist thinking.

Contemporary forms of action-oriented research place emphasis on a full integration of action and reflection, so that the knowledge developed in the inquiry process is directly relevant to the issues being studied, creating a form of knowledge useful to the actor and the point of action. There are many ways of approaching action research and action learning, and there are certain important characteristics of action research which distinguish it from more traditional forms of social research and make it particularly useful for evaluation.

First, while the primary purpose of academic research is to contribute to an abstract body of knowledge available to third-persons, it could be argued that the primary purpose of action research is to develop communities of practice.

Second, action research has a collaborative intent: a primary value of using action research methods is to increase people's involvement in the creation and application of knowledge about them and about their worlds.

Fundamentally, if one accepts that human persons are agents who act in the world on the basis of their own sense-making, and that human community involves mutual sense-making and collective action, it is no longer possible to do research on persons. It is only possible to do research with persons, including them both in the questioning and sense-making that informs the research, and in the action which is the focus of the research.

Of course, this collaboration between persons is not something which can be produced at will. Relationships emerge over time, and it may require careful facilitation for them to emerge at all.

In many ways we can say that the development of organizations and communities able to inquire into and learn from their experience is the primary purpose of all action research strategies.

Third, traditionally most forms of academic research separate the knower from what is to be known, and conduct their research from a distance (through surveys and question-naires, for example). Action research is rooted in each participant's in-depth, critical and practical experience of the situation to be understood and acted in.

This leads the fourth characteristic of action research, that truth is not solely a property of formal propositions, but is a human activity that must be managed for human purposes which leads action research practitioners to take into account many different forms of knowing – knowledge of our purposes as well of our ideas, knowledge that is based in intuition as well as the senses, knowledge expressed in aesthetic forms such as story, poetry and visual arts as well as propositional language, and practical knowledge expressed in skill and competence.

Finally, action research aims to develop a theory which is not simply abstract and descriptive but is a guide to inquiry and action in present time. A good theory arises out of practical experience, articulates qualities of practice to which we aspire, and challenges us, moment to moment in our professional and personal lives, to discover ways to realize these qualities in action.

Thus we can highlight the radical shift between the basic aims of most managerial research and participatory action inquiry: the former aims at universalizable, valid certainty in reflection about particular pre-designated questions, participatory action inquiry aims at timely, voluntary, mutual, validity-testing, transformative action at all moments of living.

Storytelling or narrative (Snowdon and Kurtz 2003) has gained new prominence within organizational studies in recent years and many organizations are finding uses for this ancient skill (Denning 2001). Storytelling in an evaluation context can be used as an action research method or a more traditional qualitative research method.

Despite the academic hostility to narrative, storytelling is pervasive in our lives. It has been at the heart of our communications since the beginning of the human race. Long before we had PR agencies, communications strategies and media training we had stories. Through stories, our values and principles have been passed from one generation to another. Storytelling brings people together in a common perspective, and stretches everyone's capacity to empathize with others (Denning 2001). In this way stories have been used to strengthen culture (Weick and Browning 1986).

In recent work in the ex-mining communities of County Durham storytelling has been used successfully to engage with communities and stakeholders that had undergone several evaluations. The approach not only unearthed the key issues in the areas but also challenged the stories that the community and the agencies serving it told about themselves that had become self-limiting.

The naturalistic approach of storytelling is ideal for community-based evaluation as it frees participants of the need to talk in anything other than their natural language. It allows the participants to spark off one another and to feel as if they have genuinely engaged in some form of process.

SOCIAL NETWORK ANALYSIS

Social Network Analysis (SNA) is a tool which has been around since the 1930s but has recently re-emerged from the backwaters of academia to be popularized in knowledge management and organizational development circles. Its re-emergence coincides with access to high-power computing at relatively low cost which means that the elaborate networks which can be generated through this tool can be visualized easily.

SNA is based upon the importance of relationships amongst interacting units. There are some central principles which distinguish SNA from other social research approaches (Wasserman and Faust 1994) and these distinctions are why it is particularly useful for evaluating regeneration projects. Specifically within SNA:

- Actors and their actions are viewed as interdependent rather than independent, autonomous units;
- Relational ties (linkages) between actors are channels for transfer or 'flow' of resources (either material or non-material);
- Network models focusing on individuals view the network structural environment as providing opportunities for or constraining individual action;
- Network models conceptualize structure (social, economic, political and so forth) as lasting patterns of relations among actors.

Most regeneration professionals would tacitly acknowledge the power of informal networks and networking in general. In fact some would go as far as to say that the influencing and reconfiguration of networks is *the* critical success factor in most regeneration projects. However, it is difficult to measure and evaluate this, so the most common approach is either to ignore it altogether or use traditional quantitative or qualitative techniques as proxy measures.

Social Network Analysis provides us with a mechanism to bridge this gap.

The network perspective has a long track record of success but is not as well established in the mainstream as some other techniques. Some landmark studies applicable to regeneration include:

- The impact of urbanization on well-being (Fischer 1982)
- Community elite decision-making (Laumann *et al*. 1977)
- Community (Wellman and Wortley 1990)
- Consensus and social influence (Friedkin and Johnsen 1990)

SNA has a rigorous mathematical basis and therefore, in a world where evidence-based policy-making and tangible metrics hold sway, it is a highly useful tool. In addition it can provide deep insight into why regeneration initiatives do and don't work as well as allowing us to utilize fundamental principles of network mathematics (such as hubs, centrality, path length) to design better interventions.

For example, if we envisage the management board of a Local Strategic Partnership in a hypothetical ex-mining community. Given the need, quite rightly to incorporate the local population into the decision-making process, the board is likely to be constituted of local elected members and other community worthies. If we were to use network analysis to look at the social network of these people we would probably find out that their networks were small and quite densely packed with only very weak ties stretching beyond the wider community network. Therefore, we can assume that their decision-making and strategic thinking would be heavily influenced by the configuration of this network. If we require the decision-making body to think outside of the box and to introduce hugely novel solutions to their problems then it is likely that we will have to influence this network in some way.

REGENERATION AND CULTURE

Imagine you are at the helm of one of the UK's Regional Development Agencies or another regional or national body charged with affecting some sort of service or change in a particular area. One of the areas that we see often ignored or glossed over (probably due to the difficulty in measuring it) is the impact of culture on regeneration.

We would argue that a serious attempt at mapping the culture of an area prior to planning regeneration initiatives would allow interventions to be far better designed and targeted. For example, many of the groups labelled as socially excluded have emergent cultural forms which should be understood before embarking on any programme.

To quote from Midgley (2000):

There is a normative assumption in some thinking about social exclusion that the excluded should participate in the mainstream institutions of society at all costs. Of course, issues of cultural diversity and choice are raised here: there are some individuals and groups who choose a position in the margins. To complicate matters further, some of the choices made by excluded individuals and groups are not taken freely.

Any regeneration initiative should at the very least attempt to understand this cultural aspect in order to have a hope of successfully designing and evaluating the success of projects.

In reality, due to the dynamic nature of culture, it can never really be fully understood. In addition attempting to understand culture can be a messy and is not a straightforward task – it can't easily be surveyed. Therefore, regeneration professionals who are working in a mechanistic or reductionist paradigm will often ignore cultural issues.

ORGANIZATIONAL BEHAVIOUR AND AN UNHEALTHY OBSESSION WITH FUNDING

Whilst accepting that the money (or rather funding) does have a critical role to play in regeneration initiatives, we argue that an unnecessary focus on chasing resources (in the form of funding and people) becomes a distraction for many organizations and also a self-limiting argument which can prevent the design of good projects or constrain innovative thinking.

The science of complexity teaches us that small interventions in a complex system can lead to much larger system level changes. This idea was popularized by the work on self-induced criticality by Per Bak (1991) and also through chaos theory and the famous 'butterfly effect'.

If we accept that the systems with which we are working in regeneration are complex systems, could it not be that we can be smarter in the way we design regeneration interventions, e.g. not entirely focused around funding but around maximal impact?

Consider this question; 'If a regeneration company is to be successful should its one strategic aim be to put itself out of business?', that is, to have succeeded to such an extent that its work is done?

In terms of distributing scarce public funds this is a key question. For example it could be argued that in certain parts of the north east there are not just three tiers of local government but also several tiers of regeneration governance. These tiers arise for two main reasons: (1) the attempt to distribute monies directly to those that require it is always tempered by the need for control and accountability therefore the main mechanism for moving monies closer to the recipient is to create smaller devolved bodies at arm's length from the large funders (central, local government and RDAs); and (2) the need to retain sufficient flexibility in setting specific targets without local scrutiny through existing local government institutions.

129

However, the effect of this is that you have a multiplication of organizations who all need housing, administrative overhead, internal governance etc. Thus a slice of the monies intended for the front line is creamed off to sustain the delivery organization. The more delivery organizations there are the more the slices required.

CONCLUSION

As we have sought to explain in this chapter, the world now inhabited by regeneration managers and professionals, service class personnel and consultancy firms becomes ever more complex. Not only does central government have a strong desire to encourage the alignment of local priorities with nationally determined targets, as recent initiatives such as LAAs demonstrate, but the scale of new programmes emanating largely from ODPM, DTI and other departments, means that HM Treasury is continually 'shifting the goalposts' on how to measure effectiveness. Local actors have to make sense of this shifting agenda, and choose from the plethora of available mechanisms for measurement. Competing agendas, conflicting objectives, different programme timeframes and an inability to mainstream, coupled with insufficient clarity or guidance on what is required to develop their own metrics (but ones that will inevitably be audited by central state) forces them to rely on external expertise or consultancy firms that have one size fits all approaches. Either that, or they revert to benchmarking their activities to other programmes, and this is fraught with difficulty due to the many problems we have outlined earlier.

The obsession with tangible targets and measures within the UK regeneration context and the professionalization of regeneration, combined with the prevalent reductionist/ mechanistic worldview which pervades much of the public sector is in our opinion a major factor in why regeneration initiatives can fail, rather than succeed. In the pursuit of efficiency over effectiveness, which again is driven by targets at the expense of the intangible elements of regeneration, the sustainability of the initiatives once the funding has gone must also be questioned. We have argued that a complexity informed approach or an augmented toolset, from the selection we introduced, are more suitable to help regeneration agencies and communities to design better interventions and to understand how they can be effective, as well as spending their funds more efficiently.

Part Four

New challenges and gaps

KEY THEMES

■ Understanding the significance of an ethical framework for reflection.
■ Developing an explicit commitment to equality and diversity in regeneration management practice.
■ Enhancing our learning from the European Union and trans-national practice.

LEARNING POINTS

By the end of Part Four we hope that you will be able to:

■ Begin to develop an ethical approach to regeneration management practice.
■ Identify the ways in which equality and diversity are absent from some regeneration practice.
■ Reflect upon the extent to which the European experience is embedded in UK regeneration management.

CONTEXT SETTING

This final set of chapters shifts the focus from exploring present practice to identifying the gaps or challenges in our knowledge and practice. We feel that there are two significant gaps in current practice. First, there is a need to reassert the value (and necessity) of acknowledging the absences from much regeneration practice. There are two strands to this debate explored here. Marjorie Mayo and her colleagues draw upon their own empirical work by discussing the need for an ethical foundation within which regeneration professionals can reflect upon their practice. The absence of an ethical and emotional framework in contemporary practice can lead to choices and outcomes which were either not intended or were not even considered. Their chapter highlights some of these unintended outcomes by drawing upon the experiences of practitioners.

Stuart Speeden discusses the way in which questions of equality and diversity have often been marginalized in regeneration practice. He makes the case for reasserting the centrality of these debates in regeneration management. Specifically, he examines the potential of developing frameworks and processes to enable managers to reflect upon their practice.

Secondly, the role of the EU is undervalued.

David Silbergh and Calum MacDonald explore the impact of EU practice and policy on UK regeneration management practice. Whilst there has been an emphasis on learning from what works, they argue that there is still much for practitioners to learn from the EU experience.

Chapter 10

Capacities of the capacity-builders

Should training frameworks include ethical and emotional dimensions?

Marjorie Mayo, Paul Hoggett and Christopher Miller

INTRODUCTION

From New Labour Policy Action Team 16's (PAT 16) report on 'Learning Lessons' onwards, there has been increasing government recognition of the importance of training – and retraining – professionals and decision makers as well as communities and their representatives, if regeneration and neighbourhood renewal programmes are to be effective. PAT 16 concluded that in addition to their finding that 'community leaders do not get the support and encouragement they need' it was also the case that 'professionals are often not equipped to operate effectively in poor neighbourhoods; and that civil servants lack a full understanding of the communities they are trying to influence' (SEU 2000: 6). The answer lay in improved basic training to make it more relevant, together with improved opportunities for people with community experience to obtain access to these types of professional jobs; there should also be greater emphasis upon 'promoting cross-sectoral thinking and working' (SEU 2000). As the Learning Curve also recognized, partnership working with stakeholders places particular demands on professionals and this means 'helping residents, civil servants, practitioners and organisations gain the skills and knowledge they need to deliver real change' (NRU 2002: 1). Since then, there have been a number of initiatives to strengthen the capacities of the capacity-builders as well as to promote capacity-building and active citizenship within communities, including 'Futurebuilders' An Investment Fund for Voluntary and Community Sector Public Service Delivery, 2004, 'ChangeUp' the Capacity Building and Infrastructure Framework for the Voluntary Sector, and the Home Office Civil Renewal Unit's programme for Active Learning for Active Citizenship (ALAC) (Home Office 2004).

However welcome this increasing recognition, this chapter will argue that improved technical training will not be sufficient. Professional education needs to provide an ethical foundation for reflexive practice. Moreover, front-line professionals need continuing support if they are to combine flexibility with principle in an increasingly complex arena of professional and cross-professional activity. Whilst regeneration provides the context for the research upon which this paper draws, ethics and ethical dilemmas have emerged as issues of increasing interest in the human services more generally.

This interest may reflect wider concerns about increasing individualization – the demise of community according to communitarians – 'liquid modernity' in Bauman's terminology (Bauman 2000). Declining religious beliefs have also been cited as a causal factor, leaving professionals with 'neither training nor value system to guide them' when confronted with everyday dilemmas (Horner 1999: 184) – although this might seem problematic as an explanation, in face of the rise of religious fundamentalisms. Is there an identifiable public service ethic or ethos, in the current context, then, and if so, is this at risk, from marketization, 'modernization' and the new public management? There has been a shift, it has been suggested, away from a collective morality, with a value-orientation of community benefits (utilitarian ethics), to a personal-competence morality of individual benefits (egoistic ethics).

In his review of the literature on altruism Julian Le Grand concluded that there was indeed research evidence that altruistic behaviour still exists in the public service sector. Public service employees report a greater concern for serving the community and helping others than private sector ones, and this holds true across a range of international contexts (Le Grand 2003). Financial incentives can affect this motivation, however. Commitment to the public sector can be eroded if professionals feel unable to provide a quality service, and professional motivation can be further undermined by excessive regulation, feeling undervalued and mistrusted. The public service ethos may still be alive, then, but its continuing survival is not to be taken for granted.

The paper will summarize findings from recent studies before drawing upon current research, exploring the ways in which front-line regeneration professionals and their managers identify and cope with the ethical dilemmas that are inherent in working with communities in the context of the new public management. As an expanding and still relatively fluid arena, regeneration poses particular challenges for training and for continuing professional development. Some of these challenges, including the challenges inherent in working across professional boundaries, may have wider relevance, however, in the current policy context.

AN EXPANDING – AND INCREASINGLY COMPLEX – ARENA OF PROFESSIONAL ACTIVITY

The number of front-line staff being paid to engage in work with communities has increased significantly in recent years. Since 1997 a trickle of programmes to involve communities and service users has turned into a veritable flood of initiatives to promote participation, capacity-building and partnership working. A survey carried out by CDF/ SCCD (with government support) between 2001–2003 began by estimating that some

14,000 were employed in this area by the beginning of the twenty-first century, compared with some 5,000 such staff in the 1980s (Glen *et al.* 2004) (although precise numbers were difficult to obtain, this type of employment being something of a moving target in the current context, characterized as it is by the increasing use of short-term contracts to work in short-term projects). The National Training Organization PAULO put their estimate as high as 146,000. The majority of posts in the CDF/SCCD survey were dependent upon central or local government funding, either directly or indirectly via special initiatives, although over half the staff were actually employed in the voluntary sector (raising questions, perhaps, about the sustainability of some of these projects in the voluntary/community/not-for-profit sectors).

Whilst welcoming this expansion of official support, the survey raised a number of concerns about the quality of jobs being created to work with communities. Only just over half of the staff had permanent contracts, with some indication that there has been a decline of the proportion of permanent posts. The pay was modest to say the least and women were disproportionately likely to be amongst the lower paid in what was becoming an increasingly feminized workforce (around two-thirds of the workforce was female compared with just over half in the mid-eighties). This casualization – and the associated deterioration in professional conditions – was the cause of some concern. As one of the participants at one of the subsequent workshops commented 'initiatives come and go so quickly – (it) undermines community confidence and community development is harder than ten years ago'. Community groups become tired of the constant turnover of staff (Glen *et al.* 2004: 18), and there were stresses inherent in trying to combine professional values with the requirements of the 'contract culture'. Workers commented on the need for more strategic approaches – with more emphasis upon professional values (Glen *et al.* 2004).

This commitment to values emerged amongst the unpaid workers interviewed in the SCCD survey. The report concluded that there was a strong allegiance in many interviewees 'to the value of community, social justice and the importance of working with community members. These values were clearly defined and there was an overall idealism or belief system about community involvement that was clear and distinct from personal motivations, perhaps for social contact or personal interests in a particular area' (Gaffney 2002: 8). Typically for these unpaid workers, this commitment – often fuelled by personal experiences of social injustices and/or poor local conditions/services – led them from one form of involvement to another. Whilst many were involved in very demanding work, the report expressed serious concerns about the level of training and support available in too many cases, leading to 'a substantial risk in some situations for alienation and burn out in those most likely to operate in facilitation roles' (Gaffney 2002: 20).

There were grounds for similar anxieties about the risk of burnout for paid staff. The job of paid workers was seen as having become more complex, involving a range of issues from regeneration and local economic development to community safety and crime reduction, from anti-poverty strategies and social inclusion to health, housing and planning and regeneration via community arts. Three-quarters were involved in capacity-building and two-thirds were involved in facilitating or supporting self-help and/or consultation (compared with just over a third who were involved in advocacy and over a third who spent less than 25 per cent of their time working directly with communities). These jobs typically involved complex roles with competing pressures, but supervision was all too often found to be inadequate. 'There is no time to receive supervision' commented one worker 'as we're delivering targets' (Glen *et al.* 2004: 37). Even when supervision was forthcoming, this was not necessarily being delivered by colleagues with the relevant expertise. A quarter of the respondents in the SCCD/CDF survey were being supervised by someone with no direct experience of working with communities and 40 per cent were being supervised by someone not currently practising community development work. As one of the respondents commented 'Workers can be left in the middle without strategic thinking or direction' (Glen *et al.* 2004: 38).

In the current policy context, however, professional supervision is becoming even more important, along with continuing professional development to build upon initial training. Like professional social workers and youth workers (Banks 1995, 1999), community workers and other front-line professionals may expect to face more ethical issues and dilemmas as professional ethics come under pressure from:

- Increasing marketization and the New Public Management
- Increased fragmentation and competition between communities and community groups in local areas
- Increasing pressures for consumer rights and user/community-determined priorities on the one hand and the requirements for rationing scarce resources on the other
- Increasing decentralization of responsibilities without this necessarily being accompanied by commensurate powers and resources
- Increasing pressures for centralized controls of targets and outputs and
- Increasing pressures to work across professional boundaries, involving varying codes and practices.

Faced with all these, it has been argued, professionals need to start with a knowledge and critical understanding of ethical issues (Freidson 2001), and then have the time and safe space for reflection/self-reflection along with professional supervision and non-managerial support. These are in addition to the resources that they themselves bring to the job due to their own personal history, upbringing, cultural mores, motivation and professional commitment. Together, these should help them to cope most effectively and with the least anxiety and guilt (Bailey and Schwartzberg 1995). Without these coping mechanisms, it has been suggested, professionals are at increasing risk of burnout.

This was the starting point for our research. How are front-line professionals coping in this context of increasing ethical uncertainty, shifting professional boundaries and increasing pressures from modernizing/New Public Management agendas? How do they hold on to their professional ethics whilst responding to new situations flexibly, avoiding total moral relativism on the one hand and/or terminal burnout on the other?

The approach to our research was psycho-social, using a series of biographical interviews to explore the origins of workers' values and motivations, semi-structured interviews based upon work-based diaries/logs which identified the dilemmas and strategies adopted and finally inquiry groups which encouraged exploration of the implications for professional training and support as well as for policy development more widely. We have been conducting this field work in two urban sites chosen (in part) for the range of initiatives and the number of highly experienced professionals in a position to reflect and to compare and contrast their experiences over time. At this point it should be emphasized that this is a qualitative study. Our findings have certainly been thought-provoking for the team – but we would absolutely not seek to exaggerate the claims that can be made for these findings, let alone to make firm statements about how far they might be replicated more generally.

With these caveats firmly in mind, the following section sets out to summarize the issues that have been emerging from the interviews so far.

FRONT-LINE PROFESSIONALS' OWN VALUES AND COMMITMENT

At the outset, we anticipated that front-line staff might face a range of dilemmas, challenging their professional ethics and their professional expertise. Community development work has tended to involve inherent tensions in any case. Community workers have been described as insiders as well as outsiders: 'In and Against the State' in previous teminology (London Edinburgh Weekend Return Group 1979), negotiating and facilitating bridges within and between communities and the agencies responsible for addressing their needs. There are inherent tensions here as well as potential strengths. In the current context of the new localism, with responsibilities being increasingly passed down the line to communities – without necessarily including the requisite resources – front-line professionals may be facing increasing challenges and dilemmas as they engage with managing forms of 'Indirect Rule'. Hiving off policy implementation effectively depoliticizes issues that should arguably be resolved democratically and transparently, it has been said, leaving workers to cope with the resulting anxieties as best they can, as they attempt to deal with intractable policy conflicts which get passed down the line from government (Hoggett 2005).

We anticipated that professionals would also express concerns about increasing technical challenges, such as coping with complex systems for monitoring and evaluating progress against milestones and targets, accounting to different funders in the context of the New Public Management whilst striving to remain responsive to local priorities and needs. Working in partnerships across organizational and professional boundaries was expected to add to these potential challenges and dilemmas.

137

Given all these pressures, we had anticipated that we would encounter expressions of anxiety, if not actual demoralization amongst some at least of these front-line public service professionals. In some ways they might be seen as exemplifying the pressures associated with increasing demands for 'emotional labour' more generally, the skills of demonstrating empathy, intuition, persuasion, even manipulation – in the context of increasing competition in the service sector, coupled with organizational forms that place more responsibility on the individual employee in the front-line (Bunting 2004: 19, referring to the writings of Hochschild). The emotional labour together with the ethical dilemmas involved in front-line professionals' work were expected to raise particular issues in terms of the implications for professional training, continuing professional development, supervision and non-managerial support.

The responses of our interviewees have been rather different, however, very different in many cases – although the analysis is still to be finalized. Professionals seem only too aware of the inherent stresses and the potential ethical dilemmas involved. We have come across cases where individuals have had to take time off with stress-related illnesses, but we have identified few if any comments that would indicate burnout in the sense of absolute demoralization or loss of concern with the work per se. On the contrary, in fact, professionals who have been engaged in this type of work for some considerable time speak of their continuing commitment. Several have specifically commented that they have decided *not* to go for promotion, in fact, if this promotion would take them away from the face-to-face work. Someone working to promote young people's participation spoke of the satisfaction of working directly with the young people themselves, their liveliness and willingness to engage 'makes your head jump' she commented. This type of response seems to be a recurrent theme amongst workers who have stayed in the field over a number of years.

There might, perhaps, be generational differences here. Certainly some of the more experienced professionals have expressed the view that those coming into the field bring different approaches based upon values and perspectives that tend to be less sharply defined (influenced, perhaps by postmodernist critiques of grand narratives?). On the basis of the evidence from the interviews themselves, however, less experienced professionals emerge as no less committed, although this commitment may, perhaps, vary in some ways, motivations and commitments being shaped, at least in part, through varying experiences in different contexts and times.

The biographical interviews give us clues, we think, to help to understand the strengths of these continuing commitments. There were wide variations in the professional trajectories of front-line professionals. Some had embarked on other job/career paths, shifting in response to external events (such as being made redundant) or simply finding their regular job uninspiring (the manager for example, or the qualified motor mechanic both of whom became youth workers focusing upon young people's participation and young people's voice). Others found that working with communities provided a fulfilling way of using their existing talents and skills (the young art student who discovered community arts work, for example). In some cases, key individuals

138

played a deciding role – role models who encouraged others to have the confidence to pursue a career in this field.

The professional trajectories were very varied then – not at all the coherent paths that might have been expected to emerge from biographical accounts. (It has been suggested that respondents can feel that they are being expected to provide coherent narratives to account for their present positions – a form of response that has been suspected of being associated with this particular research method.) So far, in addition to the impact on these trajectories of life-changing events and/or the influence of key individuals, we have identified the following:

- Early influences (such as parents or other relatives with strong values related to public service values and/or concerns with social justice whether directly or indirectly) the influences of neighbourhood, and social context (such as growing up in a strong working class community and/or faith community).
- Influences from the wider social context (such as growing up in the context of wider political struggles – the miners' strike was mentioned here, along with second-wave feminism and anti-racist struggles in the aftermath of the New Cross fire in south-east London in the 1980s; more recent examples included the influences of environmental campaigns and animal liberation).

These early and subsequent influences emerged when people talked about their values and how these values had developed and been re-enforced over time, linking these accounts with their commitment to working with communities.

Whilst the professional trajectories were varied, however, common themes have been emerging too. Several interviewees saw powerful connections between their work and their emotional lives. For example, one worker explained that adolescence had been a painful experience for her. As she now recognized she had become involved in working with young people in communities, in part, at least, because of the wish to turn this negative experience around – to be for others the type of role model/support that she would like to have experienced, personally. This notion of community and youth work as 'reparation' has emerged from a number of accounts. When emerging themes have been reflected back to participants to stimulate further discussion it has also been noticeable that many have added further examples from their own experiences. This particular theme cuts across class boundaries. Our participants came from a variety of backgrounds, many from working class families with personal experiences of some of the problems associated with urban regeneration and neighbourhood renewal. Other participants have come from professional middle class backgrounds. The notion of reparation, the desire to repair past damage, seems to have had just as much resonance for a number of them.

These biographical/emotional factors may – or may not – be explained in terms of psychoanalytical theories of reparation. The point of emphasizing them here is simply this – that front-line public service workers' professional values would seem to have

139

powerful emotional roots. This may help to explain their continuing commitment in the face of increasingly pressurized employment situations. The point is not to suggest that we are interviewing an army of knights in shining armour, community guardian angels, let alone to suggest that professionals necessarily translate such commitments into reflexive practice. On the contrary, the point is simply to emphasize the relevance of understanding workers' emotional investments in their professional roles – and for professionals to be reflexively aware of these emotional roots themselves through their training and continuing professional development, as well as having the training to discharge their more practical duties. The significance of these values may need to be more fully recognized, together with the need to recognize how much could be at stake if public professional values were to be further undermined in the current policy context.

FRONT-LINE PROFESSIONALS' DILEMMAS AND COPING STRATEGIES

Before moving on to the potential implications for training and continuing professional development, professionals' own perspectives on their dilemmas and coping strategies need to be summarized. We had anticipated that a number of dilemmas would be identified, relating to the inherent tensions and increasing pressures already identified above. Unsurprisingly, perhaps, individuals interpreted these in varying ways, depending upon their own particular perspectives and experiences. Common themes did emerge, but also differences of emphasis and interpretation.

Dilemmas associated with the potential tensions between being both an 'insider' and an 'outsider' emerged for example. A number of participants have been exploring their feelings of ambivalence – sometimes in general as well as in their professional roles more specifically. So, for example, people have referred to themselves as feeling on the margins of the mainstream, or feeling like an outsider as a working class student in an elite university setting, or feelings of not belonging, and/or having been a bit of a rebel, now feeling under pressure to become 'poacher turned gamekeeper' as a public service professional. This notion elicited a number of responses when reflected back to participants for further discussion. For some, these feelings of marginality represented sources of potential discomfort/continuing tensions in their professional roles.

For others, however, this insider/outsider tension was not only seen as inherent in the role – it was also identified as a source of potential strength. Having strong roots in the community was identified as a source of legitimacy when negotiating with formal organizations – a source of strength when negotiating for service improvements for example. Interestingly, for one relatively younger professional, being an outsider had actually represented a key coping strategy – as a consultant she was brought in on short-term contracts, so she could, if she so chose, simply move on to another contract, leaving

140

others to deal with any remaining conflicts. On further reflecting however, she was in the process of deciding (and subsequently did decide) to take up a more permanent post, feeling that this would be ultimately more satisfying, whatever the additional problems in the short term.

There were a number of dilemmas that related to questions around boundaries more generally, many of which were seen to be increasing in the current policy context. For example, professionals described some of the tensions that could arise when residents and other unpaid activists became employed as staff on projects. There were potential tensions for managers, and indeed for other residents, if such new staff members pushed the boundaries and/or broke the rules (as in the case of young people employed to work with their peers, if boundaries, such as those around alcohol or substance misuse, were pushed beyond the limits). When and how to intervene – or not to intervene – in such cases could be problematic, and not least when contained within relatively small neighbourhoods and closely knit communities. Such dilemmas could be compounded if boundaries of race and/or social class were also involved (young black residents/ employees being managed by white middle-class professionals answerable to adults in the community as well as to funders).

Dilemmas associated with the boundaries of race and class emerged very powerfully in a number of ways, in fact, especially, but by no means exclusively, in the London context. There were examples of dilemmas experienced by black workers when white managers failed to address the issues that they raised, including disciplinary issues involving other black workers. Managers (and local councillors) could be so nervous about possible allegations of racism, it was suggested, that they were reluctant to pursue personnel issues involving black staff, even if these issues were being raised by black team leaders. Conversely too, there were instances of black workers expressing frustration, feeling undervalued and undermined by white managers.

Class boundaries posed challenges for middle-class professionals practising in working class neighbourhoods just as operating in middle-class professional contexts could pose challenges for professionals from working class backgrounds. Gender issues emerged less clearly however, except, in relation to the dilemmas inherent in maintaining a reasonable balance between the pressures of work and the need to safeguard personal space for relationships and for caring responsibilities. Whilst both men and women raised these as continuing dilemmas, it was women who provided examples of how these dilemmas had actually impacted upon their employment choices (e.g. leaving a particular job because the hours were simply incompatible with childcare responsibilities).

Working with young people, in the current policy context, emerged as a relatively significant source of tensions and dilemmas in its own right. A number of professionals spoke about this with passion. Young people were being criminalized as a result of government policies, it was suggested, and workers experienced dilemmas when attempting to convince funders of the case for resourcing provision for young people. Unless they colluded with such stereotypes, presenting the young people as potential criminals in need of treatment, it was argued, resources were unlikely to be forthcoming.

141

Participants also commented on the increasing technical pressures that they faced in their professional roles. These included the problems associated with coping with complex systems for monitoring and evaluating progress against milestones and targets and accounting to different funders whilst aiming to hold on to local definitions of needs and priorities for addressing these. Competition for targets was identified as one more source of pressure for professionals working in different projects and sectors. This was unsurprising. A number of participants also reflected on the importance of accountability, however, commenting, in several cases, on the inadequacies of particular accountability systems in the past. There seemed a notable lack of nostalgia for the so-called 'golden era' of community work. Whilst some participants referred to their greater freedom to support advocacy and campaigning, previously, there were also comments about the lessons to be learnt and the need to separate professional from political agendas (distinctions that had, perhaps, been less clearly delineated by some activists turned professionals in earlier times). Whilst targets and complex accountability systems have emerged as problems, then, these have not necessarily been identified as being amongst the more difficult dilemmas. Professionals seem to have accepted these as simply coming with the job.

There were, in addition, some surprises around which issues and dilemmas professionals experience as being most stressful personally. We started from the assumption that professionals would identify a number of dilemmas associated with the decentralization of decision-making – having to find ways forward in this context, having considerable discretion without necessarily having commensurate guidance, let alone commensurate powers or resources. In fact it emerged from the inquiry group discussions that professionals can be just as, if not even more, stressed in situations where they feel that they have less rather than more professional autonomy. Professionals expressed powerful feelings about situations in which they felt that they had little if any choice about how to act. Even if they personally agreed with particular procedures, they could still feel disquiet about their outcomes. Examples included concerns about the impact upon individuals disciplined for failing to follow procedures, as in the case of residents/workers who had failed to respect official boundaries, or fellow workers who had been disciplined for failing to focus upon agreed targets. Feelings of powerlessness compounded professionals' feelings of disquiet in such circumstances, even when they accepted the logic of the formal procedures involved.

There were more concerns, it seemed, around partnership working and the shifting boundaries of the voluntary and community sectors, themselves. There is a growing literature on the problems associated with partnership working including the tensions associated with relationships and inequalities of power (Glendinning *et al.* 2002; Taylor 2003). Front-line professionals may feel particularly vulnerable in this context, potentially caught between the competing pressures of official agencies and the differing interests that are being articulated – or not being articulated – within communities.

Examples of dilemmas identified with partnership working, and working in area-based programmes more generally have included the following:

142

- Dilemmas associated with working with people's cynicism/disillusion and mistrust of official agencies – encouraging people to participate, despite this scepticism, only to experience further let-downs and disappointments, leaving the professional to take the flak for decisions and/or lack of action taken/not taken elsewhere. These relate to some of the more general dilemmas associated with short-term interventions, with top-down targets versus the need for longer-term interventions to develop trust, agree priorities and work towards sustainable outcomes.

- Dilemmas inherent in working with conflicts within and between different groupings and interests within the voluntary and community sectors, including the specific dilemmas associated with 'troughing' (a local London term deriving from the expression 'snouts in the trough' – i.e. when individuals or groups exploit regeneration resources for their own individual or sectional interests) and dilemmas associated with issues of representation – who may legitimately claim to speak on behalf of whom, and what to do if 'representatives'/'local leaders' appear to be failing to represent constituents' interests democratically and/or inclusively (dilemmas potentially compounded by differences of class and/or race).

The research provided examples of sophisticated coping strategies, as front-line professionals find ways of negotiating between and around these competing demands, aiming to work flexibly across professional boundaries without losing their own professional identities and values. From the perspectives of participants in our study, partnership working is particularly problematic, however, in that the professionals involved may find themselves effectively coping 'on their own'. For example, one participant gave a (highly confidential) account of his dilemmas when another agency consistently failed to deliver to the partnership as promised. The participant came to understand the complex reasons for this block but felt unable to address these. Taking the issues up formally via line managers could simply jeopardize the fragile relations between the agencies in question. So the worker felt that he had no option but to cope as best could, unsupported.

SUPPORT STRUCTURES AND COPING STRATEGIES

This lack of support has been emerging as an issue more generally. We interviewed very few people who identified their line manager as key in terms of support. One participant commented that supervision and support in their previous post in the voluntary/community sector was non-existent – but that he was now very much enjoying the experience of professional supervision (in a not-for-profit organization in the health promotion sphere). In other cases, professional support was effectively non-existent. Two respondents were actually paying for non-managerial supervision from their own pockets!

This lack of support seems to run across the statutory and voluntary/community sectors. There may be additional problems for those working in small voluntary/community sector organizations and agencies, however. For example, one participant explained that she had been faced with a complex issue amongst their own small staff group (one worker was alleged to have been behaving in discriminatory ways). This case raised issues of employment law as well as of issues around equalities procedures and practices. In a large formal organization, the participant would have had access to specialist advice, for example from human resources and/or legal departments. In this case, the participant was on her own.

Participants have been speaking of the support systems that they have been developing for themselves, emailing a former colleague to share dilemmas, for example, or testing out potential solutions informally with trusted colleagues in neighbouring areas. Participants have also commented on their personal coping strategies – going to a football match, playing computer games, going for a drink with friends – as ways of turning off at the end of a particularly stressful day. Somehow people *are* finding their own ways of coping – but typically they are doing this on their own, without professional support.

Meanwhile the changing boundaries between sectors in an increasingly marketized economy of welfare would seem to be exacerbating the pressures on front-line professionals. Some of the most painful dilemmas that have been recounted so far relate to the tensions arising *within* the voluntary/community sector as a result. Participants have spoken of the 'brutalism' that can occur when voluntary/community sector agencies compete for resources, fighting for their own organizational survival in the context of increasingly short-term contracts and increasingly casualized labour. Others have spoken of the dilemmas inherent in being a public service sector worker in such situations. They often feel blamed for the shortcomings of the public sector in its entirety by professionals from the voluntary sector who present themselves as the only true representatives of the community (whilst pursuing competing agendas for their own organizational survival). The role of insider/outsider may have its potential advantages, but this would seem less evident with the role of scapegoat/public enemy number one – without the right of reply.

This, it may be argued, comes with the job, being able to take the pressure from all sides, responding flexibly to maximize the potential benefits from particular programmes without losing sight of the values that underpin front-line professionals' commitments in the first place, but this also raises questions about the education and training of front-line professionals, together with their continuing management support. Whether or not the next generation of front-line professionals may have different ways of identifying and addressing these dilemmas, however, there is no reason to suppose that they will need less rather than more support.

TOWARDS CONCLUSIONS

Whilst we have been exploring conclusions with stakeholders and policy makers, a number of areas of potential concern have been emerging. First, there would seem to be issues emerging around the education and training of front-line professionals. Training needs to focus more on the development of the 'moral imagination' (Whitebrook 2002) and a greater understanding of differing approaches to professional ethics, not taught abstractly but practically. This would enable them to be more confident in making difficult choices as reflexive practitioners, critically aware of their own values and emotional motivations, aware of themselves and their personal baggage as well as of the personal resources that they bring to the role and tasks. Second, there are a number of implications for the management and support of front-line professionals, so many of whom seem to be so seriously under-supported at present. There are implications too for the training and continuing professional development of managers and policy makers in these fields. And finally there would seem to be wider issues for public policy and politics, issues with particular relevance in the context of debates around the new localism. Dumping the problems of inadequate service delivery, unresolved policy conflicts or symbolic and knee-jerk responses to moral panics onto front-line professionals may be just as stressful – and ultimately just as problematic – as expecting them to resolve the problems associated with the democratic deficit through programmes to promote community participation and empowerment. Whilst these issues have not emerged in the forefront, they would seem relevant, nevertheless, for those concerned with public policy to facilitate user and community involvement more generally.

Chapter 11

Equality and regeneration

Managing conflicting agendas for social inclusion

Stuart Speeden

The development of the National Strategy for Neighbourhood Renewal (SEU 1998, 2000, 2001) marked a significant reorientation of urban policy in Britain in which social inclusion became a key element within urban regeneration. The benefits of a renewal strategy based on investment in physical and economic infrastructure had, it was argued, generally failed to reach deprived neighbourhoods and persistent patterns of social exclusion continued to exist alongside successful renewal projects. The recognition of the failure to address poverty and social exclusion led to a greater emphasis on social regeneration with attention focusing on community involvement, 'joined-up' services and partnership working (Taylor 2000).

The National Strategy for Neighbourhood Renewal (NSNR) was developed as a comprehensive strategy to address poverty and social exclusion in deprived neighbourhoods. The approach sought to overcome the weaknesses of service delivery at the local level by dealing with the fragmentation of policy initiatives and the failure to consult and involve local communities. It was also concerned with building capacity and 'social capital' (Putnam 1995) within deprived areas as a way of harnessing the benefits of physical and economic improvement. It was argued (Putnam 1995) that social capital is essential for economic renewal as 'the glue that bonds the benefits of economic and physical capital into marginalized communities' (ibid.: 308). In effect a new discourse of regeneration based on the principles of social inclusion has been developed. The strong identification between the processes of regeneration and social inclusion are now evident throughout the policy initiatives of New Labour and through a proliferation of regeneration and social inclusion strategies at a local level.

In parallel with the emerging policy discourse on social inclusion and regeneration, two further discourses of 'inclusion' have emerged around equality and cohesion. These policy discourses address aspects of exclusion and deprivation, which appear separate from social inclusion. They are pursued by different government departments and have developed a range of distinctive policies and practices. The following discussion explores the relationship between these policies, and examines the political and management frameworks through which the policies are mediated through local governance. The discussion is itself informed by qualitative material drawn from a number of interviews conducted with a range of offices and policy makers across the public sector.

SOCIAL INCLUSION AND DISCRIMINATION

The policy discourse around social inclusion and regeneration has developed principally around the notion of social deprivation and social exclusion. A broad definition of social exclusion (SEU 2004) emphasizes a range of linked problems leading to social exclusion 'Social exclusion is a shorthand term for what can happen when people or areas suffer from a combination of linked problems such as unemployment, poor skills, low incomes, bad health and family breakdown.' In an earlier report, the SEU (1998) identified 'key features of poverty and social exclusion' as follows:

- Lack of opportunities to work
- Lack of opportunities to acquire education and skills
- Childhood deprivation
- Disrupted families
- Barriers to older people living active, fulfilling and healthy lives
- Inequalities in health
- Poor housing
- Poor neighbourhoods
- Fear of crime
- Disadvantaged groups.

The conclusions of the SEU show that patterns of deprivation can lead to a cycle of social exclusion which:

happens when people or places suffer from a series of problems such as unemployment, discrimination, poor skills, low incomes, poor housing, high crime, ill health and family breakdown. When such problems combine they can create a vicious cycle.

(SEU 1998)

These patterns of exclusion:

can happen as a result of problems that face one person in their life. But it can also start from birth. Being born into poverty or to parents with low skills still has a major influence on future life chances.

The definitions of exclusion presented by the SEU focus on deprivation as the key component of exclusion; it emphasizes the multifaceted character of deprivation and it

147

highlights the importance of background and locality in shaping the opportunities of people born into poverty. Policies for inclusion and regeneration have been developed to address these patterns of social exclusion. Within this framework, issues of diversity have not been addressed as major policy consideration.

A study conducted for the Joseph Rowntree Foundation (Brownhill and Darke 1998) concluded that race and gender were neglected within regeneration. The report found that:

- Women and ethnic minorities are over-represented in areas undergoing regeneration. However, race and gender are rarely prioritized as major strategic issues within regeneration policy at the national, regional or local level.
- The nature of poverty and exclusion in regeneration areas is different for different groups. For example, women may be excluded by lack of confidence, domestic responsibilities and economic discrimination. Ethnic minorities face stereotyped attitudes and in some cases barriers of language or custom.
- There is evidence of a variety of approaches placing race and gender in the mainstream of regeneration. Universal strategies prioritize issues such as exclusion; others prioritize race and/or gender as specific policy targets. Research suggests that projects will need a mixture of universal and specific targets if the needs of specific groups are to be met.

More recent research undertaken with managers involved in regeneration and social inclusion[1] showed a greater sensitivity to race and gender issues. However, the common assumption was that there is an *implicit* equality focus within regeneration and social inclusion policy and practice. This is expressed through policies, objectives and targets for social inclusion. Specific objectives addressing the needs of ethnic minorities, women, young people or the elderly were present within many regeneration projects.

The presence of specific projects addressing the needs of women and black and minority ethnic (BME) groups shows an awareness of diversity as a factor in social exclusion that requires specific interventions, but it is not clear how these issues are examined on a consistent or systematic basis. Managers referred in some cases to the importance of community consultation and involvement in the identification of diverse needs, but there was no use of equality impact assessment as a technique for gathering evidence of the impact of policies on diverse groups. In practice, whilst there was a growing awareness of the need to include projects to meet specific diversity needs, this fell short of a 'mainstreamed' understanding of discrimination and equality.

The presence of specific targets and objectives to address the needs of women or BME communities may have a positive effect in addressing aspects of exclusion. They will be inadequate if the effect of other regeneration activity being undertaken within a renewal area, say, for physical redevelopment or economic development, is having a negative effect. The research evidence on regeneration policies (Tyler et al. 2000) shows that 'market effects' play an important role in the complex construction of social exclusion and there is strong evidence that the unintended effect of social policies, such as housing policy can produce discriminatory effects that create disadvantage and exclusion (Khakee *et al.* 1999). For example, the consequences of housing redevelopment, designed to improve housing quality and remedy aspects of social exclusion for a BME community, may have a number of unintended consequences that impact negatively on the lives of women or young people within that community. At present social inclusion policies do not, generally, address the impact of market forces, the policy outcomes or the discriminatory effects that may affect social groups such as women, black and ethnic minorities or the disabled.

In dealing with diversity and equality it seems there are assumptions in regeneration and social inclusion practices that equality and diversity issues can be dealt with through the existing framework and practices for social inclusion. In short we appear to have a discourse based upon the alleviation of deprivation which *contains* an approach for addressing equality. However, there is no clear methodology in use for understanding the way in which *discrimination and prejudice* produce patterns of exclusion. This problem arises because the policy discourses dealing with social exclusion, as deprivation, have developed separately from the policy discourse around equality and diversity.

EQUALITY AND DIVERSITY: AN EMERGING POLICY DISCOURSE

Alongside the social exclusion/inclusion framework that has been driven by the government's Social Exclusion Unit there have been separate policy discourses dealing with social inclusion that focus on diversity, equality and discrimination. This policy framework is rooted in the social movements and social theory that have shaped understanding of identity and difference since the 1960s. Anti-discrimination law was established through the Race Relations Act (1965), the Equal Pay Act (1970) and the Sex Discrimination Act (1975) and has gathered pace since the mid-1960s with new legislation to tackle institutional discrimination through the Race Relations Amendment Act and the extension of law to cover discrimination on grounds of disability, sexual orientation, age and religious belief (Collier 1998). Convergence has begun to take place around both law and policies to address discrimination so that a common framework for equality has begun to emerge for race, gender and disability. This framework would be extended further by the proposed Commission for Equality and Human Rights and by a single equality act. In practice, equality policy has been shaped across a number of government departments (the Home Office, Department of Trade and Industry and Work and Pensions) and through three equality commissions. Its expression as a coherent *equality* strategy is most clearly developed in the work of local government and NHS Trusts.

A recent NHS report makes the case for Equality and Diversity in the NHS, explaining, 'Equality is about *creating a fairer society* where everyone can participate and has the opportunity to fulfil potential. It is backed by legislation designed to address unfair discrimination based on membership of a particular group.' The goals identified are to:

■ Ensure public services are fully accessible and responsive to the diverse needs of all the groups and communities they serve
■ Promote equality and diversity in public sector employment.

The field of operation for equality policy is defined in legislative terms to cover race, gender and disability and is extended through the Human Rights Act 1998 and the European Union Employment Directive to address discrimination with regard to sexual orientation, religion and belief and discrimination on the grounds of age.

Thus we have an equalities agenda that is concerned with *equal opportunity* and *equal access*. However, following the findings of the Stephen Lawrence Enquiry, it is also concerned with institutional discrimination and the idea of *equal outcome* for public services as measured across the equality strands.

The emphasis on outcome is apparent in the development of the system of race equality schemes and race equality impact assessment as a basis for implementing the requirements of the Race Relations Amendment Act (2000). The principles are taken further and applied more widely to gender and disability through the Equality Standard for Local Government (Speeden and Clarke 2001). Assessment of policies and actions to explore discriminatory and adverse impact on diverse social groups is an important feature of these systems.

EQUALITY IN SOCIAL INCLUSION AND REGENERATION

Policies to address discrimination, and the inequalities they generate, gained considerable momentum through the findings of the Stephen Lawrence Inquiry. The phenomenon of institutional discrimination has been recognized through a body of research in housing and urban policy stretching back over four decades. These studies provide evidence of policies producing discriminatory effects through bureaucracies and markets that lead to inequality and disadvantage for women and for black and minority ethnic groups. I want to argue that the discriminatory effects of urban policy have been conflated with *disadvantage* in policy discourse for social inclusion and regeneration. As a consequence there has been little consideration of the role that bureaucracies and markets play in discrimination and exclusion applied to race, gender, disability, sexual orientation, belief and age.

Across these two areas of emerging policy it will be evident that social exclusion (SEU 2003) has focused on the *lack* of access and opportunity that lead to social exclusion and it focuses on raising these levels. Equality policy is concerned with *equality* of access and opportunity. Clearly, policies that address lack of opportunity and access (social exclusion) will, generally, operate in support of equal access and opportunity (equalities) but there are many aspects of equality policy that they will not address. In the same way, equality policy does not, generally, address class, income and poverty and therefore does not address all aspects of social exclusion.

At the heart of this discussion is the question of convergence. Can these policies be brought together within a single unified framework? The question arises because each of the discourses adopts a separate *universal* principle which seeks to place disadvantage or equality (of access and opportunity) as the core value of a policy framework. More than this they seek to make each of these values *integral* to all aspects of policy and service delivery. The pressures to integrate policy is explicit within each of the policy frameworks in terms of coordination, joined-up policy-making and mainstreaming; they also provide an overlapping rhetoric that competes to give meaning to the notion of inclusion. These tendencies mean that in practice these policy discourses interact at the level of front line services and they are not simply complementary. They do in fact create conflicting objectives that can prove difficult to resolve.

Current policies focusing on employability and social exclusion provide an illustration of the potential conflict between social exclusion and equality policies. A strong and growing feature of the government's approach to social exclusion is to see engagement in the labour market as a central component of policies for inclusion. Emphasis is placed on employability and skill levels for 'excluded' people alongside efforts to address the social, cultural and economic barriers that may prevent people from taking up work. Employment is therefore a key measure of achievement in dealing with excluded communities and projects across neighbourhood renewal areas are targeted to improve employability for women, BME communities and disabled people as part of the policy commitment to social inclusion.

These policies for employability, while they may address social inclusion, do not automatically address issues of equality. Equal access, equal treatment should stand alongside access to employment as measures of social inclusion. Equality can be regarded as a measure of social inclusion but it is not generally treated as a central performance measure within regeneration and social inclusion. For convenience it is useful to think of social exclusion and equalities as overlapping policy agendas where the overlap will contain common policy objectives but where neither field of activity is simply subsumed by the other.

The importance of the new equality agenda is that it emphasizes mainstreaming and requires that all activities should be examined for their equalities impact and not just those activities that are directed at a disadvantaged or excluded group. It is therefore important that regeneration managers engage with equality management as a distinctive focus of activity.

COMMUNITY COHESION

A further complication to this picture arises in relation to the Government's commitment to Community Cohesion. Community Cohesion policy has emerged from debate following the tensions and conflicts that surfaced in a number of northern towns and cities in 2001. The tensions in towns such as Oldham, Burnley and Bradford centred on the relationship between white and ethnic minority communities raising questions of difference and cohesion: differences in culture, religion, differences between generations and genders were seen to contribute to divisions and mistrust (Cantle 2001, 2005).

Following a report of an independent review team, the government has established a Community Cohesion Unit and a policy agenda for promoting greater Community Cohesion. A cohesive community, it is argued, is one where:

- There is a common vision and a sense of belonging for all communities
- The diversity of people's backgrounds and circumstances is appreciated and positively valued
- Those from similar backgrounds have similar life opportunities
- Strong and positive relationships are being developed between people from different backgrounds in the workplace, in schools and within neighbourhoods.

This forms the framework for wide-ranging policy activity that overlaps with Social Exclusion and Equality and Diversity policy in that it works at the interface between equality strands and the activity is often focused in renewal areas where there are high levels of social exclusion.

The overlapping fields of activity and the potential for interaction and conflict between these policy agendas is increasingly important at the level of policy implementation. The interaction between these agendas is, however, not simply a question of coordination. There are more fundamental problems to overcome because these agendas do pursue different goals, they develop their own discourses and interpret evidence in different ways. This means that within the overlapping areas of policy activity there is the potential for policy objectives that are pulling in different directions.

An illustration of conflicting objectives was identified in the interviews with regeneration managers. An area of older housing that was occupied by a largely BME community had been identified for redevelopment. The redevelopment would improve housing quality and tackle housing poverty, an aim that was seen as consistent with social inclusion. However, a number of issues began to arise. First, the rehousing proposals brought about a reaction from the mostly white community in the area for proposed rehousing. Second, there was opposition to the proposal from the BME community, homeowners, who were concerned about the impact of the proposals on the community and the threat of racial harassment following rehousing. Further work in the BME community showed a deep division within the BME community between younger members of the community and the elders, who were perceived as 'community leaders' and were, therefore, the main point of contact for consultation with the council.

While the redevelopment proposals met a number of social inclusion objectives, they failed to address community cohesion. The problems could have been overcome by examining the community cohesion impact of what was essentially conceived as a social inclusion measure.

Similar conflicts can occur across a range of regeneration activity. A new supermarket built in an inner-city neighbourhood may have a positive impact for economic regeneration and create opportunities for social inclusion. It may also be perceived as a 'social seam', promoting interaction between diverse communities, thereby building social cohesion. However, if the supermarket leads to a decline in local BME retailing there is a negative equality impact to be balanced against the *gains* for cohesion and inclusion.

The policy fields of equality, cohesion and inclusion are, in general, managed separately. At the level of central government, dedicated units in different government departments handle these policy discourses.[2] The response at the level of local authorities and local partnership has been to treat them as separate agendas. The danger, in this situation, lies at an operational level where activities on the ground may be pulling in different directions and where adverse impacts may be generated.

The ability to resolve these policy conflicts within regeneration and other areas of local policy development is essential for good practice in public service provision but, more than this, resolution is essential if the principle of mainstreaming for equality is to be achieved. It is important to consider *how* these conflicts are identified and resolved. A framework for identifying the conflicts and the race equality impact of cohesion and inclusion is essential to meet the requirements of the Race Relations Amendment Act. Moreover, the explicit exploration and recognition of conflicts between policy objectives can provide a basis for community involvement and local accountability in conflict resolution and decision-making.

MAINSTREAMING AND EQUALITY MANAGEMENT

The principle of mainstreaming is becoming a central feature of equality management. It represents a desire to place equality principles at the heart of public service decision-making, policy development and delivery. Although the idea has been present within equality practice since the 1980s, the importance of mainstreaming and the means for realizing its implementation have developed in the last few years.

The importance of mainstreaming has been emphasized by the debate that followed the Stephen Lawrence Inquiry into the London Metropolitan Police. The findings of the inquiry pointed to racism within the police force which, was described as 'institutionally racist'.

'Institutional Racism' consists of the collective failure of an organisation to provide an appropriate and professional service to people because of their colour, culture or

153

ethnic origin. It can be seen or detected in processes, attitudes and behaviour which amount to discrimination through unwitting prejudice, ignorance, thoughtlessness, and racist stereotyping which disadvantage minority ethnic people.

(McPherson 1999)

It has been increasingly recognized that these characteristics of institutional racism may be located in the practices and embedded culture of all public service organizations and may lead to an unconscious discrimination and unfairness in service delivery and employment (Speeden and Clarke 2004). The recognition of this problem within public service delivery is expressed in legislation through the Race Relations Amendment Act (2000), which established the Race Equality Scheme and Race Equality Impact Assessment as a statutory requirement. The Equality Standard for Local Government (Speeden and Clarke 2001) recognized the wider implications of institutional discrimination for equality in race, gender and disability[3] and it was designed as a systematic approach for changing the embedded discriminatory culture of public service organization.

In addition to dealing with embedded cultures, the Equality Standard recognized the cross-cutting nature of equality issues and the importance of this in shaping service delivery. There are intersections between the equality strands that shape the patterns of discrimination. For example, the combination of racial discrimination and gender discrimination together shape the experience of women from BME backgrounds. For Muslim women their experience is further shaped by religious discrimination. Policy and service delivery needs to be sensitive to the way in which the patterns of discrimination are interwoven, the way in which this creates 'substantively different experiences' (Weber 2001). By working within a common framework for addressing equality the Standard provides an opportunity to explore the intersectionality between discriminatory processes.

Equality Impact Assessment and Equality Performance Management are integral to the Equality Standard and it combines with the Race Relations Amendment Act and other equality legislation to provide the most comprehensive programme for mainstreaming in public services. These management tools will be given additional authority with the implementation of proposals to extend public sector duties around disability and gender and with the broadening of the agenda to include sexuality, belief and age.

It will be clear that the objectives of mainstreaming require that policies and practices for social exclusion and community cohesion should be assessed to consider their equality impact. Impact assessment is a procedure that has been adopted within the RRAA Code of Practice and in the Equality Standard for systematically examining both policy and practice within service delivery to assess their *outcome* or *likely outcome* in relation to equality. Through impact assessment (and throughout the equality improvement process set out in the Equality Standard) a framework is being established that increasingly requires managers to consider the interaction between equality, social inclusion and community cohesion policies and the competing policy objectives they produce within regeneration.

154

THE EQUALITY STANDARD FOR LOCAL GOVERNMENT

The new management of equalities requires:

- The development of information and monitoring procedures to provide a strong evidence base for assessing policies and procedures;
- The development of a research culture amongst managers that will encourage reflection on policy outcomes;
- A move way from narrow targets for evaluating projects to ones that embrace broader corporate values, e.g. equality;
- A performance management system that will assure continuous assessment and improvement.

This approach is illustrated by the Equality Standard for Local Government, which is designed to embed a number of management processes that promote the continuous improvement of equality within local governance. The Standard is designed around five levels of achievement.

Level 1 – Commitment

At this level an organization establishes commitment to equality through the development of a Comprehensive Equality Policy. Commitment involves a shared understanding of the policy and its aims throughout the organization and an action plan for implementation through further levels of the standard.

Level 2 – Assessment processes

A number of core processes are established at this level. Equality impact assessment provides a framework for evaluating all activities within the organization to assess their impact on race, gender and disability and develop equality objectives. A system of self-assessment based on the principle of Total Quality Management provides a basis for continuous improvement. Consultation processes are put in place to support the development of impact assessment and self-assessment.

Level 3 – Equality objectives

Working with the systems established at level 2, managers establish equality objectives based on the knowledge from Equality Impact Assessment, consultation and corporate objectives for equality. These objectives are operationalized through business planning and performance management systems and monitoring procedures will be put in place to support the self-assessment of progress.

155

Level 4 – Monitoring

At this level the systems established through the preceding levels should be operating effectively and data will be available to assess progress against the performance measures associated with equality objectives. Progress should be assessed and this would lead to the review of performance indicators and equality objectives.

Level 5 – Outcomes

This level is reached when a local authority can show outcomes that demonstrate an improvement in equality performance across the organization. The achievement of this level will be an affirmation that the systems and processes are in place and producing real change in equal outcomes for employment and service provision. An authority would be expected to maintain work at this level on a continuing basis to sustain their commitment to equality.

The Equality Standard provides a systematic methodology and a toolkit for managing change and improving equality outcomes. These tools and processes can also provide a framework through which managers may examine the conflicting policy objectives raised by commitments to equality, social inclusion and community cohesion.

The broad aims of social inclusion and community cohesion can be brought inside the standard from level 1, where a clear understanding of these commitments would be established. Conflicting aims may become apparent at level 1 through deliberation but the impact assessment process provides the real key to identifying policy conflicts.

Equality Impact Assessment provides a framework for reviewing the existing policies and practices within an organization to measure and assess their effect on employment and service delivery. The aim of the process is to examine how procedures and policies may influence equality outcomes to see whether there is an adverse impact and to explore whether a change in procedures could make a positive contribution to equality. The equality impact process could readily be used to examine the impact of policies and procedures on social inclusion and community cohesion. This would be an important step towards mainstreaming these commitments and would create an improved understanding for managers about their interaction.

The purpose of carrying out an impact assessment is to provide information that will assist managers (policy makers and the community) in developing equality objectives that can rectify inequalities and promote good equality practice. Again, the system can be readily extended to develop objectives that promote social inclusion and community cohesion. At the objective-setting stage there is a further opportunity to consider conflicts between these commitments.

Monitoring, review and self-assessment provide a basis for maintaining a continuous approach for managing and reviewing conflicts within the policy agenda.

In itself, therefore, the systems for managing equality can provide a framework through which regeneration managers can examine overlapping and interactive policies for addressing equality, social exclusion and community cohesion. Within regeneration management, the method of impact assessment can be adapted to examine the impact of policy on equality, exclusion and cohesion in a combined process. The tricky problem arises where the assessment process does identify conflict. Where there is evidence of an adverse impact that is unlawful in equality legislation, remedial action will be necessary. In other cases the conflict may focus on operational conflicts and the challenge for managers and decision makers will be how these conflicts should be resolved.

RESOLVING CONFLICT IN 'INCLUSION' POLICIES

The conflict in policy discourse that has been described may be resolved at a national level through government or through the establishment of the Commission for Equality and Human Rights. In the interim, decisions are made at a local level to resolve the conflict between these discourses by prioritizing objectives and actions. The interviews with managers suggest that the decision-making takes place in a number of ways. One source of resolution takes the form of *executive* decision-making by managers involved in regeneration where certain objectives are given priority over others. Prioritization takes place through managerial decisions informed by discussions in project teams, partnerships and through consultation. In some cases, key decisions may be resolved through the political process at committee or council level.

The pattern described is consistent with the development of a managerialist approach to public services (Newman 2001). Audit, performance management and evaluation are clear features of the managerial approach adopted in the modernization of local governance (Clarke *et al*. 2000) and methodological problems have been raised about the way in which these management tools deal with conflict. Clarke *et al*. (2000) argues, 'each stage of evaluation involves potentially contested processes of social construction. There are potential conflicts over the definition of objectives; over the choice of indicators; over the attribution of causal effects; and over how comparison is affected'. The dangers posed by bringing equality, social inclusion and cohesion together within all-embracing framework are that it will locate key decisions on contested discourses inside the management process.

The Equality Standard seeks to counter managerialist tendencies in its application by building in a strong emphasis on scrutiny and community involvement. The effectiveness in developing a more democratic approach to objective-setting and conflict resolution, however, depends upon the realization of new structures for local democracy that shift real decision-making power to communities. The survey of managers suggests that scrutiny and consultation are not well developed as frameworks for conflict resolution. The scrutiny processes that are being developed by local councils can play a developing role in the conflict resolution process but in regeneration activity the local community needs to be involved. Consultation processes have a role to play here (Del Tufo and Gaster 2002) but in many authorities, consultation has developed as an information

157

collection process to serve managerial decision-making rather than as a tool for resolving conflicts within local democratic forums.

CONCLUSION

The view, commonly held within regeneration management, that equality is already included in the regeneration discourse needs to be questioned. Equality is dealt with partially through the social exclusion objectives within regeneration, but this falls short of mainstreamed equality practice. It is important that practitioners working within regeneration recognize the salience and distinctive contribution of working on equality issues and engaging with the procedures for equality management. An evidence-based approach for identifying and understanding the conflict between policies for equality, social inclusion and community cohesion can be achieved using the tools and processes for managing equality. By extending the scope of equality impact assessment, objective-setting and performance management, regeneration managers can develop a coherent approach for managing policy. However, conflict resolution within the policy agenda raises some broader issues about democracy and community involvement that can only be addressed through a more radical restructuring of power within regeneration management.

NOTES

1   These interviews have been undertaken as part of ongoing work associated with the implementation of the Equality Standard for Local Government.
2   The Social Exclusion Unit is located in the Office of the Deputy Prime Minister, the Community Cohesion Unit is located in the Home Office and equalities policy is the responsibility of the Department of Work and Pensions, the Home Office and the Department of Trade and Industry.
3   The development of the Equality Standard took into account discrimination on sexual orientation, religion and belief and age but the first published Standard focused on race, gender and disability.

Chapter 12

Policy transfer

Learning from the European Union

David Silbergh and Calum Macleod

This chapter considers the scope for transferring policy learning from the European Union (EU) to domestic arenas. It focuses on the experience of managing European regional policy through the distributive instrument of Structural Funds in support of the EU's efforts to promote economic and social cohesion. It is important to note from the outset that the EU's emphasis when promoting cohesion is predominantly on the regional as opposed to the city level. However, we contend that this regional experience of managing regeneration can provide fruitful and illuminating lessons that may be applicable and transferable to the city context.

We trace the evolution of the EU and, within this broader context, map the development of its regional approach to securing cohesion. We go on to discuss the use of Structural Funds as the EU's main implementation mechanism in this respect.[1] Specifically, we identify five key elements that have been influential in shaping the management of regeneration within the EU. These elements are:

1 Regionalization;
2 Partnership and programming;
3 Administrative innovation;
4 Financial constraint; and
5 The mainstreaming of cross-cutting themes.

Each is discussed in turn and conclusions are drawn as to their applicability and value in the city context.

THE EVOLUTION OF THE EUROPEAN UNION

The European Economic Community (EEC) was established in 1957 following the negotiation of the Treaties of Rome. Its antecedents lay in the social and political upheaval wrought in Europe in the aftermath of the Second World War and the desire of Western European liberal democracies to secure sustained peace on the continent. Increasingly, economic integration was viewed as central to securing this aim. It was for this reason that Belgium, West Germany, Luxembourg, France, Italy and the Netherlands established the European Coal and Steel Community (ECSC) in 1951. This forerunner to the EEC transferred decision-making responsibilities concerning the coal and steel industries in these countries to an independent, supranational organization titled the 'High Authority' (Wæver 1995).

By 1957 the integrative ambitions of the ECSC's Member States were such that they signed the Treaties of Rome. These created the European Atomic Energy Community (EURATOM) and the EEC. The latter was central to furthering economic, and ultimately political, integration between its Member States by establishing a common market through removal of internal trade barriers. Institutional integration occurred in 1967 through the creation of a single European Commission and Council of Ministers and the establishment of a European Parliament.

The 1970s marked the first of several enlargements of the Community's membership with the accession of the United Kingdom, Ireland and Denmark. These enlargements continued in the 1980s, first with the accession of Greece in 1981, followed by that of Spain and Portugal in 1986. The following year the Single European Act was ratified, paving the way for completion of the Community's single market in 1992. This project, envisaged in the original Treaty of Rome, further reinforced the role of the Community as a cohesive and integrated economic unit through removal of internal barriers to the 'four freedoms' in relation to the movement of services, people, goods and capital. The drive towards economic integration was given still further impetus in 1992 with the decision to establish economic and monetary union (EMU) by introducing a single European currency under the control of a European Central Bank. This single currency was introduced on 1 January 2002 with the euro replacing national currencies in 12 of the EU's then 15 Member States:[2] 1992 was also the year in which the European Community was transformed into the European Union, with the passing of the Maastricht Treaty (Wæver 1995). This added inter-governmental forms of cooperation, for example, in the fields of defence, justice and home affairs to the scope of the Union's activity. The Treaty of Amsterdam in 1997 then established sustainable development and equal opportunities as key areas of policy priority across the Union.

As the preceding demonstrates, the European Community (and latterly Union) has exerted increasing influence on a wide range of Member States' domestic policy concerns in the half century since its creation. Much of this influence has been driven by an economic imperative as the Union seeks to define itself as the leading player in a global economic system. At the same time, the Union seeks to balance this ambition by further developing its strategic perspective on policy issues complementary to its main economic objectives. These complex relationships are encapsulated in the EU's so-called Lisbon and Gothenburg Agendas.

In 2000 at their Lisbon Summit, the EU's Member States outlined an agenda designed to make the EU the most competitive and dynamic knowledge-driven economy by 2010. To meet this objective, the EU aims to increase investment in research and development, promote entrepreneurship and achieve an EU employment rate of 70 per cent of the eligible workforce. At the Gothenburg Summit of 2001 EU leaders set out a strategy for sustainable development to complement the aims of the Lisbon Agenda. It focused on limiting climate change and increasing use of clean technology, addressing threats to public health, managing natural resources more responsibly and improving the transport system and land use.

Against this general background, the next section focuses on the development and functions of European regional policy.

European regional policy

The primary area of European policy of relevance to those engaged in the management of cities is regional policy. Although the origins of a European regional policy can be traced to the Treaty of Rome, the creation of a *specific* regional policy instrument in the form of the European Regional Development Fund (ERDF) did not occur until 1975 (Armstrong 1989). Moreover, regional policy between the mid-1970s and mid-1980s has been characterized as driven by national (not European Commission) initiatives, with an emphasis on subsidy rather than strategic imperatives (Mannin 1999). However, a combination of events helped to transform the role and focus of regional policy in the late 1980s. First, successive enlargements of the Community occurred. Left to their own devices the new Member States' relatively underdeveloped economies threatened to undermine the economic and social cohesion of the Community as a whole. The problem of regional economic and social disparities risked further exacerbation with the imminent activation of the EU's single internal market in 1992, following the Single European Act of 1987 which paved the way for completion of the single market by removing barriers to the free movement of goods, people, services and capital (Lenschow 1999). However, there was widespread recognition amongst Member States and the European Commission that an unfettered single market risked further concentrating economic growth in the EU's richer regions, thereby paradoxically undermining the Community's cohesion objectives (Mannin 1999).

For practical and political reasons linked to the above, regional policy therefore underwent a radical reform in terms of both resources and focus in 1988. The 1988 reform also introduced the following principles which were to underpin a new approach to regional policy (Armstrong 1989):

- *Concentration* – whereby funds would be targeted at regions facing the greatest structural disparities;
- *Partnership* and *programming* – whereby regional policy would be implemented through management structures encompassing a wide range of regional institutional actors within a framework of multi-annual regional programmes;
- *Additionality* – whereby regional EU assistance was to result in at least an equivalent increase in total EU and national assistance in Member States rather than acting as a substitute for national regional assistance.

These reforms were developed in subsequent programming periods (1994–2006) and further consideration will be given to the most significant of these innovations and their implications for development within cities later in this chapter.

Structural Funds today

Today the Structural Funds (including ERDF) are one of the best-known mechanisms by which the European Union's policy aims are implemented in Member States. The purpose of these Structural Funds is (Keating 2005: 151) to 'secure economic, social and territorial cohesion across the Union' and more specifically, to 'bring lagging regions up to a state in which they can compete within the single market, by investing in infrastructure, human capital and business services'. The distribution of these Funds is mainly managed along regional lines, based on the notion that whilst cities have certain distinctive characteristics, they should be managed and developed in a manner that takes account of relationships with their hinterlands. This regional approach has of course been a long-standing policy commitment of the Union, to the chagrin of some city authorities who wish to see the development of a stronger European urban policy (this issue that will be addressed more fully later in this chapter).

Structural Funds represent the second-largest component of the European Union's budget after intervention in agriculture and, at the time of writing, it is anticipated that Structural Fund expenditure will be in the order of €40 billion in 2006, rising to circa €50 billion per annum to help address the special needs of the ten new Member States when the Union's new budgetary cycle starts in 2007 (European Commission 2004). There are four main policy and budgetary divisions, which currently account for approximately 95 per cent of Structural Fund expenditure, complemented by four 'Community Initiatives'. Table 12.1 gives an oversight of the main Structural Funds, of which the European Regional Development Fund and the European Social Fund are of most relevance to those involved in urban development and managing cities.

The Structural Funds are, at the time of writing, spent in accordance with three Objectives, two of which have a strong regional dimension:

- Objective 1 – the vast majority of Structural Funds (*c.* 70 per cent) are spent against this Objective, which is to develop those regions of the Union significantly lagging in terms of their economic performance (in keeping with the Union's concentration principle);
- Objective 2 – funds distributed under this Objective (*c.* 12 per cent) are to assist with restructuring in areas that have economies in transition, e.g. decline of heavy industry or agriculture;
- Objective 3 – this Objective effectively maps to the European Social Fund and is therefore non-territorial in nature. Approximately 13 per cent of Structural Funds are distributed under this Objective.

Table 12.1 *European Structural Funds*

Fund	Support for
European Regional Development Fund (ERDF)	An integrated and healthy European economy by encouraging economic and physical development in defined regions.
European Social Fund (ESF)	Training and learning for the employed and the unemployed and other socially excluded groups (non-territorial funding).
Guidance Section of the European Agriculture Guidance and Guarantee Fund (EAGGF)	Rural development/diversification of the rural economy/links to other aspects of the Common Agricultural Policy.
Finance Instrument for Fisheries Guidance (FIFG)	Fishing and aquaculture – especially the restructuring of these industries in line with the Common Fisheries Policy.

It is expected that revised Objectives will be in use from 2007, although the main themes of lagging regions, regions in transition, social need and regional cooperation will continue to guide the allocation of Structural Funds. For further information on these new Objectives (the proposed names are Convergence, Competitiveness and Cooperation) please see European Commission (2005).

ERDF (with its regional rather than city focus) and ESF (with its non-territorial focus) are, despite the fact that neither is wholly focused on an urban agenda, the two European funding sources that cities are most likely to benefit from as a simple consequence of the sheer scale of the funds distributed. As previously noted, the European Union has devoted approximately five per cent of its Structural Funds budgets to tackling four priorities through Community Initiatives. The four Community Initiatives are summarized in Table 12.2, and one of these, the URBAN Initiative, has as its name suggests, is a clear focus on issues relevant to cities.

As can be seen from Table 12.2, however, the URBAN Initiative does not itself represent a full-scale coherent cities policy on the part of the EU and should not be thought of as such. Rather, URBAN is best seen as an attempt to address the very real issues of urban decay faced by some cities, but firmly within the context of an overarching regional policy approach. Less than one half of one per cent of the total Structural Fund budget is allocated to URBAN, and this figure gives an immediate sense of the fact that URBAN can play only a small part in achieving the overall aim as regards the sustainable regional development of a cohesive Union.

Table 12.2 Community Initiatives

Initiative	Support for
URBAN	Tackling urban decay and decline through regeneration – both physical redevelopment and social projects.
LEADER	Sustainable development actions in the rural areas of the Union and cooperation between these areas.
EQUAL	Anti-discrimination actions associated with the promotion of equal opportunities for all throughout the Union.
INTERREG	Inter-regional cooperation within and across Member States, with a special focus on border regions.

POLICY TRANSFER FROM EUROPEAN PROGRAMMES

The introduction to this chapter noted that the EU exerts a powerful influence on regional policy at Member State level through the distributive mechanism of Structural Funds. In this section, we identify and discuss key ways in which these funds have acted as a conduit for policy transfer to the regional, and by extension city, levels of governance. In particular we explore the effect of management structures and processes introduced to regional development via the EU. We also discuss the significant role played by the EU in promoting sustainable development and equal opportunities as key horizontal or cross-cutting themes in regeneration.

Regional focus

The first area of policy transfer from the EU of relevance to the management of cities has already been mentioned, i.e. that the Union strongly promotes a regional rather than a city-based view of development. The EU does acknowledge the vital role played by cities in regions but, other than through the limited URBAN Initiative, its policies do not encourage an explicit focus on cities. The Union uses the term 'City-Region', which acknowledges the need for vitality in cities as 'drivers of economic competitiveness, social inclusion and environmental quality' (Dutch Ministry of Interior and Kingdom Relations 2005: 1). The concept of the City-Region does however allow the Union to resist attempts to move from a fundamentally regional policy (which includes the URBAN programme to address the most serious of cities' problems). There are of course good reasons for this, as articulated below:

In many member states the administrative boundaries of cities are often much smaller than their economic boundaries, creating working difficulties. Ministers emphasise the value of adopting the city-region concept in this area. This city-region concept encourages integrated territorial development involving the important principle of partnership and collaboration working across the wider economic territory beyond narrow administrative boundaries.

(Dutch Ministry of Interior and Kingdom Relations 2005: 4)

This position has been challenged by pressure groups such as 'Cities for Cohesion',[3] which has argued that the European Union's City-Region approach tends to 'hide' large-scale economic and social problems, especially in those inner-city areas that may nevertheless be found at the heart of relatively wealthy regions. They have called for 'a genuine urban dimension in future EU regional policy' (Cities for Cohesion 2003: 12), noting:

The indicator currently used by regional policy – regional GDP – has shown itself to be inadequate outside Objective 1, as it does not highlight sub-regional disparities, which need to be taken into account. These disparities not only demonstrate the socio-economic cohesion gaps within a region, but also act as barriers to regional – and therefore European – competitiveness, hampering the capacity of a region to develop to its full potential. GDP in large urban areas can be considerably inflated by commuters, and disposable income is a much more helpful indicator, given the costs of transport and housing in these urban areas.

Such criticisms are not new. Keating (1988) documents the lack of engagement of the City of Glasgow in domestic regional development planning agendas in the late 1960s and early 1970s. Thus, although prior to the UK's accession to the EU, similar concerns played their part then. What differs today, however, is that city managers have little choice but to engage with the City-Region agenda if they are to seek financial support from Structural Funds (other than the relatively small sums available via URBAN). An alternative middle way has been suggested by Turok (2005) who has proposed that it may be most appropriate to undertake ERDF-type infrastructure projects at a regional level but to focus on cities in relation to the delivery of social projects.

On balance, however, it is likely that the EU will continue to encourage strategic oversight and promote regional development rather than adopting a focus on, for example, urban or rural issues. It is apparent from speeches delivered at the European Week of Regions and Cities held in Brussels in October 2005 that the UK Presidency of the Union, the European Commission and the Committee of the Regions are all as one on this issue (see respectively Prescott 2005; Hübner 2005; Galeote 2005). This explicitly regional focus is the first clear example of the Europeanization of the policy agenda.

165

Partnership and programming

The second area of policy transfer from the EU relates to the 1988 Structural Funds reform principles of partnership and programming. These principles have significantly altered the focus and scope of Union policy, providing momentum for the creation of a regional policy landscape in which strategic developmental priorities have been determined largely by regional stakeholders rather than centrally imposed by national governments (Mannin 1999). In Scotland for example, the development of a 'differentiated' system of managing Structural Funds can be attributed to the impetus provided by the 1988 reforms and by a desire on the part of key local policy stakeholders to inhabit a regional policy space which central government was increasingly disinclined to occupy. Thus, over the last decade, custom-built partnerships (consisting of a wide variety of public and third sector organizations[4]) have developed and managed successive Structural Fund programmes through independent administrative units. To reiterate, this programmed partnership approach has reinforced the setting of strategic economic development priorities at the regional, not national, level. These priorities are thematic in nature. In Scotland for example, Structural Fund programmes address infrastructure developments, support to enhance the competitiveness of SMEs, community development and training and learning, especially for the socially excluded. Arguably, none of these themed priorities can be easily addressed other than in partnership. One clear consequence of Structural Fund programmes has therefore been to encourage a move away from the delivery of stand-alone regeneration projects towards joined-up regionally based strategic initiatives.

The Structural Fund emphasis on partnership and programming has exerted what is probably *the* most significant influence of all on domestic policy. Partnership and programming are inextricably linked and have arguably resulted in a broad shift in UK regional policy over the last 15 years from a highly centralized to a devolved approach. Some commentators contend such partnerships to be the product of a concerted collective effort by regional policy actors to 're-engineer' administrative processes, thereby ensuring that policy more closely reflects their own development priorities (Mannin 1999). Certainly within a Scottish context, the differentiated partnership system used for managing Structural Funds has concentrated significant (but not exclusive) influence regarding policy formulation and delivery at the regional level. Thus, while operating within constraints of eligibility determined by the European Union, Scottish Structural Fund partnerships have enjoyed considerable autonomy in determining the scope and content of their individual programmes. This is a clear example of the Europeanization of the policy landscape, and one which may be usefully learned from, even if European funding were to cease.

Administration

The third area of policy transfer from the EU of relevance relates to administrative matters. As previously indicated, the introduction of stand-alone, partnership-run programmes has sharpened the focus of European financial assistance by setting strategic objectives and identifying thematic priorities for support. Moreover, these programmes' multi-annual characteristic means that projects can receive support for up to three years at a time. This provides financial stability for projects over an extended period. It simultaneously allows the programme partnerships themselves a sufficiently long time period (seven years) to realize their strategic objectives of enhancing economic and social cohesion.

Aside from the above, Structural Fund programmes exhibit a range of features not always evident in other domestic regional development programmes. These perform various administrative but policy-linked functions and include:

1 *Core project selection criteria* to be addressed by each application for project funding. Such criteria enable partnerships to set minimum requirements for funding and assess project validity against these requirements. Below in Table 12.3 is an example of such criteria, as used by the East of Scotland ERDF Objective 2 Partnership (ESEP):

Table 12.3 *ESEP core project selection criteria*

Net additional jobs	Evidence of demand
Leverage	Infrastructure impact
Resource efficiency	Environmental impact
Access and opportunity	Local added value
Capacity building	Social inclusion
Strategic integration	Durability and feasibility

2 *Programme targets and indicators* designed to measure funded project (and ultimately programme) contribution to the development objectives identified by the partnerships. Such targets and indicators tend to focus on outputs rather than outcomes. 'Number of individuals trained' would for instance be an example of such an output indicator.

3 *The 'N+2 rule'*, as enshrined in the Structural Funds regulatory framework. Programmes have spending targets to meet at particular intervals throughout their lifespans. In practice, any funding not claimed by applicants within two years of its allocation will be de-committed from the relevant Programme and clawed back by the European Commission for reallocation elsewhere. This creates an administrative environment in which avoiding politically damaging de-commitment of funds becomes a central concern for partnerships. In turn, N+2 acts as a catalyst for the efficient allocation of Structural Funds.

167

Once again, even if European funding were to cease, there is scope for domestic policy actors to learn lessons from the positive effects of all of the above administrative innovations.

Additionality and State Aids

This fourth area of policy transfer from the European Union as regards the management of cities is highly technical and legalistic. Despite the generally challenging nature of issues concerning 'Additionality' and 'State Aids', these are an important part of the framework of policy in all Member States and are a clear example of the effect which EU policy has had on the development agenda.

Additionality and State Aids place restrictions respectively on how European money and domestic money can be used. As previously noted, Additionality means that Structural Funds must not be used simply as a substitute for Member State activities that would have happened anyway. Such rules have been ever-more strictly enforced over time, because of a legacy of problems in this area from the past. For example Armstrong (1989: 180) noted:

> The EC, not unnaturally, is keen to see its spending being used in an 'additional' manner and not for member states simply to view it as a convenient means of financing their own budgets. Vigorous EC attempts to persuade states to use ERDF aid in a truly 'additional' manner have, unfortunately, in many cases been met simply by deception . . . Considerable substitution has clearly occurred and directly undermines the ERDF's effectiveness.

Whereas rules on Additionality seek to place constraints on the use of European funds, rules on State Aids seek to place a further set of constraints on the use of domestic resources. As expressed by the European Commission (1998: 1):

> One of the cornerstones of the Community is economic and social cohesion . . . It aims at reducing disparities between the levels of development of the richer and poorer regions in Europe . . . Article 87 (formerly Article 92) of the treaty establishing the Community stipulates that aid granted by the Member States is incompatible with the common market.

However, the European Union does allow for derogations from this standard policy in two cases, which are (European Commission 1998: 1):

- Aid to promote the economic development of areas where the standard of living is abnormally low or where there is serious underemployment [Article 87(3)(a)];
- Aid to facilitate the development of certain economic activities or certain economic areas, where such aid does not adversely affect trading conditions to an extent contrary to the common interest [Article 87(3)(c].

168

Both derogations therefore allow for some domestic regional development monies to be spent by Member States outside the Structural Funds policy framework, but there are strict limits placed on this in terms of geography, type of activity, timescale for support and level of investment. These limits vary from case to case and the mechanisms for calculating what is and what is not allowable are complex and can give rise to tensions between the Union and Member States. Thus, to summarize, rules on Additionality place controls over what European resources can and cannot be used to support in terms of regeneration. Conversely, rules on State Aids control what domestic resources can be used to finance and are a further clear example of the Europeanization of the policy agenda.

Mainstreaming of horizontal themes

The fifth and final of the main areas of policy transfer from the European Union is the expectation for mainstreaming of horizontal themes in all actions. The Union has, over time, made a number of commitments to tackle certain issues in all of its activities, which have become known as 'horizontal themes' as they cut across all policy areas. For example, the EU has decided that sustainable development will not be pursued simply through one policy, programme or project but is to be an aim for all. The implication of this is that sustainable development is to be considered by all policy actors before undertaking a given action. This will seem eminently reasonable to most readers, but one difficulty is that there is no easily accessible, overarching and definitive list of what all of these horizontal themes are.[5] The commitments to these themes have been made in different places at different times and have differing degrees of legal status. For example, the 1997 Treaty of Amsterdam established a constitutional basis for sustainable development as a horizontal theme, but many of the other themes have less solid foundations.

Needless to say, this range of horizontal themes can cause confusion and, whilst all of the themes are undoubtedly relevant to the effective management of a city, it can be difficult for managers to integrate all of these issues within a single project, for example, building a new road. In practical terms, guidance is always issued at programme and project level on which horizontal themes are most appropriate in that particular bailiwick, which does simplify implementation considerably.[6] In a recent study of mainstreaming, Wells *et al.* (2004) concluded:

> Current UK Objective 1 programmes have adopted horizontal priorities as a means of both embedding wider EU policy concerns . . . experience to date has been a varied one. This has not been helped by the added complexity and burden that they have brought to an already intricate system . . .

The EU's twin focus on its Lisbon and Gothenburg agendas means that the emphasis on mainstreaming, like that on regional rather than urban policy, is unlikely to change in the near future. The EU's mainstreaming agenda is undoubtedly challenging. However, as Macleod (2005) notes in relation to sustainable development, mainstreaming has been instrumental in raising stakeholders' awareness of the concept and its relevance to their activities. It is incumbent upon city managers to cope with the requirements of mainstreaming in the best way that they can, having regard to the guidance of which- ever European programme they are engaged with. Therefore, even if European funding were to cease, there are valuable lessons that could be learned from Structural Fund experiences of mainstreaming complex policy aims for application in the context of cities.

CASE STUDIES

In this section we outline some examples of the type of project made possible by Structural Fund support. As the authors both work in Scotland, a decision has been taken to use case studies from there. At a basic level, concentration of resources on regions exhibiting greatest need has enabled greater levels of financial assistance to be channelled to some of Scotland's most economically and socially disadvantaged urban environments (all the more so in light of the Additionality principle of Structural Funds). Thus, matching European funds with domestic budgets delivers financially larger-scale pro- jects than otherwise possible. In Scotland, cities such as Glasgow, Dundee, Stirling and Inverness have benefited from often large-scale Structural Fund investments in a wide range of eligible project activities supported through: the Scottish ERDF Objective 2 Programmes in eastern and western Scotland; the Highlands and Islands Special Transitional Programme; the Lowlands Scotland ESF Objective 3 Programme and the Community Initiatives. These range from business support initiatives, physical infra- structure investments, community development projects and human resource/training initiatives. Table 12.4 provides examples of such initiatives.

CONCLUSIONS

An underpinning theme of this chapter has been that the EU's policies and actions do not have a clearly defined focus on cities. That said, they do nevertheless have relevance for the effective management and regeneration of urban areas. What then are the potential lessons to be applied within the context of city regeneration as a result of policy transfer from the EU? Perhaps the most significant of these is the influence exerted by the delivery mechanisms adopted to implement Union policy. For example, the differentiated partnership model used in Scotland to manage Structural Funds has acted as a catalyst for linking diverse policy perspectives and institutional actors within a strategic regional framework. In turn, the programming approach to allocating funds, with its emphasis on broad thematic priorities for action, has allowed the partnerships themselves to engage

Table 12.4 *Case study projects*

I   Gardyne's Land Project – Tayside Building Preservation Trust

Project part-funded by East of Scotland ERDF Objective 2 Programme Partnership to regenerate the historic heart of Dundee city centre. The project's aims are to:

- Conserve derelict buildings in the city's main shopping area, preserving sixteenth-century built heritage and improving amenity in line with horizontal theme of sustainable development;
- Seek to reuse the conserved buildings as a modern youth hostel, expanding the city's attractiveness as a tourist destination and thereby generating new income flows and employment opportunities.

II   Edinburgh Women's Training Course – Nisus Scotland

Project part-funded by Lowlands Scotland ESF Objective 3 Programme. This project, run in Leith – a dockland area of Edinburgh that is undergoing large-scale regeneration – has been in receipt of financial support from the European Union since its inception in 1986. The project aims to:

- Provide training opportunities for women with poor or outdated skills to enter or re-enter the workforce (approximately 95 per cent of participants have gone on to work or further education);
- Place a special emphasis on information technology skills, providing training for qualifications ranging from the basic European Computer Driving Licence to advanced courses in hardware and multimedia;
- Ensure that trainees entering/re-entering the labour market gain experience of the world of work through undertaking a work placement with one of 60 local partner companies.

III   Building Brighter Futures – West Dunbartonshire Council

Project part-funded by the Clyde Waterfront URBAN II Programme to engage with the citizens of the depressed ex-industrial South Clydebank area and encourage greater community participation in the area's regeneration. Project aims include:

- Capacity-building to increase input from local people into decision-making processes as regards the regeneration of their area;
- Providing training programmes (both generic and tailored) to encourage the development of grass-roots regeneration projects;
- Job creation and improving the employment prospects of local citizens who are out of work;
- Tackling social exclusion through strengthening local community identity;
- Identifying (and seeking to plug) gaps in local service provision.

in joined-up decision-making in ways that would not be possible with more traditional models of delivery.

The European partnership approach has been able to encourage meaningful action to be taken on the large canvas of the City-Region. There is, however, considerable scope

171

for lessons to be drawn from this larger canvas in relation to the management of the smaller scale of the city itself. We propose that adoption of the following, drawn from the European Structural Fund experience, could be of significant benefit to city authorities in their endeavours to manage regeneration initiatives:

- *A thematic priority-based approach* to be used when addressing complex activities such as regeneration (for example, business development, infrastructure, community development) replacing narrower, professionally defined approaches (e.g. planning, roads, social services);
- *An innovative, practically orientated approach towards mainstreaming* complex yet fundamentally important cross-cutting policy issues such as equal opportunities and sustainable development. For example, the strategic emphasis on cross-cutting themes at programme level (along with capacity-building initiatives) give these a profile with stakeholders not always encountered in existing domestic policy regimes. This can ensure that stakeholders consider the practical implications of their actions in relation to these issues;
- Administrative processes that provide for *enhanced transparency, accountability and efficiency* on the part of both the funder and the projects that they support. From a city-based partnership's perspective, working with clearly defined core selection criteria should enable robust, balanced and transparent evaluation of the strategic merits of particular projects. An equivalent of the 'N+2' Rule would provide administrative discipline in terms of allocating funding timeously. Projects would also benefit from an open selection process and from transparency as regards project monitoring and reporting requirements.

Structural Funds have been of significant value in terms of tackling disadvantage in the UK. They are however by their very nature transient, and act as a fixed-term pump-primer for cohesion. Nevertheless, as the preceding demonstrates, there are important lessons to be derived from the experience of managing these Funds which could form the basis of a lasting legacy within the context of city management.

NOTES

1 At time of writing, Structural Funds are about to enter a period of significant change. The current funding period ends in 2006. Following recent enlargement of the EU to the east, budgetary and management arrangements for the next funding period (2007–2013) have yet to be finalized.
2 Further enlargement had taken place in 1995 when Austria, Sweden and Finland became Members.
3 Cities for Cohesion represents Amsterdam, Barcelona, Berlin, Brussels, Copenhagen, Frankfurt, Helsinki, Liverpool, London, Malmo, Manchester, Paris, Prague, Stockholm, Tallinn, Turku and Vienna.

4 For example: local authorities; economic development agencies; higher and further education institutions; social economy organizations; statutory environmental agencies etc.
5 Commonly cited horizontal themes include (in alphabetical order): (1) community involvement; (2) crime; (3) employability; (4) equal opportunities; (5) information technology; (6) innovation; (7) lifelong learning; (8) social inclusion; and (9) sustainable development.
6 Although this does not fit logically nor sit easily with the Union policy priority that *all* horizontal themes are to be mainstreamed.

Conclusion

John Diamond and Alan Southern

REVISITING THE THEMES

We have claimed throughout this collection of essays that contemporary UK regeneration practice has entered a significant phase of transition. Whilst we have attempted to anticipate and identify knowledge and practice gaps in understanding we cannot, of course, be certain of the precise nature of the regeneration experience over the next decade.

The fault lines running through the management of regeneration over the past 40 years can be encompassed by recognizing that:

- Regeneration practice has been decontextualized from the communities and localities within which it takes place;
- Regeneration management practitioners have lacked the capacity to learn from previous initiatives;
- The policy- (and political-) making processes have suffered from short-termism.

Despite this, it is possible to note new and potentially innovative developments. In the preceding chapters we have attempted to describe and point to examples where these developments are taking place. In our view they include:

- A more nuanced and reflective assessment of the benefits and disadvantages associated with collaboration and partnership working;
- A new approach to evaluation;
- A more proactive process of knowledge transfer exchange and learning;
- A more systematic and explicit process of embedding the experience and practice of managing complex initiatives within structures and systems of accountability and governance;
- The potential to place the central issues of equality and diversity within the context of regeneration initiatives;
- The recognition that practitioners working with local communities need more developed and robust systems of personal as well as professional support.

174

We discuss each of these themes below. We believe that they illustrate the ways in which our received knowledge and understanding of the processes associated with the management of cities and communities can be changed, so that our systems and structures of local governance are more open and inclusive.

The decontextualization effect

At first glance this would appear to be a perverse reading of the past 40 years. By definition all regeneration initiatives are located within a defined geographic area. Indeed, since the introduction of the Urban Programme, all initiatives take as a given the spatial construction of a specific place. The criteria used to secure external funding and the commitment of resources derive from an assessment of need based upon a calculation of deprivation itself derived from the characteristics of a local population.

Our point is that the process involved in defining what additionality particular initiatives bring has been an exclusive process undertaken by external agencies. As a consequence, we have observed how local community organizations, individuals and even local state agencies feel disconnected from the processes associated with defining needs and identifying what support or interventions are required. In particular, there remain real concerns that local residents are not sufficiently engaged with the evaluation processes.

We have tried to show that this experience of alienation can impact directly on the capacity of local statutory/state agencies to engage with local communities. In effect the multiplicity of initiatives (both over time and within a relatively narrow time frame of a decade) can leave local communities confused at best, and at worst, suspicious or antipathetic to new initiatives. A recurring theme in the policy literature is that local communities either lack the capacity to engage or that local community actors are 'unrepresentative' of their neighbourhoods. Whilst both may be true, it also follows that local managers and agencies may not fully understand the needs of local communities or lack the capacity (or willingness) to listen to local communities.

These concerns were well articulated in the initial projects associated with the Urban Programme in the late 1960s/early 1970s. Our reason for rehearsing these concerns now is to point to the accumulated consequences over time of not engaging with local communities. It is not that each initiative is experienced by local communities as a unique intervention. On the contrary there is a greater breadth/depth of experience contained within many of our cities than that which is contained in new initiatives sponsored by central or local government.

Failure to transfer learning

A recurring theme in the policy papers prepared to introduce the New Labour initiatives on neighbourhood renewal stressed the need to learn from existing practice and to share that learning across and between practitioners. Whilst this commitment to learning demonstrates a significant change (and we explore its implications below) it is important to explore the context within which it is taking place.

The absence of a structured approach to learning and understanding illustrates another example of the ahistorical or atheoretical approach to regeneration management in the UK. We are not suggesting that there was a 'golden age' of learning and the promotion of critical self-reflection before 1997. On the contrary we want to argue that from the late 1960s to the late 1990s there were separate but interrelated processes in play. Nevertheless, we would claim that the processes of that period were more theoretically informed.

There was in fact an explicit rejection of the theoretical and conceptual framework which was articulated by the Community Development Programme (CDP) initiative. Rather than address the causal and structural factors which underpinned inequality and racial and social disadvantage, successive governments adopted quasi-market solutions to the physical/economic decline of inner cities or peripheral estates. The CDP model was marginalized as being too radical in its thinking, it was replaced by an approach which emphasized a combination of physical/infrastructure renewal with that of attracting corporate business investment and support. The examples of the London Docklands renewal initiative or the Albert Dock project in Liverpool illustrate this.

The consequences of this model for urban regeneration practitioners was a separation of professionals into those engaged in planning/economic development and those involved in direct service delivery. There was an additional consequence. This separation at a local and central level by department/organization was reinforced by a further division in terms of the language or discourse in which regeneration initiatives were constructed. Local agencies concerned with specific front line services (health, education, housing or work with young people) were perceived as less important in the hierarchy of regeneration professionals and so were less able to shape the policy and practice context.

During the 1980s and 1990s the context of further and higher education changed radically. The capacity of training/education providers to shape the professional content of programmes or to develop new ones which explicitly addressed the need to learn, to reflect and to share practice were themselves conditioned by the financial/resource economies of the sector. As the sector became more market-driven, programmes needed to respond to these pressures and the capacity of institutions to sustain alternative programmes was constrained.

The primary reservoir of knowledge and experience was held by voluntary sector agencies or charitable bodies (such as Joseph Rowntree). Whilst they were (and remain) significant sites of collected knowledge, experience and insight, their capacity to shape the external political, professional or policy environment was dependent upon their access to key 'actors'. It is interesting and significant that many of the current Government's policies (from 1997 to the present) can be traced back to successive reports for the Rowntree Trust and similar agencies or organizations. In one sense

176

we can say that the national voluntary organizations and the charitable trusts (large and small) have acted as the collective memory or resource bank for current practitioners.

Finally, the impact of professional segregation, the marginalization of an explicit practice of community development processes and the relatively quick resurgence in regeneration management have resulted in many practitioners lacking the conceptual language to reflect upon new initiatives or to learn from past ones.

Short-termism and its consequences

A familiar criticism of UK regeneration initiatives introduced by successive governments has been that they are usually either for a fixed period of time or that new initiatives are announced before any evaluation or assessment has been made of previous schemes. In part this process of multiple initiatives being 'live' can be understood by recognizing that the political/decision-making processes are shaped by time frames which are relatively short (two–three years). As a consequence decisions made in Westminster/Whitehall are tied to the national election cycle rather than linking their decisions to the needs of specific localities or the capacity of agencies to respond to new initiatives.

This pattern of short-term thinking can be illustrated by noting that from 1997 to the present some neighbourhoods were the site of:

- Single Regeneration Budget initiatives
- New Deal for Communities
- Education Action Zones
- Health Action Zones
- Neighbourhood Renewal initiatives
- Neighbourhood Management Pathfinders
- Sports Action Zones.

In addition agencies working in these areas would be engaging with new initiatives aimed at reducing antisocial behaviour and community safety, as well as liaising with other 'new' initiatives launched under the labels of Sure Start, Connexions and the Children's Service process. Local authority staff would also be working with a range of agencies as they negotiate Local Area Agreements with the Government Office for the Region (GOR) and developing policies/processes to report to their Local Strategic Partnership (LSP).

We have discussed the complex nature of these relationships throughout this edited collection. Our concern here is to identify the potentially disruptive impact that waves of different initiatives can have on the capacity of both statutory and voluntary agencies to absorb the requirements and demands set by central government. Our secondary concern has been to argue that the concurrency of the initiatives can shape the organizational structure and focus of local agencies which then have to adjust to respond to the next initiative. This may have the unintended consequence of marginalizing the

177

significance of evaluation processes and any lessons learnt which might influence new policies over a larger time frame.

Identifying gaps: enhancing understanding of partnership dynamics

We have attempted to demonstrate that our understanding of and appreciation of partnership working requires a more nuanced and intellectually sophisticated approach than is evident in much of the existing literature. We have shown that it is possible to advance our understanding by examining, describing and analysing the dynamics of partnerships within the broader context. Whilst partnerships involve formal collaboration between different agencies, it is, of course, located in an external environment where discussions about the partnership originate. It is important that this is perceived to influence the dynamics within the partnership, but we must not assume that this is significant. As we have shown, a further level of analyses is possible which enriches our understanding of the efficacy of different partnerships.

Within any one partnership there will be a set of dynamics derived from interactions of different types which will directly impact on the outcome.

This approach enables us to extend the debate on partnership working to explore the ways in which differences in personal power (by status or occupation) interact and are reactive to questions of (inter alia), gender, race, social class and disability. These interactions and the ways in which they get played may aid our understanding of the value of collaborative working in ways which go beyond the conventional because they also point to gaps in skills, knowledge and training for practitioners.

Learning from experience

There are a number of important developments which suggest that the processes associated with (and the promotion of) knowledge transfer, exchange and learning have assumed greater significance. The Labour Government's sponsorship of the Academy for Sustainable Communities or the British Urban Regeneration Association (BURA) programme of learning are important, but the increased interest by both the further and higher education sectors in programmes for practitioners at undergraduate degree level or as foundation degrees signal a new development. The development of various 'leadership' initiatives appears to indicate an awareness of the need to enhance the capacity/skill of local residents and practitioners.

It is too early to assess the impact or quality of these developments. We can, however, observe growing networks of practitioners with overlapping membership who are sharing ideas and discussing ways of applying knowledge and understanding in highly proactive ways.

We acknowledge that, in part, this interest and provision stems from external factors and the more explicit policy initiatives from the ODPM, but such networks, by their very nature, cannot be centrally managed or directed.

178

The value of these emerging and existing networks lies in their capacity to shape agendas to meet their needs and to extend collaborative practice beyond whatever initial remit or goals may be set. It is within these networks (some of which will have a specific life expectancy) that we can see the development of a reservoir of knowledge and experience which has the potential to influence practice with local communities.

Embedding experience and accountability

The plethora of initiatives at a local or subregional level has resulted in a confusing mix of agencies which are accountable to local government and many which operate on a stand-alone basis and appear to be accountable to no one. Over the past decade there has been a growing awareness that there is a democratic deficit. This is, perhaps, best illustrated by reference to the ways the management and delivery of services at a local level are organized.

As we have shown, there is now a much more lively debate concerning the ways in which local residents and service professionals can cooperate in designing and setting up local trusts or partnership boards to provide systems of scrutiny and monitoring. Whilst this debate is ongoing we would want to argue that the core defining principle should be one which provides for local resident involvement and participation. The growth in partnership boards or arrangements for local residents to sit on local boards is a necessary first step but is not sufficient. The experiences of partnerships described and analysed in an earlier chapter suggest that local resident participation needs to be accompanied by an explicit commitment to enhancing their capacity to act as equals with service professionals and, at the same time, for service professionals to receive sufficient support so that they too can engage effectively with local residents.

The risk associated with the growth in such boards and/or trusts is the emergence of a new cadre of 'trust professionals' who become effective managers of these agencies but lack sufficient knowledge and experience to relate to or listen to local residents. If LSPs do act as the new key local body we are still concerned that the reforms to local government indicated in speeches by ministers may not pay sufficient attention to the needs of local communities.

Equality and regeneration

We would maintain that this remains one of the core outstanding tasks confronting local public service managers in the UK. It represents 'unfinished business' rather than a work in progress. Despite legislation and successive reports and initiatives there is no doubt, in our view, that the questions of race and social class have seemed less significant to policy and decision makers than they were 30–40 years ago.

The introduction of the Equality Standard for Local Government is welcome, but it remains only the step in a much broader programme of change. We have discussed some of the elements of that programme in this collection.

However, we remain concerned that, as with measures to restore local involvement in service management, design and delivery, there is a risk that the standard becomes a new norm to which agencies aspire (or even achieve) without reflecting upon the ways in which organizational cultures can act against the experiences and aspirations of black minority communities.

Indeed, the presence of such a discussion illustrates how temporary or fragile initiatives which aim to achieve progressive outcomes can be. We can observe an apparent contradiction in the process. Whilst there is a rich evidence base which highlights structural inequality and the availability of training programmes to promote equality and diversity, there is still a gap in the extent to which agencies or organizations are able to accommodate to change. We believe that this debate should be at the centre of policy and practice discussions over the next five years.

Support needs of practitioners

The practice and experience of those working with and within local communities illustrates an additional gap in our received knowledge and understanding. They too, point to a much broader discussion which will impact upon the management and delivery of local services. The extent to which those engaged in community work practice receive support in developing their emotional and ethical skills and practice has been neglected. Yet the growth in skills and training programmes for professionals working in regeneration initiatives or alongside regeneration practitioners has never been higher.

The growth in these programmes has, usually, focused upon the development of a range of technical skills underpinned by some basic levels of knowledge and awareness. The concern we have is that they concentrate on a defined set of skills or knowledge which often exclude the issues of emotional or ethical literacy. The pressures on local workers to reconcile professional or agency demands with those of local people can create personal pressures for staff. The issues raised are not just about improving line management support or improving the quality of professional/personal supervision but also about enhancing the status of emotional and ethical frameworks within which workers operate. This remains, for us, one of the key knowledge and understanding gaps in current practice.

SUMMARY

The themes outlined represent our contribution to a discussion on the ways in which practitioners, policy makers and decision makers can inform and shape appropriate professional development. The task, we suggest, is a significant one. The gaps in knowledge and practice are profound ones. We feel that this collection of essays marks one important contribution to the next phase of regeneration and city management debates. The recognition that we are in a phase of transition is, we believe, a necessary

180

first step in understanding the task in hand. The collective experience of practitioners and residents provides a significant reservoir of knowledge which we need to draw upon. By defining and articulating this notion of transition we are seeking to draw attention to the knowledge and experience we have and to identify the real and significant gaps which need attention.

Bibliography

'A Single Equality Body: Lessons from abroad', December 2002, http://www.info4local. gov.uk/searchreport.asp?id=13370&heading=e-mail+alert.

'A Single Equality Body?', December 2002, http://www.info4local.gov.uk/searchreport. asp?id=13584&heading=e-mail+alert.

Abels, P. (2005) *Distance Education in Social Work: Planning, Teaching and Learning.* Springer Publishing Co Inc., U.S.

Accreditation Guidance, Neighbourhood Renewal Unit, http://www.neighbourhood.dtlr. gov-uk/partnerships/accred/index.htm.

Acheson, C. (1998) *Community Sector Participation in the Regeneration of East Belfast,* Belfast: Greater East Belfast Partnership.

Aidt, T. and Tzannatos, Z. (2002) *Unions and Collective Bargaining: Economic Effects in a Global Environment,* Washington DC: The World Bank.

Aitken, K. (1997) *The Bairns O'Adam: The Story of the STUC,* Edinburgh: Polygon.

Ambrose, P. (2001) Thumbs down is the key indicator. *New Start* 3 (134): 15.

Amin, A. (1999) An institutionalist perspective on regional economic development. *International Journal of Urban and Regional Research* 23: 365–78.

Apostolakis, C. (2004) Citywide and local strategic partnership in urban regeneration: Can collaboration take things forward? *Politics* 24 (2): 103–12.

Armstrong, H. (1989) Community regional policy. In Lodge, J. (ed.) *The European Community and the Challenge of the Future,* London: Pinter, pp. 167–85.

Arnstein, S. (1969) A ladder of citizen participation. *American Institute of Planners Journal* 35, 216–24.

Atkinson, R. (1999) Discourses of partnership and empowerment in contemporary British urban regeneration. *Urban Studies* 36, 59–72.

Audit Commission (2003) *Community Leadership – learning from comprehensive performance assessment: briefing 1,* London: HMSO Audit Commission (2005) *Governing Partnerships: Bridging the Accountability Gap,* London: HMSO.

Austrin, T. and Beynon, H. (1997) *Masters and Servants: Class and Patronage in the Making of a Labour Organisation,* London: Rivers Oram Press.

Audit Commission (2005) *Governing Partnerships: Bridging the Accountability Gap*, London: HMSO.

Baccaro, L., Carrieri, M. and Damiano, C. (2003) The resurgence of the Italian confederal unions: will it last? *European Journal of Industrial Relations* 9 (1): 43–59.

Bache, I. and George, S. (1999) *Towards Inclusion: Trade Union Participation in EU Structural Fund Partnerships*, Sheffield, Department of Politics, University of Sheffield.

Bailey, D. and Schwartzberg, S. (1995) *Ethical and Legal Dilemmas in Occupational Therapy*, Philadelphia, PA: Davis.

Bailey, J. (1975) *Social Theory for Planning*, London: Routledge and Kegan Paul.

Bailey, N. (2003) Local strategic partnerships in England. The continuing search for collaborative advantage, leadership and strategy in urban governance. *Planning Theory and Practice* 4 (4): 443–57.

Bailey, N., MacDonald, D. and Barker, A. (1995) *Partnership Agencies in British Urban Policy*, London: UCL.

Bains, M. (1972) *The New Local Authorities: Management and Structure*. London: HMSO.

Bak, P. and Chen, K. (1991) Self-organised criticality. *Scientific American* January 46–54.

Balls, E. (2000) Britain's new regional policy: sustainable growth and full employment for Britain's regions. In Balls, E. and Healey, J. (eds) *Towards a New Regional Policy*, London: The Smith Institute.

Banks, S. (1995) *Ethics and Values in Social Work*, London: Macmillan.

Banks, S. (ed.) (1999) *Ethical Issues in Youth Work*, London: Routledge.

Bauman, Z. (2000) *Liquid Modernity*, Cambridge: Polity Press.

Beck, U. and Gernsheim, E. (2002) *Individualization*, London: Sage.

Berghman, J. (1995) *Beyond the Threshold*, Bristol: Policy Press.

Blackman, T. (1991) *Planning Belfast – A case study of public policy and community action*, Avebury: England.

Boddy, M and Fudge, C. (eds) (1984) *Local Socialism?*, London: Macmillan.

Boland, D. (2000) Pragmatist with hope for a better Belfast, *Irish Independent* 25 September, p. 3.

Booth, C. (2001) *Mainstreaming Diversity in the Planning Process: An Examination of the Planning Inspectorate*, Town and Country Planning Summer School, University of Exeter, September. Available at http://www.planningsummerschool.com/main_ site/planningpapers.html.

Bore, A. (2004) The local authority perspective – city governance in Birmingham. In Smith Institute (ed.) (2004) *Making Sense of Localism*. London: The Smith Institute, pp. 33–42.

Brownhill, S. and Darke, J. (1998) *Rich Mix: Inclusive strategies for urban regeneration*, Bristol/York: The Policy Press/JRF.

Brownhill, S. and Darke, J. (1998) *Race, Gender and Urban Regeneration*, Bristol: Policy Press.

Bunting, M. (2004) *Willing Slaves: How the overwork culture is ruling our lives*, HarperCollins.

Cabinet Office (1999) *Modernising Government*, London: The Stationery Office.

Cabinet Office/DTLR (2002) *Your Region, Your Choice: Revitalising the English Regions*, London: The Stationery Office.

Cameron, A, and Palan, R. (2004) *The Imagined Economies of Globlization*, London: Sage.

Cantle, T. (2001) *Community Cohesion, A report of the Independent Review Team*, London: Home Office.

Cantle, T. (2001) *The Report of the Community Cohesion Team*, London: Home Office.

Cantle, T. (2005) *Community Cohesion: A new framework for race and diversity*, Basingstoke: Palgrave Macmillan.

Carley, M., Campbell, M., Kearns, A. and Wood, M. (2000) *Regeneration in the 21st Century*, Bristol: Policy Press.

Castells, M. (1972) *The Urban Question: a Marxist approach*, London: Edward Arnold.

CEC (1996) *At Regional Level on Behalf of Europe's Regions: developing a new field of trade union activity*, Luxembourg: Office for the Official Publications of the European Communities.

Cities for Cohesion (2003) *A Stronger EU Intervention in Large Urban Areas*, Brussels: Cities for Cohesion.

Clarke, J., Gerwitz, S. and McLaughlin, E. (eds) (2000) *New Managerialism, New Welfare?* London: Sage.

CLES (1999) Coming in from the cold: trade unions in economic development partnerships. *Local Work* 11(March) 1–4.

Clough, B. (1997) Union partnerships for lifelong learning. *Local Economy* 3(12): 262–7.

Coaffee, J. (2004) Re-scaling regeneration – experiences of merging area-based and city-wide partnerships in urban policy. *The International Journal of Public Sector Management* 17 (5): 443–61.

Coaffee, J. and Healey, P. (2003) My voice my place: tracking transformations in urban governance. *Urban Studies* 40 (10): 1960–78.

Coaffee, J. and Johnston, L. (2005) The management of local government modernisation – area decentralisation and pragmatic localism. *International Journal of Public Sector Management* 18 (2): 164–77.

Cohen, A. (1985) *The Symbolic Construction of Community*, London: Routledge.

Colenutt, B. and Cutten, A. (1994) Community empowerment: in vogue or vain? *Local Economy* 9, 236–50.

Collier, R. (1998) *Equality in Managing Public Services*, Buckingham: Open University Press.

Cooke, P. (1985) Class practices as regional markers: a contribution to labour geography.

184

In D. Gregory and J. Urry (eds) *Social Relations and Spatial Structures*, New York: St Martin's Press, pp. 213–41.

Copeland, R. and Philo, P. (2000) *Strengthening Co-operation between University Research Institutions and Trade Unions*, London: Centre for Trade Union Studies, University of North London.

Copus, C. (1998) Representing a locality and party group. *Local Governance* 24 (3): 215–24.

Copus, C. (2003) Re-engaging citizens and council. The importance of the councillor to enhanced citizen involvement. *Local Government Studies* 29 (2): 32–51.

Corrigan, P. (2000) *Starting to Modernise: local solutions: a practical guide to neighbourhood forums and area committees*, London: New Local Government Network.

Corry, D. and Stoker, G. (2002) *New Localism Refashioning the Centre-local Relationship*, London: New Local Government Network.

Coulson, A. (2005a) A plague on all your partnership: theory and practice in regeneration. *International Journal of Public Sector Management*, 18 (2): 151–63.

Coulson, A. (2005b) Partnerships: managing discretion and accountability. In *Regeneration Management: Essays on Working with Complexity*, Manchester: Centre for Local Economic Strategies.

Coulson, A. (2005c) Partnership overload in north-west Birmingham. *Public Policy and Administration* 20 (3): 90–105.

Craig, G. and Taylor, M. (2002) Dangerous liaisons: local government and the voluntary and community sectors. In Glendinning, C., Powell, M. and Rummery, K. (eds) *Partnerships, New Labour and the Governance of Welfare*, Bristol: The Policy Press, pp. 131–47.

Cross, M. (1993) *Racism, the City and the State*, London: Routledge.

Crouch, C. (2000) *Coping with Post-Democracy*, Fabian Ideas 598, London: Fabian Society.

Darwin, J. (2002) *Networks, Partnerships and Alliances*, Working Paper, Centre for Individual and Organisational Change, Sheffield Hallam University.

Davidoff, P. (1965) Advocacy and pluralism in planning. *American Institute of Planners Journal* November, 331–8.

De Castella, T. (2000) Open to the public debate. *Planning* 10 March, 27.

De Castella, T. (2001) LSPs are dominated by councils, says research. *Regeneration and Renewal*, April 6: 2.

Denning, S. (2001) *The Springboard, How Storytelling Ignites Action in Knowledge-Era Organisations*, London: Butterworth Heinemann.

Del Tufo, S. and Gaster, L. (2002) *Evaluation of the Commission on Poverty, Participation and Power*, York: Joseph Rowntree Foundation.

Department of Local Government and the Regions (2001) *A New Commitment to Neighbourhood Renewal-National Strategy Action Plan*. London: HMSO.

185

Department of Transport, Local Government and the Regions (2001) *Strong Local Leadership – quality public services*, London: HMSO.

DETR (1998a) *Modern Local Government: in touch with the people*, London: HMSO.

DETR (1998b) *Modernising Local Government: Local Democracy and Community Leadership*, London: HMSO.

DETR (2000a) *Co-ordination of Area-Based Initiatives (Research Working paper)*, London: HMSO.

DETR (2000b) *Out Towns and Cities: The Future*. CMN 4911. London: HMSO.

DETR (2001) *Local Strategic Partnership: Government Guidance*, London: HMSO.

DETR (2001) DETR Local Strategic Partnerships Government Guidance Summary. Available at http://www.local-regions.detr.gov.uk/lsp/guidance/index.htm.

DfES (2003) *21st Century Skills – Realising Our Potential: Individuals, Employers, Nation*. London: HMSO.

Diamond, J. and Liddle, J. (2005) *The Management of Regeneration: choices, challenges and dilemmas*, London: Taylor and Francis, Routledge.

Dickinson, S. (2005) Urban regeneration in an era of well-being. *Local Economy* 20 (2): 224–9.

DTLR (2001) Special Grant Report no 78, March. DETR.

Duffy, K. and Hutchinson, J. (1997) Urban policy and the turn to community. *Town Planning Review* 68, 347–62.

Dunleavy, P. (1991) *Democracy, Bureaucracy and Public Choice*, London: Harvester Wheatsheaf.

Dunlop, J. (1994) *Report and Recommendations of the Commission on the Future of Worker-Management Relations*, Washington, DC: US Department of Labour/US Department of Commerce.

Dutch Ministry of Interior and Kingdom Relations (2005) *Urban Policy – cities empower Europe – conclusions of the Dutch Presidency 2004*, Den Haag: Dutch Ministry of Interior and Kingdom Relations.

Egan, J. (2004) *The Egan Review: Skills for Sustainable Communities*, ODPM: London.

Ellem, B. and Shields, J. (1999) Rethinking regional industrial relations: space, place and the social relations of work. *Journal of Industrial Relations* 41 (4): 536–60.

Equality and Diversity in the NHS – Progress and Priorities Human Resource Directorate October 2003 http://www.gov.uk/comrace/cohesion/.

Etherington, D. (1997) Trade unions and local economic development – lessons from Denmark. *Local Economy* 3 (12): 267–74.

European Commission (1998) *Guidelines on National Regional Aid*, Luxembourg: Office for Official Publications of the European Communities.

European Commission (2004) *Cohesion Policy: the 2007 Watershed*, Brussels: European Commission Directorate-General for Regional Policy.

European Commission (2005) *Cohesion Policy in Support of Growth and Jobs: Community Strategic Guidelines 2007–2013* COM(2005) 0299, Luxembourg: Office for Official Publications of the European Communities.

Fainstein, S. S., Gordon, I. and Harloe, M. (eds) (1992) *Divided Cities: New York and London in the contemporary world*, Blackwell: Oxford.

Fischer, C. S. (1982) *To Dwell Among Friends: personal networks in town and city*, Chicago, IL: University of Chicago Press.

Flynn, R., Williams, G. and Pickard, S. (1996) *Markets and Networks: contracting in community health services*, Buckingham: Open University Press.

Foley, K. (2002) Local economies and the impact of the privatization of public services. *Local Economy* 17 (1): 2–7.

Forester, J. (1993) *Critical Theory, Public Policy and Planning Practice: toward a critical pragmatism*, New York: State University of New York Press.

Fothergill, S. (2001) The true scale of the regional problem in the UK. *Regional Studies* 35 (3): 241–6.

Fraser, N. (1995) From redistribution to recognition? Dilemmas of justice in a post-socialist age. *New Left Review* 212: 68–93.

Frazer, H. (1991) Integrated approaches to development. In Rees, V. *et al.* (eds) *A Survey of Contemporary Community Development in Europe*. The Hague, October.

Frazer, H. (1994) *The Importance of Community Involvement in Integrated Local Development Initiatives*, Seminar Report, N.I Voluntary Trust, December.

Freidson, E. (2001) *Professionalism*, Chicago, IL: University of Chicago Press.

Friedkin, N. E. and Johnsen, E. C. (1990) Social influence and opinions. *Journal of Mathematical Sociology* 15, 193–206.

Furedi, F. (2005) *Politics of Fear: Beyond Left and Right*, London: Continuum.

Gaffney, M. (2002) *Change from the Inside: a study of unpaid community workers*, London: CDF/ SCCD.

Galeote, G. (2005) Regions and cities: key players of regional policy and the Lisbon Agenda paper presented to *European Week of Cities and Regions*, Brussels, 12 October.

Garlick, S. (2001) Editorial, *Regeneration and Renewal* March 3: 15.

Geddes, M. and Newman, I. (1999) Evolution and conflict in local economic development. *Local Economy* 13 (5): 12–25.

Glen, A., Henderson, P., Humm, J., Meszaros, H. and Gaffney, M. (2004) *Survey of Community Development Workers in the UK*, London: CDF.

Glendinning, C., Powell, H. and Rummery, K. (2002) *Partnerships, New Labour and the Governance of Welfare*, Bristol: Policy Press.

Goos, M. and Manning, A. (2003) McJobs and MacJob: The growing polarisation of jobs in the UK. In Dickens, R., Gregg, P. and Wadsworth, J. (eds) *The Labour Market Under New Labour: The State of Working Britain 2003*, London: Palgrave, pp. 85–105.

187

Granovetter, M. (1992) Economic action and social structure: the problem of embededness. In Granovetter, M. and Swedberg, R. (eds) *The Sociology of Economic Life*, Oxford: Westview Press, pp. 53–81.

Greenwood, D. J. and Levin, M. (1998) *Introduction to Action Research: Social Research for Social Change*. Sage Publications: USA.

Grint, K. (1997a) *Fuzzy Management Contemporary Ideas and Practices at Work*, Oxford: Oxford University Press.

Grint, K. (ed.) (1997b) *Leadership, Classical, Contemporary and Critical Approaches*, Oxford: Oxford University Press.

Hastings, A., McArthur, A. and McGregor, A. (1996) *Less than Equal? Community and estate regeneration partnerships*, Bristol: The Policy Press.

Henderson, P. and Mayo, M. (1998) *Training and Education in Urban Regeneration: a framework for participants*, Bristol/York: JRF/The Policy Press.

Herod, A. (2001) *Labor Geographies: Workers and the Landscapes of Capitalism*, New York: Guilford Press.

Herod, A., Peck, J. and Wills, J. (2002) *Geography and Industrial Relations*, London: Unpublished Paper, Department of Geography, Queen Mary and Westfield College, University of London.

Heselden, L. (2001) Coming in from the cold: the role of trade unions on public policy bodies at a regional level, with a focus on London, the southeast and the east of England. *Antipode* 33 (5): 753–62.

Hill, D. (1984) *Citizens and Cities: Urban Policy in the 1990s*, London: Harvester Wheatsheaf.

Hill, D. (1994) *Citizens and Citizens*. Hemel Hempstead: Harvester Wheatsheaf.

Hirschman, A. (1970) *Exit, Voice and Loyalty. Responses to decline in firms, organisations and states*, London: Harvard University Press.

HM Treasury (2001) *Productivity in the UK: 3 – The Regional Dimension*, London: HM Treasury.

Hochschild, A. (1983) *The Managed Heart: the commercialisation of human feeling*, Berkeley, CA: University of California Press.

Hoggett, P., Beedell, P., Jimenez, L., Mayo, M. and Miller, C. (2006) Identity, life history and commitment to welfare. *Journal of Social Policy, forthcoming*.

Hogwood, B. and Gunn, L. (1984) *Policy Analysis for the Real World*, Oxford: Oxford University Press.

The Home Office's Civil Renewal Unit (2004) *Active Learning: Active Citizenship*, London: Home Office.

Horner, J. (1999) Ethical codes. In Parker, M. (ed.) *Ethics and Community in the Health Care Professions*, London: Routledge, pp. 172–87.

Hubbard, P. (2003) Fear and loathing at the multiplex: everyday anxiety in the post-industrial city. *Capital & Class* 80, 51–75.

188

Hübner, D. (2005) *Regional Policy for Growth and Jobs: Meeting the Expectations of Citizens.* Paper presented to *European Week of Cities and Regions,* Brussels, 13 October.

Huby, M. and Dix, G. (1992) *Evaluating the Social Fund,* London: HMSO.

Hudson, R. (1998) Restructuring region and state: the case of northeast England. *Tijdschrift voor Economische en Sociale Geografie* 89: 15–30.

Huxham, C. (1996) *Creating Collaborative Advantage,* London: Sage.

Hyman, R. (1994) Theory and industrial relations, *British Journal of Industrial Relations* 32 (2): 165–80.

Jessop, R. (2002) *The Future of the Capitalist State,* Cambridge: Polity.

Johnston, C. (2005) Strategic superboards: improved network management processes for regeneration. *International Journal of Public Sector Management* 18 (2): 139–50.

Johnston, L. (2005) Waking up the sleeping giant – change management, policy transfer and the search for collaboration. *Public Policy and Administration* 20 (3): 69–89.

JRF (1995) *Inquiry into income and wealth, volume 1,* York: Joseph Rowntree Foundation.

JRF (1999) *Developing Effective Community Involvement Strategies: guidance for single regeneration budget bids, Summary 169,* York: Joseph Rowntree Foundation.

Kanter, R. M. (1989) *When Giants Learn to Dance,* London: Simon and Schuster.

Kanter, R. M. (1994) Collaborative advantage: the art of alliances – successful partnerships manage the relationship, not just the deal. *Harvard Business Review* July–August, 96–108.

Keating, M. (1988) *The City that Refused to Die – Glasgow – The Politics of Urban Renewal,* Aberdeen: Aberdeen University Press.

Keating, M. (2005) *The Government of Scotland: Public Policy Making after Devolution,* Edinburgh: Edinburgh University Press.

Kelly, J. (1998) *Rethinking Industrial Relations,* London: Routledge.

Khakee, A., Somma, P., Thomas, H. (eds) (1999) *Urban Renewal, Ethnicity and Social Exclusion in Europe,* Aldershot: Ashgate.

Kooiman, J. (ed.) (1993) *Modern Governance: new government-society interactions,* London: Sage.

Lasch, C. (1979) *The Culture of Narcissism: American Life in An Age of Diminishing Expectations,* New York: W. W. Norton.

Laumann, E. O., Marsden, P. V. and Galaskiewicz, J. (1977) Community elite influence structures: Extension of a network approach. *American Journal of Sociology* 83, 594–631.

Le Grand, J. (2003) *Motivation, Agency and Public Policy,* Oxford: Oxford University Press.

Lenschow, A. (1999) The greening of the EU: the Common Agriculture Policy and the Structural Funds. *Environment and Planning C: Government and Policy* 17, 91–108.

Levitas, R. (1998) *The Inclusive Society? Social exclusion and New Labour*, Basingstoke: Macmillan.

Liddle, J. (2001) RDAs, Sub-Regional Partnerships and Local Regeneration. *Local Economy*, Vol. 16, No. 4: 312–3.

Local Government Act (2000). London: HMSO.

London Edinburgh Weekend Return Group (1979) *In and Against the State*, London: London Edinburgh Weekend Return Group.

Loney, M. (1983) *Community against Government: The British Community Development Projects 1968–1978*, London: Heinemann.

Lovering, J. (1999) Theory led by policy: the inadequacies of the 'New Regionalism' (Illustrated from the case of Wales). *International Journal of Urban and Regional Research* 23 (2): 379–95.

Lovering, J. (2001) The coming regional crisis (and how to avoid it). *Regional Studies* 35 (4): 349–55.

Mackintosh, M. (1992) Partnerships: issues of policy and negotiation. *Local Economy* 7 (3): 210–24.

Macleod, C. (2005) Integrating sustainable development into Structural Funds programmes: an evaluation of Scottish experience. *European Environment* 15, 313–31.

Maginn, P. (2004) *Urban Regeneration, Community Power and the (in) Significance of Race*, Ashgate: Aldershot.

Mannin, M. (1999) *The politics of Structural Funding: arenas and agendas*. In Carr, F. and Massey, A. (eds) *Public Policy in the New Europe*, Cheltenham: Edward Elgar, pp. 67–81.

Manning, A. (2002) Unions and devolution. In Benneworth, P. and McInroy, N. (eds) *Our Regions, Our Choices: debating the future for the English regions*, Manchester: Centre for Local Economic Strategies (CLES), pp. 28–32.

Marion, R. and Uhl-Bien, M. (2001) Leadership in complex organizations. *The Leadership Quarterly* 12: 389–418.

Marion, R. and Uhl-Bien, M. (2002) *Complexity theory and Al-Queda: examining complex leadership*. Presented at Managing the Complex IV: A Conference on Complex Systems and the Management of Organisations, Fort Meyers, Florida.

Martin, R. (1999) Institutional approaches in economic geography. In Barnes, T. and Sheppard, E. (eds) *Companion to Economic Geography*, Oxford: Blackwell, pp. 1–28.

Martin, R., Sunley, P. and Wills, J. (1996) *Union Retreat and the Regions: The Shrinking Landscape of Organized Labour*, London: Jessica Kingsley.

Martin, S. (2003) Engaging with citizens and other stakeholders. In Bovaird, T. and Loeffler, E. *Public Management and Governance*, London: Routledge, pp. 189–202.

Massey, D. and Painter, J. (1989) The changing geography of trade unions. In J. Mohan (ed.) *The Political Geography of Contemporary Britain,* London: Macmillan, pp. 130–50.

Maud, J. (1967) *Report of the Committee of the Management of Local Government.* London: HMSO.

Mayo, M. (1994) *Communities and Caring: The Mixed Economy of Welfare,* Basingstoke: Macmillan.

Mayo, M. and Taylor, M. (2001) Partnerships and power in community regeneration. In Balloch, S. and Taylor, M. (eds) *Partnership Working: Policy and Practice,* Bristol: The Policy Press, pp. 39–56.

McClean, E. (2003) *Voices From the Margins: a study of social exclusion and urban regeneration in Belfast Northern Ireland and Halifax Nova Scotia,* Belfast: Queens University Belfast, July. Conference Paper.

McKay, I. (1999) *The Road to Devolution,* Unpublished Paper, London: Unions 21.

McPherson, Sir W. (1999) *The Stephen Lawrence Inquiry,* London: HMSO.

Midgley, G. (2000) *Systemic Intervention: Philosophy, Methodology, and Practice.* New York: Kluwer Academic.

Milliband, D. (2005) The Politics of Community. Speech at the launch of the North West Improvement Network, Manchester, October 24.

Minford, P. (1985) *Unemployment: cause and cure,* Oxford: Blackwell.

Morgan, K. and Rees, G. (2001). Learning by doing: devolution and the governance of economic development in Wales. In Chaney, P., Hall, T. and Pithouse, A. (eds) *Post-Devolution Wales: New Governance – New Democracy?* Cardiff: University of Wales Press.

Myerson, J. (2005) The 10 best ways to waste councillor's time. *Society Guardian* April 27.

National Audit Office (1991) *The Social Fund,* London: HMSO.

National Audit Office (2004) *English Regions: an early progress report on the New Deal for Communities programme,* London: The Stationery Office.

National Strategy for Neighbourhood Renewal (2000) Policy Action Team PAT 16 *Learning Lessons,* London: HMSO.

NEA (2002) *Strengthening Accountability in the North East,* Newcastle Upon Tyne: North East Assembly (NEA).

Northern TUC (2002) *Trade Unions and Regional Government: Grasping the Opportunity,* Newcastle Upon Tyne: Northern TUC.

Neill, W. J. V. (1995) Lipstick on the gorilla? Conflict management, urban development and image making in Belfast. In Neill W., Fitzsimons S. and Murtagh B. (eds) *Reimaging the Pariah City,* England: Avebury.

Newman, J. (2001) *Modernising Governance, New Labour, Policy and Society,* London: Sage.

Niskanen, W. (1971) *Bureaucracy and Representative Government*, Chicago, IL: Aldine.

Nolan, J. L. Jr (1998) *The Therapeutic State: Justifying Government at Century's End*, New York: New York University Press.

NRU (Neighbourhood Renewal Unit) (2002) *The Learning Curve*, London: Office of the Deputy Prime Minister.

NRU (Neighbourhood Renewal Unit) (2004) *Transformation and Sustainability. Future support, management and monitoring of the New Deal for Communities programme*, London: NRU.

O'Brien, P. (2001) *Devolution and the Trade Union Movement: the key issues*, Newcastle Upon Tyne, Centre for Urban and Regional Development Studies (CURDS): University of Newcastle Upon Tyne.

O'Brien, P., Pike, A. and Tomaney, J. (2004) Devolution, the governance of regional development and the Trades Union Congress (TUC) in the North East Region of England. *Geoforum (Special Issue: New Geographies of Trade Unionism)* 35: 59–68.

O'Brien, P., Pike, A. and Tomaney, J. (forthcoming) Devolution, the Governance of Regional Development and the Trades Union Congress (TUC) in the North East Region of England. *Geoforum (Special Issue): Geographical Challenges and the Future of Organized Labour)*.

O'Brien, P. and Stirling, J. (2001) *Bread and Roses: Trade Unions and the Newcastle/ Gateshead Capital of Culture Bid 2008*, Newcastle Upon Tyne: Northern TUC.

Office of the Deputy Prime Minister (2004a) *Local Area Agreements: A Prospectus*. London: ODPM.

Office of the Deputy Prime Minister (2004b) *The Future of Local Government: Developing a 10 year Vision*. London: ODPM.

Office of the Deputy Prime Minister (2004c) *Assessing the Impacts of Spatial Interventions: regeneration, renewal and regional development: The 3Rs guidance*, London: ODPM.

Office of the Deputy Prime Minister (2005a) *Research Report 16: Improving delivery of mainstream services in deprived areas – the role of community involvement*, London: HMSO.

Office of the Deputy Prime Minister (2005b) *LSP Evaluation: interim report*, London: HMSO.

Office of the Deputy Prime Minister and Department for Transport (2006) *National Evaluation of Local Strategic Partnerships: formative evaluation and action research programme 2002–2005, Final Report*, London: ODPM.

Osborne D. and Gaebler, T. (1992) *Reinventing Government: how the entrepreneurial spirit is transforming the public sector*, Reading, MA: Addison-Wesley Publications Co.

Perri 6 (1997) *Holistic Government*, London: Demos.

Paddison, R. (2001) Communities in the city. In Paddison R. (ed.) *Handbook of Urban Studies*, London: Sage.

Patel, A. (2004) Regeneration can bridge race divide (development of the Government's cohesion and race equality strategy). *Regeneration & Renewal,* 20.8.04.

Peck, J. and Tickell, A. (1994) Too many partnerships . . . the future for regeneration partnerships. *Local Economy* 9 (3): 251–65.

Percy-Smith, J. (ed.) (2000) *Policy Responses to Social Exclusion,* Buckingham: Open University Press.

Perulli, P. (1993) Towards a Regionalisation of Industrial Relations. *International Journal of Urban and Regional Research* 17: 98–113.

Pierson, J. (2002) *Tackling Social Exclusion,* London: Routledge.

Pike, A. and O'Brien, P. (2000) *The North Can Make it: a strategy for modern manufacturing,* Newcastle Upon Tyne, Centre for Urban and Regional Development Studies (CURDS), University of Newcastle Upon Tyne.

Pike, A., O'Brien, P. and Tomaney, J. (2002) Regionalisation, devolution and the trade union movement. *Antipode* 34 (5): 819–28.

Pike, A., O'Brien, P. and Tomaney, J. (2004) Trade unions in local and regional development and governance: the Northern Trades Union Congress in North East England. *Local Economy* 19 (2): 1–15.

Pike, A., O'Brien, P. and Tomaney, J. (2006) Devolution and the Trades Union Congress in North East England and Wales. *Regional and Federal Studies* 16 (2): 157–78.

Pike, A., Rodriguez-Pose, A. and Tomaney, J. (2006) *Local and Regional Development,* London: Routledge.

PIU (Performance and Innovation Unit) (2000) *Wiring It Up: Whitehall's Management of Cross-cutting Policies and Services,* London: Cabinet Office.

Porter, M. (1990) *The Competitive Advantage of Nations,* New York: Free Press.

Powell, M. and Hewitt, M. (2002) *Welfare State and Welfare Change,* Buckingham: Open University Press.

Pratchett, L. (ed.) (2000) *Renewing Local Democracy? The modernisation agenda in British local government,* London, Frank Cass and Company Ltd.

Prescott, J. (2005) *Strong Cities, in Strong Regions, in a Strong Europe.* Paper presented to the European Week of Cities and Regions, Brussels, 12 October.

Pressman, J. and Wildavsky, A. (1973) *Implementation. How great expectations in Washington are dashed in Oakland; or why it's amazing that federal programs work at all, this being a saga of the economic development administration as told by two sympathetic observers who seek to build morals on a foundation of ruined hopes,* Berkeley, CA: University of California Press.

Putnam, R. (1995) Bowling alone: America's declining social capital, *Journal of Democracy,* 6 (1): 65–78.

Putnam, R. D. (2000) *Bowling Alone: The collapse and revival of American community,* New York: Simon and *Schuster.*

Randle, A. (2005) *Councils Embracing Localism: Lessons from Birmingham, Wakefield and West Sussex,* London: New Local Government Network.

193

Rhodes, R. A. W. (1996) The New Governance: governing without government, *Political Studies* 44, 652–67.

Rhodes, R. A. W. (1997) *Understanding Governance: policy networks, governance, reflexivity and accountability*, Buckingham: Open University Press.

Richards, P. (2000) *Is the Party Over: New Labour and the Politics of Participation*, Fabian pamphlet 594, London: Fabian Society.

Robinson, F. (2002) The north east: a journey through time. *City* 6 (3): 317–34.

Robinson, F. and Shaw, K. (2000) *Who Runs the North . . . Now?* Durham: Department of Sociology and Social Policy, University of Durham.

Rogers Hollingsworth, J. (1995) A strategy for Labour. *Industrial Relations Journal* 34 (3): 367–81.

Rose, R. (1993) *Lesson Drawing in Public Policy: a guide to learning across time and space*, Chatham, NJ: Chatham House.

Rowe, M. (1999) Joined-up accountability: bringing the citizen back in. *Public Policy and Administration* 14, 91–102.

Rowe, M. (2002) Discretion and inconsistency: implementing the Social Fund. *Public Money and Management* 22 (4): 19–24.

Rowe, M. (2003) *Communities Beyond Regeneration: sustaining capacity once the money runs out.* Presented to Regional Studies Association Annual Conference, Pisa, March.

Rowe, M. (2004) *Abusive Partnerships: new forms of governance, new forms of abuse?* Paper presented to Managing Regeneration V, Liverpool, June.

Rowe, M. (2005) *Bending the Mainstream: evaluation and learning in regeneration.* Paper presented to Managing Regeneration VI, Durham, June.

Rowe, M. (2005) Abusive partnerships. In McInroy, N., MacDonald, S., Diamond, J. and Southern, A. (eds) *Regeneration Management: Essays on Working with Complexity*, Manchester: Centre for Local Economic Strategies.

Rowlinson, M. (1997) *Organisations and Institutions*, Basingstoke: Macmillan.

Sadler, D. (2000) Organising European labour: governance, production, trade unions and the question of scale. *Transactions of the Institute of British Geographers* 25: 135–52.

Sadler, D. and Thompson, J. (2001) In search of regional industrial culture: the role of labour organisations in old industrial regions. *Antipode* 4 (33): 660–86.

Sandercock, L. (1998) *Towards Cosmopolis*, Chichester: John Wiley and Son.

Schedler, K. (2002) Keynote speech at the International Symposium of Public Sector Research, University of Edinburgh, April 2002.

Sennett, R. (1998) *The Corrosion of Character*, New York: Norton.

SEU (1998) *Bringing Britain Together: A National Strategy for Neighbourhood Renewal*, London: Social Exclusion Unit.

SEU (2000) *National Strategy for Neighbourhood Renewal: A Framework for Consultation*, London: Social Exclusion Unit.

SEU (2001) *A New Commitment to Neighbourhood Renewal: National Strategy Action Plan*, London: Cabinet Office.

SEU (2003) *Tackling Social Exclusion Achievements, Lessons Learned and the Way Forward*, London: ODPM.

SEU (2004) *Breaking the Cycle of Social Exclusion*, London: Social Exclusion Unit.

Shaw, K. (1993) The development of a new urban corporatism: the politics of urban regeneration in the north east of England. *Regional Studies* 27, 251–9.

Short, J. (1989) *The Humane City*, Oxford: Basil Blackwell.

Short, J. (1996) *The Urban Order: an introduction to cities, culture and power*, Oxford: Blackwell Publishers.

Skelcher, C., Navdeep, M. and Smith, M. (2004) *Effective Partnership and Good Governance: lessons for policy and practice*, Birmingham: Institute of Local Government Studies.

Skelcher, C., Navdeep, M. and Smith, M. (2005) The Public Governance of Collaborative Spaces: Discourse, Design and Democracy. *Public Administration* 83 (3): 573–96.

Snowden, D. (2002) Complex acts of knowing. Paradox and descriptive self-awareness. Special edition of *Journal of Knowledge Management* 6 (2): 68–88.

Snowden, D. and Kurtz, C. (2003) The new dynamics of strategy, sense making in a complex-complicated world. *IBM Systems Journal*, 42 (3): 462–83.

Southern, A. (2003) The management of regeneration: processes and routes to effective delivery. *Local Work* April, 50: 1–3.

Speeden, S. and Clarke, J. (2001) *The Equality Standard for Local Government*, London: Employers Organisation for Local Government.

Speeden, S. and Clarke, J. (2004) *From Adverse Impact to Positive Action: beyond institutional discrimination*. Paper presented to the Mainstreaming Equality Conference, Liverpool, April.

Speeden, S., Clarke, J., Ackah, W., Chesters, G., Diamond, J., and Leeming, K. (2001) *Multicultural Britain, Making it Work Locally*. A Research Brief commissioned by the Commission for Racial Equality. London: CRE, unpublished.

Stacey, R. D. (1996) *Strategic Management and Organisational Dynamics*, London: Pitman.

Streeck, W. (1992) *Social Institutions and Economic Performance*, London: Sage.

Stoker, G. (2004) *Transforming Local Governance: from Thatcherism to New Labour*, London: Palgrave.

Sullivan, H., Smith, M., Root, A. and Moran, D. (2001) *Area Committees and Neighbourhood Management: increasing democratic participation and social inclusion*, London: Local Government Information Unit.

Sullivan, H. and Skelcher, C. (2002) *Working Across Partnerships: collaboration in public services*, Palgrave Macmillan.

Taussik, J. and Smalley, J. (1998) Partnerships in the 1990s: Derby's successful City Challenge bid. *Planning Practice and Research* 13, 283–97.

Taylor, M. (2000) Communities in the lead: power, organisational capacity and social capital. *Urban Studies* 37 (5–6): 1019–35.

Taylor, M. (2000) *Top-down Meets Bottom-up: neighbourhood management,* York: Joseph Rowntree Foundation.

Taylor, M. (2003) Neighbourhood governance: Holy Grail or poisoned chalice? *Local Economy* 18 (3): 190–5.

Taylor, M. (2003) *Public Policy in the Community,* Basingstoke: Palgrave.

Taylor, R. (2000) *The TUC: From the General Strike to New Unionism,* Basingstoke: Palgrave.

Taylor, F. and Gaster, L. (2001) *In the Neighbourhood: area decentralisation and new political structures,* London: Local Government Association.

Teague, P. (1995) Europe of the Regions and the future of national systems of industrial relations. *Economic and Industrial Democracy* 16 (3) 327–52.

Thompson, G. (1993) Network coordination. In Maidment, R. and Thompson, G. (eds) *Managing the United Kingdom,* London: Sage, pp. 51–74.

Tomaney, J. (2002) The evolution of regionalism in England. *Regional Studies* 36 (7): 721–31.

Northern TUC (2001) *Barriers to Skills and Learning,* Newcastle Upon Tyne: Northern TUC.

Northern TUC (2002) *Women at Work: Gender Inequality in the North East Labour Market,* Newcastle Upon Tyne: Northern TUC.

TUC (2002a) *Half the World Away: Making Regional Development Work,* London: TUC.

TUC (2002b) *The Need for Regional Government – Response to the White Paper 'Your Region, Your Choice: Revitalising the English Regions',* London: TUC.

Wales TUC (n.d. a) *An Agenda for Prosperity.* Cardiff: TUC

Wales TUC (n.d. b) *Economic Development and Regeneration.* Cardiff: TUC.

Wales TUC (2003) *Transforming Wales Together: Annual Report 2002–2003.* Cardiff: TUC.

Tufts, S. (1998) Community unionism in Canada and labor's (re)organization of space. *Antipode* 30: 227–50.

Tullock, G. (1965) *The Politics of Bureaucracy,* Washington, DC: Public Affairs Press.

Turok, I. (2005) Making Scotland competitive and cohesive. Paper presented to Scotland the EUconomy: Regional Competitiveness Beyond 2007, Glasgow, 11 November.

Tyler, P. with Dabinett, G. Lawless, P. and Rhodes, J. (2000) *A Review of the Evidence Base for Regeneration Policy,* Department of the Environment, Transport and the Regions. London: HMSO.

UNISON (2000) *Towards Regional Government,* London: UNISON.

Waddington, J. and Hoffman, R. (eds) (2000) *Trade Unions in Europe,* Brussels: ETUI.

Wæver, O. (1995) Europe since 1945: crisis to renewal. In Wilson, K. and van der Dussen, J. (eds) *The History of the Idea of Europe* (revised edn), London: Routledge, pp. 151–214.

Wasserman, S. and Faust, K. (1994) *Social Network Analysis, Methods and Applications*, Cambridge University Press.

Weber, L. (2001) *Understanding Race, Class, Gender and Sexuality: a conceptual framework.* Boston, MA: McGraw Hill.

Weick, K. E. and Browning, L. D. (1986) Argument and narration in organizational communication. Yearly Review of Management. *Journal of Management* 12 (2): 243–5.

Wellman, B. and Wortley, S. (1990) Different strokes for different folks – community ties and social support. *American Journal of Sociology* 96, 558–88.

Wells, P., Gore, T., Escott, K. and Booth, C. (2004) *The Implementation of the Horizontal Priorities in the 2000–2006 Structural Funds Programmes: what happens after the rhetoric of policy making?* Paper presented to Europe at the Margins: EU Regional Policy, Peripherality and Rurality, Angers, 15–16 April.

Whitebrook, M. (2002) Compassion as a political virtue. *Political Studies* 50: 529–44.

Wills, J. (1998) Taking on the Cosmocorps: experiments in transnational labor organizations. *Economic Geography* 74: 111–30.

Wills, J. (2001) Community unionism and trade union renewal in the UK: moving beyond the fragments at last? *Transactions of the Institute of British Geographers* 26, 465–83.

Wills, J. (2002) *Union Futures: Building Networked Trade Unionism in the UK*, London: Fabian Society.

Wills, J. and Cumbers, A. (2000) The workplace at the millennium: new geographies of employment. *Environment and Planning* A 32 (9): 1523–8.

Wilson, D. and Game, C. (3rd ed) (2002) *Local Government in the United Kingdom*, London: Palgrave/Macmillan.

Wilson, J. Q. and Kelling, G. L. (2004) Broken windows: the police and neighbourhood safety. In Stelzer, I. (ed.) *Neoconservatism*, London: Atlantic Books, pp. 151–66.

Wilson, P. (1997) Building social capital: a learning agenda for the 21st century. *Urban Studies* 34, 745–60.

197

Index

198

INDEX